Raging Rivers
Stormy Seas

TERRY STORRY
Marcus Bailie & Nigel Foster

The Oxford Illustrated Press

The Oxford Illustrated Press

© 1989 Terry Storry, Nigel Foster, Marcus Bailie as credited.

ISBN 0 946609 60 8

Published by:
The Oxford Illustrated Press Limited, Haynes Publishing Group,
Sparkford, Nr Yeovil, Somerset BA22 7JJ, England.

Distributed in the United States of America by: Sheridan House Inc.,
145 Palisade Street, Dobbs Ferry, New York 10522, USA

Printed in England by:
J.H. Haynes & Co Limited, Sparkford, Nr. Yeovil, Somerset.

British Library Cataloguing in Publication Data
Storry, Terry
  Raging rivers, stormy seas.
  1. Canoeing.
  I. Title II. Foster, Nigel   III. Bailie, Marcus
  797.1'22
  ISBN 0-946609-60-8

Library of Congress Catalog Card Number
  88-83914

Contents

Dedication

For Callum
That he may understand the child in the man

Acknowledgements

Liz Colhurst, Marcus Bailie, Dee de Mengel, Alun Hughes, and Marty Kelly for their diaries.

John Barry and Jim Hargreaves for the inspiration.

Julie for reading the manuscript, telling me when it did not make sense, and correcting the spelling when it did.

All my paddling friends, on trips remembered and forgotten.

Philippe Simoens for who he was.

Photographs
As credited

Maps
By Terry Storry

Other books by Terry Storry
North Wales White Water (with Jim Hargreaves), 1980
Alpine White Water, 1982
Snowdonia White Water Sea and Surf, 1986

Introduction

'Sole, Lundy, Fastnet, Irish Sea, west backing south-west, 7 to gale 8, rain, moderate! A poor shipping, and indeed sea canoeing, forecast; but on the western coasts and hills of Britain, the surf will be up and the river banks full, so many canoeists are rubbing their hands in anticipation. *'Vingt-sept degrés à Briançon ce matin';* the radio promises a good day's sunbathing for south-eastern France, but canoeists will be donning wetsuits and cagoules to catch rivers swollen by snow and glacier melt. 'The tide races off Anglesey North and South Stack are dangerous for boats', the Admiralty chart for Wales warns, yet sea canoeists go there to play. It is an absurd, upside down world, this canoeing game. And yet, and yet, as Rat says in *Wind in the Willows,* 'there is nothing, absolutely nothing half so much worth doing as simply messing about in boats'.

Perhaps then I start with an advantage over John Barry, friend and author of *The Great Climbing Adventure,* when faced with the question, 'Why do it?' With the odd exception—like a student I overheard saying, 'I don't like much about canoes, there tends to be a lot of water underneath them'—messing about in boats is dear to every (big) kid's heart. Whether we were descended first from apes or dolphins hardly matters (although our hairless bodies and layers of subcutaneous fat suggests an answer); most feel more at home in or on water, than hanging over space. Tree climbing comes after the swimming pool. Water is a natural element.

It has weight and can support us, unlike air. It moves like fire, but unlike fire it can be held and consumed. It laughs and cries, is at peace and war, is never pedestrian like the earth, always changeable like ourselves. It does not age, nor is it staled by use or custom. As long as it is cherished it will remain for each generation to find and enjoy.

The canoe will take you anywhere on the water. You can even sleep in it, as Marcus did on the Nile. In and out of caves on rivers and sea, across shallow mud-choked estuaries, through the tightest gorges, down waterfalls and over cataracts, traversing pond and ocean, the canoe will go. Moulded in plastic the limits of its strength and durability are well beyond those of the paddler. It is the ultimate boat, as the Eskimos and Indians knew.

This book does not, however, seek to preach or convert; rather it hopes to entertain, amuse, excite, and occasionally provoke—believer and non-believer alike. In pursuit of this I believe exaggeration and embellishment is inevitable. It all happened, but after a pint, or a quarrel, round a fire, or in the midst of a party, a story can get subtly altered to meet the expectations of the audience. That is why diaries are so important. They cannot lie. Without them memory is fallible. But follow me in there if you will, in your imagination or for real, and you will know that Jugbuster and the raging Rangitata, thunderous Lava Falls and sad Busti are as I have described them, and excepting the ravages of man and nature, so they will remain.

Since I have written half the book, it is slanted towards my side of the sport, white water kayaking. I was lucky therefore, to have two friends with different interests who were prepared to put pen to paper. Nigel Foster's sea kayaking trips, and Marcus Bailie's story of Canadian canoeing down the Nile, give the book much-needed breadth. More important than this, they are also passionate about canoeing, about its essence rather than its form.

While working at Plas y Brenin I have seen thousands of canoeists, hundreds of excellent paddlers, and perhaps ten masters of the game. Of these, two stand alone, Ray Rowe and Nigel Foster. So dedicated to their sport that they remain enigmas even to close friends, they are the unsung heroes of many. Just to watch Ray paddling a pine log, or tackling extreme waterfalls, or charging up a wave-lashed lake in a racing C1, is to marvel at his balance. And because balance (and reticence) is the measure of the man I did not think he would be interested in contributing to this collection.

Nigel, on the other hand, is a man possessed. It is the northern sea or nothing, and perhaps one day it will be nothing. The Nordic genes are there in the wild blue eyes, shaggy beard, and sun-streaked blond hair. On our crossing the Bristol Channel to Lundy, I felt the hackles of my Anglo-Saxon ancestors rise as he prowled round us in his Vyneck like a Viking warrior.[1] Head fixed, body rotating to the rhythm, he shepherded us, paddling faster than any person I have seen. Occasionally he would stop and turn, as if to measure each of us against his great blue horizon.

Did hubris lead Nigel close to death in 1981 when crossing the Hudson Strait alone? Such reflections are not in his nature. He describes the storm,

---

[1] The Vyneck is an extremely fast specialist sea kayak designed by Nigel for open sea crossings.

not the sorrow, and with such vividness that we know he survived by being at one with it. Skilfully mixed in is the Faroes epic, where, responsible for students, wind and wave drive him again to the brink of disaster. The tension produced by the two stories flashing backwards and forwards across six years is only bearable because he is still here to tell of it.

First however, he gives us a reminder that even on sea canoeing trips, much more time is spent on land than on sea. The circumnavigation of Iceland in the summer of 1977 was a major undertaking, but Nigel describes a small part of the journey, where, trapped by the weather the duo's existence was stripped to the bare essentials, food, shelter, and yes, perhaps, companionship. Still always in the background is the northern sea, moodily described and overwhelming in it's presence.

Marcus Bailie smokes and drinks too much, like many of his countrymen. Pass him on the street and you would say he had been washed up. The leprechaun's myriad friends, and indeed all the lucky students who pass under his tutelage, know different. *He* is the rock on whom they brace, the shore to which they scurry in times of storm and stress. And it is all so understated. You have to read between the lines of his Nile trip to see his energy and resourcefulness pushing and pulling the team through the doldrums. He saved our trip too by pulling my shoulder back into place.

Marcus is not perhaps the master technician that Nigel is (although still a better canoeist than I am), and he may be less comfortable with words than Mr Three Degrees, but he has more to say than either of us. He is after all interested in people as well as canoeing. Travelling with him we meet the poor of Sudan and Mexico, and, across the River of Ice, Anna, fishing and hunting out of a small cabin. Perhaps one day Marcus too will disappear. Not for him a watery grave, but rather a mud hut and a shared cup that is passed round in a never-ending circle. He constantly searches for the basic essentials of the good life, and invites us to join his dreams. And the excitement and adventure is also there, a disturbingly powerful brew to set before the comfortably seated reader.

So Nigel and Marcus balance my writing by far more than their broader areas of canoeing interest. Self-centred as only a singleton can be, I do not look around me. The environment, yes, I went there once and didn't like it. Other people I like in small doses. Then I fall in love, and I am at the mercy of my passionate involvement. I have my say at the end; but if on the way you detect a little narcissism creeping in, you will know that I have been carried away again by my love of the great canoeing adventure.

Terry Storry
North Wales
August 1988

Shorebound—On Iceland by Nigel Foster

We landed tired in the bay. It had been a long day with good conditions for the first thirty miles, but as we neared Hvalnes a seemingly malevolent headwind had roared down from the mountains, blowing first hot then cold and raising lines of stinging spray from the sea. We struggled against the wind for control of our paddles. An imposing wall of mountain rose steeply ahead of us. Obscuring the summit ridge was a lively roll of cloud that had been visible in the far distance when we set off in the morning; brilliant white cloud, flowing outwards and then falling like some giant waterfall to evaporate mysteriously on its way down towards the valley below. Dwarfed by the mountains above lay a sickle blade of sand beach, its surface twisting into drifting waves of misty grey with the gusty wind. It was where the tip of this grey blade touched the rock of the headland that we sought what shelter we could find and rested our aching bodies.

Geoff Hunter groaned with the bitter-sweet pleasure of stretching hard-worked muscles; the sort of pain that makes you feel better afterwards.

'I wouldn't want to have to work any harder than I did crossing that last bay!' he confided. 'Me neither!' I agreed readily. It had been hard work and we had made painfully slow progress. I watched as a little line of spray weaved its way from the shore into the bay. 'Well! I suppose we'd better get sorted out. Do you want to change first or put up the tent?'

We decided to tackle the tent first so that we could have a hot drink brewing while we changed. The wind made it a struggle and we fought for some time with the nylon flysheet of the Force Ten that we used for shelter. Eventually we succeeded in pinning it to the ground with large boulders, but the fabric bulged and slammed in angry protest.

I took the empty water carrier from my boat and picked my way back into the broad open valley to find the stream that lay hidden by the stony terrain. The strange cloud above me was reflecting an eerie light into the valley. I paused for a moment, balancing with difficulty on a boulder while

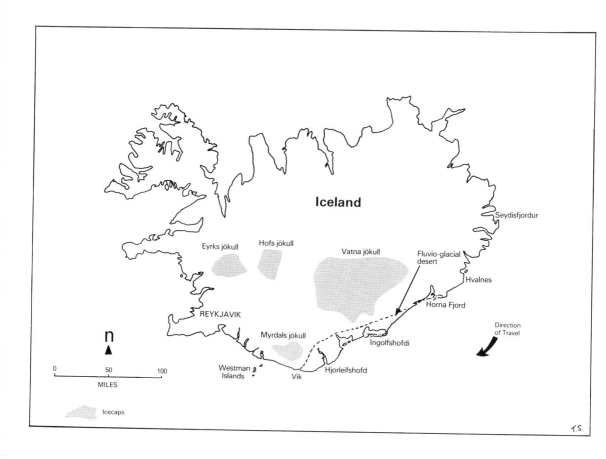

Iceland

Seydisfjordur

Eyrks jökull   Hofs jökull   Vatna jökull   Fluvio-glacial desert

Hvalnes

Horna Fjord

REYKJAVIK

Myrdals jökull   Ingolfshofdi   Direction of Travel

n

0   50   100
MILES

Westman Islands   Vik   Hjorleifshofd

Icecaps

T.S.

the wind pushed and shoved. All around me stretched gravel banks and mounds of pale brownish boulders. It looked as though the land had been stripped bare of vegetation, but of course this landscape was completely natural. Despite the desolation, or perhaps because of it, there was a strange beauty about the scene. My eyes watered in the wind and I rubbed them, cursing loudly as the salt that had dried on my face and in my eyelashes from the day's paddling stung my eyes. My eyes were just beginning to clear again when I thought I saw a movement. I looked more carefully. I must have been mistaken. I suppose it could have been a bird. It was as if a boulder had moved. I was about to turn away when my eyes caught another shift of shadow. There it was again! A reindeer! I whistled quietly through my teeth in delight. A pale phantom ghosted almost invisibly across the rocks. Suddenly I could see others! I counted six, then spotted more. Ten . . . eleven . . . a dozen at least! They were no more than 200 yards away and it seemed they had not sensed my presence yet, or perhaps I represented no threat to them at this distance. I moved gently

10

towards them, aware that the wind would carry sound and scent away. Their pale bodies floated slowly and effortlessly away as if the boulders never existed. I followed for a full ten minutes, marvelling at the almost perfect camouflage of the beasts. A stationary reindeer was almost invisible even at this range, yet they were not small animals! I recalled having read somewhere that reindeer were introduced from Norway in the eighteenth century, but I had somehow never expected to see any. It was a real treat.

I retraced my steps down the valley, filling the water container on the way, and turned against the wind to rejoin Geoff by the tent. Every step in the wind was an effort. I was glad to collapse in a heap outside the tent in the warmth of the sun. In the relative shelter of the flysheet, the petrol stove roared and hiccuped, the flame now blue, now yellow, flaring out from beneath the pot with every slam of the wind. I shut my eyes and groaned.

'Wake me up next week!' I muttered to Geoff.

Geoff and I were settling into a very flexible paddling routine along the south coast of Iceland. We hoped to circumnavigate the island and had carried our kayaks off the small Faroese ferry, the Smyril, at the east coast village of Seydisfjordur. Seydisfjordur nestles at the foot of mountains rising steeply to over 3000 ft. When we had arrived, these mountains were still white with snow. Leaving Seydisfjordur at about midnight, taking advantage of the endless daylight, we had reached the open sea at the end of the long fjord and turned south to travel clockwise around the island. Now, some 80 miles further on we had reached a turning point; a corner of Iceland where a mountain range ran straight from the great Vatnajokul icecap to the sea, presenting a solid barrier to the weather. Winds deflected by the massive icecap funnel around and over this mountain headland, speeding up and creating the strange hot and cold gusts we were experiencing. No doubt once we were clear of the headland again we would find the winds less fierce.

Our wait for lighter winds over the next few days seemed endless and we grew increasingly lethargic. Our food supply grew low and we needed to go shopping for more, but we had at least a day's paddle ahead before the next village. Sleep was fitful, with the tent making a restless shelter, and outside even standing in the wind was an effort. Not surprisingly our thoughts and conversation turned increasingly to food. 'How about roast beef, Yorkshire pudding, sprouts, roast potatoes and carrots for starters?' suggested Geoff, fuelling my hunger with tantalising fantasies.

'I'd settle for a big steak with fried onions and tomatoes, and salad . . .' I trailed off as the mental picture grew too vivid for me.

'Black forest gateau . . . or blackcurrant cheesecake,' suggested Geoff.

I suppose it is not surprising that hunger brings the conversation round to food. Stone age man sitting in his cave enjoying a quiet weekend probably discovered that he was right out of red bull meat. His inability to articulate the finer points of a three-course meal to his companions, might well have led him to draw the outlines of animals on the cave wall until desperation finally drove him out to do a spot of hunting. Geoff, with the surname of Hunter was the first to give in. 'I'm just going outside. I may be some little while,' he announced, misquoting Captain Oates.

'But there's no need to go!' I replied. 'We've got plenty of food.'

'What food have we got?'

'Why, we've got Scott's porridge, Oates!'

In truth, porridge oats, rice and onions were about all we had left, and we had a real craving for meat. Geoff disappeared from the tent entrance leaving me alone with my thoughts.

Earlier in our trip we had been paddling across a bay in warm sunshine, enjoying the freedom of movement that lighter clothing allowed, when a thick mist rolled in and a chilling breeze sprang up. An island appeared from this mist and we turned eagerly into a narrow beach and landed. Having donned some warmer clothes we decided to explore the island and set off across the hummocky ground. Then quite suddenly my foot broke through the surface turf into a puffin burrow, squashing the poor occupant underfoot. I lifted the limp body out. The smart black and white plumage was smeared now with earth, but the brightly coloured beak and mournfully expressive face were as clean and bright as in life.

Puffin meat is still eaten both in the Faroe Islands and Iceland, as indeed it used to be in Britain. Later that day we landed on a driftwood-strewn beach and lit a fire. By the time the bird was plucked and drawn the fire was roaring away. We spit-roasted the puffin and the meat proved to be superb. We picked the bones quite clean. After our meal we doused the embers of the fire and paddled on for a few more hours before stopping for the night. The memory of the tasty meat seemed to linger in my mouth now as I lay down the centre of the tent, trying to avoid the blows of the nylon as the wind kept up its battering.

Before long Geoff returned, grinning. 'Butcher's delivery service!' he announced. 'Meals on wings!' I scrambled out into the sunshine to see a plump duck lying on the grass.

'NEE-HI!' I shouted in appreciation. 'Duck! I'll light the fire!'

While Geoff prepared the bird, surrounded by an eddying whirl of feathers and down, I collected driftwood. Icelandic beaches are seldom bare of wood, despite the lack of trees on the island, and I soon had a reasonable pile gathered. I had difficulty kindling a flame onto the thinly split wood I had prepared, but once the wood was alight the gale rapidly fanned the flames into a blaze. Three boulders and the rusty rim of an oil drum that Geoff pulled out of the grass provided a suitable support for our largest pot, into which the dismembered duck just about fitted, with a couple of onions and some seasoning. Then, after setting a large stone on the lid to keep it in place, we sat down to wait.

Hours passed. The meat was becoming tender enough now to pull away easily from the bone, so we put on a pan of rice to cook. I was feeling impatiently hungry by now, and strolled away to have a pee. Having a pee in a gale was a necessary evil that was by now getting to be tedious. 'Confucious, he say: "He who pees in the wind gets his own back!"' I muttered to myself, and then swore as the fickle wind proved the prophesy correct yet again. I was in full flow when I caught sight of a bright red jeep bouncing over the boulders towards me. I felt embarrassed. But where else could I have a pee in such a wide open space?

The jeep pulled up beside the tent and two men climbed down. The elder held out his hand. 'My name is Elias Jonsson,' he announced in perfect English. 'Doctor Livingstone, I presume?' ran through my head, but I said, 'Nigel Foster, and Geoff Hunter.' Geoff stood beside me, spoon in hand. Elias introduced his son, then explained that he was a newspaper reporter from Hofn. He had read an article in an Icelandic paper about our journey and had come out to try to find us. We talked, then at length he asked, 'What are you cooking?' Geoff and I glanced at one another. We had heard that the eider duck is protected in Iceland because of the economic importance of the down, which is collected from the nests. Could we tell a newspaper reporter that we had caught a duck?

'Oh, it's just a pudding,' said Geoff, and neatly steered the conversation towards the kayaks, with their pumps and hatches. Elias was not so easily distracted. He was soon concerned about the food again.

'Will it be all right?' he asked. 'What is it that you are cooking?'

Geoff explained casually, 'Oh, it's just flour, fat and a little water with sultanas added. We call it a pudding. It needs to cook for a long time. It will be O.K.'

Conversation moved towards the Willis Jeep, with its air intake inside the cab to ease river crossings and the sturdy tyres. 'Wide tyres are best for the sands of the south coast, but for this'—Elias threw out an arm to indicate the bouldery terrain—'I did not think it worth taking off my road tyres for today. But, are you sure your food is O.K.?'

By now we were too deeply into the deception to retreat. It would surely be courteous to offer our visitors something to eat, but it would be difficult to explain the meat and bones in a steamed sultana pudding! Thankfully Elias contented himself with taking a few photographs, and then with a brief and formal 'Goodbye and good luck!' the father and son climbed back into the jeep, roused the engine and drove slowly and carefully away.

Geoff and I stood grinning at one another. Somehow the unexpected incident had cheered us up enormously. 'How about some grub then?' asked Geoff. There was no need to wait for my reply. We were soon digging into the now soggy rice and tender succulent meat. It was a meal worth waiting for!

By our last night at Hvalnes, the battering of the tent had grown so wearing that we found a hollow on the hillside in which to sleep out in the open. I slept like a log until just before 3 a.m., when I awoke to discover that the wind had died away completely. The sun was just about to emerge from behind the mountain. I got up immediately, ran down the hillside to the tent, made some coffee and carried it back with me to wake Geoff. It was great to be moving again. Without the wind every movement seemed light and easy. It was no longer an effort to stand still in one place!

Westwards from Hvalnes the most prominent headlands have become linked together with sandbanks curving gracefully from point to point, enclosing lagoons which no doubt will silt up and become marshland. Maybe in the future there will be good farmland here. To the south of the Vatnajokull icecap is an extensive fluvio-glacial plain, hemmed by a long black curve of sand that stretches 85 miles from the rock Inglfshofdi to the cliffs by the village of Vik. This was the stretch of coast that the Icelandic people that we had met were most concerned about. Heavy surf, quicksands and dust and sand storms make it an inhospitable area, and there are countless tales of shipwreck where those survivors who reached land perished in the attempt to reach help. We prepared ourselves for the 55-mile paddle to Ingolfshofdi at the last coastal town, Hofn. Hofn has grown up in the last eighty years from a single farm to an important fishing port with a population of over 800 people. Over eighty islands studding a vast salt water lagoon have been linked by gravel causeways and consolidated to create a foundation for this fascinating town. We were entertained royally by Elias Jonsson and his wife. We were invited to use the showers in the police cells, and the town's police officer drove us to a vantage point in the mountains to take advantage of the superb view of the lagoon below. We also shopped, and with much cramming and rearranging we managed to load our bulky supplies into the kayaks.

With an ebbing tide we launched into a thick wet mist and drifted rapidly towards the narrow entrance in the sand bar and the open sea. Because of the strong tide, which reputedly attains a rate of ten knots, we had no doubt that we were drifting in the right direction even though at this point we could see no land. However, our peace of mind was soon disturbed by the throbbing sound of a powerful engine. A boat was evidently approaching us, as the noise was getting louder. Geoff looked at me and I stared back. It was difficult to tell which way the boat was heading, and so it seemed best just to sit and listen in the hope that it would pass us by. Suddenly a large wooden fishing boat appeared, swept past and disappeared again. 'Phew!' I whistled. 'That was close!' My relief was short-lived. 'I can hear another one!' shouted Geoff. I turned my head and confirmed that above the din of the disappearing craft was a different note. My mind flashed back to an incident a couple of years earlier.

I had been crossing the English channel by night with a friend, and towards dawn we had run into a dense bank of fog close to the French port of Calais. Daylight was beginning to brighten the scene when out of the damp shroud had come the noise of a ship heading towards us. It was impossible to tell whether it would pass to our left or right, or indeed if it would actually hit us, but the thunder of the engines grew louder and louder. We sat, tense and worried. We turned our heads trying to pinpoint the position of the ship, but the noise grew so loud that it seemed to come from all around us. We were helpless. If we were in the way we would be hit. It was inevitable. We would not .have time to paddle clear. My stomach felt empty. It seemed to be echoing the rumble of the engines. Then it was upon us. The huge shape of a cross-channel ferry storming past, only yards away.

'There it is!' shouted Geoff. I jumped. A fishing boat was almost upon us. The painted woodwork had a grainy appearance in the mist, like a photograph enlarged so far that the individual grains in the emulsion have become visible. Peering from the side window of the wheelhouse was a pale moon-like face. It didn't move. Suddenly the boat twisted sideways towards us. It must have hit a sandbank! The powerful current pushed it over until the starboard decks were awash. The engine raced. I sat, stunned, and watched the boat lurch upright again shedding grey water from its decks. The engine note dropped to a slow rhythmical beat, but the vision faded into a shadowy shape and vanished in the fog. We could no longer see what was happening. The tide was carrying us away.

'What do you think we should do?' I asked. There really was nothing we could do. The tide would prevent us from returning.

'Do you suppose that was our fault?' asked Geoff.

'Might have been, I suppose,' I replied. 'But it sounds as though they're all right.' There was now a clanking noise together with the throb of the engine. 'Let's get away before any more come along.'

We started paddling across the path of the waves, reading them as an indication of the direction of the tide stream. Soon we could make out the shore to the west and shortly we were pitching out into the bigger swell of the Atlantic again. It was a strange experience to be paddling along the coast in these conditions. Keeping outside the surf break, we were often out of sight of the beach. It was a difficult line to follow. Every so often steep green walls of water would emerge from the fog, telling us we were getting too close to the shore, even though that shore was still hidden.

Soon we reached a rocky outcrop, linked to the mainland by the sand. We landed and choosing a bank of shingle in preference to the sand, we pitched our tent and settled in for the night. Now we were clear of the entrance to the lagoon, we could be independent of the tide again, for it is weak along the next section of coast. There was something satisfying about having as full a supply of food as we could fit in our kayaks. However, there was a stretch now of some 130 miles before the next coastal village at Vik.

It took us two days to reach the island rock of Ingolfshofdi. We had a back view of the mountains and tumbling glaciers beyond the coastal plain and the insidious chill of the night breeze pouring silently from the icecap, but most prominent was the sand. Dark grey sand, with the white wash of waves dancing constantly at its steep foot. A headwind sprang up and paddling became tedious. Salt water forced its way up my sleeves and weighed heavily at my elbows. I paused to drain the water, holding each cuff open in turn. Then I chased Geoff to recover the lost yards before settling back into a steady paddling pace. I had learnt by now that Geoff became aggravated by headwinds and I could sense his growing frustration. I kept silent for a while and withdrew into my thoughts.

It is at times like this that one questions one's reasons for being there. Is it a case of the end justifying the means, or do periods of discomfort, hard work and disillusionment actually heighten one's appreciation of the really sparkling times? You often have to suffer the rain to see the rainbows. I can remember a friend saying, 'Sea canoeing is about pain. If you don't like pain you won't like sea canoeing.' I wouldn't put it as strongly as that myself, but it does help if you have the ability to tolerate pain; the ability to escape into your thoughts, wherever they may take you, while your body gets down to a bit of hard work. Yet it is surprising how sharp the senses remain during this 'daydreaming'.

A solitary great skua broke the monotony of the sandbank. As we grew close it fluttered, half running, half flying across the sand, tripping into a heap as though it had a damaged wing. 'Shall we have a look?' I asked.

'Why not,' replied Geoff, as eager as me for an excuse to break the tedium. We sank onto the beach on the back of a dumping wave, tumbling out into the water in our haste to run up the beach before the next hungry wave had a chance to bite at us. Dragging the boats clear enough for a few minutes' stop, Geoff ran towards the apparently injured bird. But as soon as he drew close, the skua stretched its wings high, launched perfectly into the wind and flew away.

'Oh well,' I thought, 'It was a good enough excuse to land.'

We unpacked some dried fish and biscuits from our kayaks and climbed the sandbank to look out over the vast black desert that lay behind it. It was a sobering thought that much of this sand was the result of volcanic eruptions beneath the icecaps. The volcano Katla sleeps none-too-soundly beneath the Myrdalsjokul icecap, and according to my research it erupted in 1918 with such heat that the water from the melting ice rushed across the coastal plain at twice the rate of the river Amazon, carrying with it masses of ash and silt. The volcano Grimsvotn, beneath the Vatnajokull icecap, erupted in 1934, melting about 16 cubic kilometres of ice, and again producing an incredible torrent of water. I shivered, partly because of the bite of the cold wind, but also at the thought of what must have been an awesome spectacle. Hopefully we would not have a repeat performance just yet! We turned and ran down the sand slopes, long steps sliding with avalanches of sand to speed our feet towards the ocean again.

After much singing, swearing and aching, we drew near the rock of Ingolfshofdi. Noisy clouds of seabirds circled around us, and seals bobbed and splashed. Ingolfshofdi means the promontory or headland of Ingolfur. Ingolfur was, together with his foster-brother Hjorleifur, the first Norse settler in Iceland. Ingolfur arrived here on the south coast in about the year 874, later making his home in what is now the capital, Reykjavik. We parked our kayaks on the sand at the foot of the rock and scrambled the 200 feet or so to the top of the island. There we found a refuge hut, its red-painted corrugated roof emerging from the turf walls in the same way that the island itself seemed to protrude from the encroaching sand. The inside of the hut was in need of a little cleaning, but there were bunks and a roof, so we decided to stop there rather than pitching the tent. It would be a luxury for us to have so much room.

Our main requirement now was water. After some searching we discovered a well. It was lined with wooden barrels sunk into the ground, and it smelled pretty bad. The water was rather brown in colour, but it was free of salt and both of us had drunk worse. Since we boiled most of our water for hot drinks and cooking, there was unlikely to be any problem so we returned to the kayaks to collect what was necessary for our stay. All the while we were surrounded by wheeling gulls and fulmars and were easy targets for great skuas. The latter became so persistent in their attacks that it was a great relief to retreat into the hut to escape their attentions. Inside we found a long-handled fowling net, rather like a gigantic butterfly net. We were tempted to use it to put an end to the skua attacks, but they were only defending their territories and it was only right that we should avoid disturbing them. Geoff took a few practice swings in the air with the net, looked thoughtful for a moment and then strode off in the direction of the cliffs. I suppose that like most activities, fowling needs practice and what looks easy when performed by an expert is actually quite difficult for a beginner. Certainly, according to Geoff's account, one swing of the net and every bird in the area fled! His next attempt was to scale an easy section of cliff to approach some herring gulls nesting at the top. This was fraught with its own hazards; as he neared the top he discovered a fulmar sitting on her egg, and as his head drew level she spat out a jet of foul-smelling oil onto his head. When he returned from his expedition clutching two herring gulls, he was scowling and in a foul mood; all I could do was laugh as he recounted the tale.

He had regained his normal composure by the time he had found his soap, however and he hurried away towards the sea to wash his hair. Despite his attempts to rid himself of the fulmar oil, the bird had left a lingering and pungent smell that persisted for days. Geoff had the last laugh on me however. I decided to skin the birds rather than plucking them. I removed the head of one and was running my fingers around the still warm carcass between the skin and the body to ease the skin off, when the pressure of my hands forced the air out of the bird's lungs, giving out a loud squawk! I dropped the bird with a start and stared at it for a moment in disbelief. I gingerly picked it up again to resume where I had left off and was for a second time startled by a loud cry. As I began to realize what was happening, Geoff collapsed on the grass, helpless with laughter. I had evidently removed the head leaving the voice box in the neck attached to the body.

Later, we tried what was for us a new culinary experience; herring gull curry, served with rice and chapatis. Not a common dish but certainly one that proved very palatable.

It was at about this time that we started having difficulties with our tiny petrol stove. It would not burn properly, producing a weak yellow flame and a sweet sickly smell. Our attempts to dismantle the stove with a pair of pliers in the absence of a spanner only resulted in burring the edges of the brass nut. In the end, Geoff used brute strength on it and it succumbed to the pounding he gave to it with a hammer and screwdriver. Inside we found the pipes and wick choked with a thick black tar. We cleared the pipes as best we could, and the stove burned powerfully again for a while. It was not until several weeks later that we discovered the cause of the trouble. It lay with the plastic container Geoff was using to carry the fuel. It seems the petrol was dissolving the plastic, which then left the tarry residue when burned in the stove.

I stood alone on a corner of the island looking out across the dark sea of sand towards the distant mountains. I felt a certain snug security here, surrounded by thousands of sea birds. Sheep scrambling over the roof of the hut had woken us this morning, and below me now seals were cavorting with one another in the crystal clear sea. Yes, I could imagine Ingolfur standing here all those years ago thinking to himself that this rugged oasis would serve well as a home for a while. His foster-brother Hjorleifur had landed further to the west with ten slaves that he had taken in Ireland. By the following spring Hjorleifur lay dead, slain by his slaves who then fled with their wives to a group of islands. Ingolfur discovered the body of his foster-brother, and seeing that his boat had gone, guessed where the slaves had gone. He found them and killed them all. Many jumped from the cliffs to their deaths rather than face his sword. The islands have ever since been known as the Westman Islands, the 'West men' being the Irish. Ingolfur then went on to settle on the west coast of Iceland at what is now Reykjavik. Our own travels lay in the same direction. Ingolfshofdi is the last solid land before the next coastal village of Vik, eighty-five miles to the west. Between here and Vik would be just sand—black sand, with no natural shelter for the wind. Apart from the few shipwreck shelters it is unshaped by man and seldom visited. I stood and savoured the view.

Back on the move again, huge flocks of guillemots parted at our approach, skittering ahead to reform in dense groups again. The whirring sound of purposeful wingbeats accompanied the plump auks criss-crossing overhead and the calm dark eyes of fulmar petrels regarded us as they swept effortlessly past in graceful curves, almost brushing the water with their wing-tips. Then we rounded the last corner of rock and saw ahead the dark sands extending into a hazy distance. As we drew away from Ingolfshofdi, so the birds thinned until we were alone with a grey sky, grey sea and grey sand. We began to paddle by the clock. Two hours of paddling, then a short stop with a bite to eat. Another two hours of paddling and another stop, and so on. In that way we were always paddling towards a measurable goal. The scenery certainly did not change. Our charts marked river entrances, but there was no sign of them. Possibly they had been blocked by shifting sands, or had dried up. The only positive landmark we passed was a shipwreck shelter. Now after six and a half hours of paddling Geoff spotted a square object speeding along the beach. 'Can you see it?' he asked. 'What do you reckon it is? A jeep perhaps?'

I could see it, but I was also unsure what it was. We peered at it as we gradually drew nearer, in the end deciding that it must be a shipwreck shelter. The movement must have been an illusion caused by the scudding rain clouds and rolling surf. Without anything against which to judge distance or size in such a featureless landscape we were uncertain until we were quite close. The sighting was encouraging. If this was the second hut then we should reach a third one in about an hour, and there we could stop for the night. Paddling seemed a lot less tedious than I had expected. The rhythmic tune of 'Sunshine Superman' skipped along with my paddling rhythm and occasionally I burst out into song with the few words that I knew. Geoff would join in and we would end up singing a duet into the vastness of the grey day.

It was half past midnight when we spotted the hut we were looking for, seemingly speeding along the sand like the previous one. The surf was heavy, but sitting out beyond the break we could make out what seemed to be a submerged sandbank that was causing the waves to break heavily and then reform again at a more acceptable size as the water deepened again behind the bar. We skirted round the end of the bar with massive breakers rolling in to our left and then cut in behind the bar, sneakily avoiding the full power of the surf. However, after we had ploughed up onto the sand and scrambled from the kayaks we discovered that a river lay between us and the hut. Great boils of dark grey sandy water erupted as the powerful current rushed across the beach. We gingerly tested the depth and found that the bottom was scoured into deep pools and ridges, so we went well upstream, launched and paddled across, our kayaks sweeping back towards the surf as we struggled across to the security of the far bank.

We looked around for a suitable place to leave the kayaks. The almost black sand not only stretched as far as we could see along the coast in each direction but it appeared to stretch just as far inland too. Great sun-bleached logs, green glass fishing floats gleaming in the rain, fish boxes and other debris lay scattered as far as the horizon. How far up the beach would the sea reach at high tide? Would we have to carry the kayaks all the way up to the hut? We carried them a long way towards it, but it became obvious that it was even further away than it had originally appeared, so we laid the kayaks side by side and tied them together. Geoff drove a stake deep into the sand and secured the line to it. It might possibly help prevent the kayaks from blowing away in the wind, but it was more a token gesture. We trudged along the wet sand to the hut. This was a neat square structure painted bright red and supported on stilts to prevent the sand from building up around it. A pile of plastic debris had gathered in the hollow scoured out by the wind.

We climbed the open wooden staircase and opened the double doors, stepping into the stillness of a single dark room. As our eyes accustomed themselves to the light we could make out a couple of tables, benches, folding beds, survival rations, first aid kit and bible, items stored there for the use of any seamen unfortunate enough to be wrecked upon this inhospitable shore. A vision of a fishing vessel riding out a storm in the darkness of the northern winter, forced upon a shore so low and flat that

20

even radar cannot warn of its lethal proximity, flashed through my mind. The wrecks of dozens of such vessels lie buried in the ever-encroaching sands, their unfortunate crews perhaps surviving the trauma of shipwreck only to perish on the shelterless sands whilst searching for help. It was the frequency of such disasters, with often whole ships' crews found huddled together on the sand dead from exposure, that prompted shipping companies to contribute funds to build and provision a series of coastal shipwreck shelters. These have paid for themselves time and again in the saving of lives. On the wall was a mounted chart showing the position of the hut and a route to the nearest farm some eight miles inland. Geoff struck a match, and lifting the glass of a paraffin lamp, lit the wick. In the warm glow we could now see that everything was coated in a layer of grey dust. It took some willpower to turn our backs on the cosy shelter and trudge through the rain to our kayaks to fetch the necessary gear for the night, but the pleasure of dry clothes and a meal cooking in the hut banished any discomfort.

The following morning we flung open the double doors to reveal a dismal scene of heavy driving rain. The surf thundered and the low clouds, together with the dark sand, seemed to swallow the daylight. We hung out some containers to collect the rainwater that was streaming down from the roof and returned to the shelter to cook breakfast. Then with our water bottles full, there was nothing but our reluctance to keep us from leaving. 'Oh! This is gorgeous!' I shouted, as I pulled my wet and sandy fibre-pile clothing over my dry body. In truth I detested mornings like this when everything was cold and wet. I knew that I would be soaking wet for the rest of the day, and if it continued to rain like this then I would probably be cold too. My most acute discomfort now over, I stood and grinned as Geoff went through the same spasms of self-torture. Finally we gathered our bags of gear, shut the double doors behind us and meandered through the driving rain towards the kayaks.

There was little loading to do, but the rain made sandy pools in the hatches and the cockpits were inches deep in water. I cursed as cold water ran down my neck and dripped off my nose while I crouched to bail out the water, and then we carried the heavy boats down to the sea. The river seemed to have swollen since last night and was now a raging torrent with line upon line of standing waves. The sea was rough. I could not see beyond the first few massive lines of surf. We sized up the situation and decided that the river would probably help us out through the surf, although it did not seem to have any calming effect on the water.

We launched from the sand into the river and were swept rapidly down through the strange currents and head-on into the surf. For a moment, all went well, but as I struggled through successively bigger waves I found that the great grey walls of water were breaking with startling power. I was still far from open sea. I piled into a massive pillow of heavy foam and found myself carried backwards with the nose of my kayak pointing skywards. I twisted into a sideways brace and noted with relief that Geoff was not in my path. By the time I had freed myself from the wave I was back near the beach and had lost my hard-earned ground. I started paddling back out again. The steep crashing waves were breaking close behind one another. There was little time to recover after one wave before the next crest thundered down. The kayak exploded through one crest, lunged into the air and crashed down into the base of the next wave, its steepening wall about to collapse. Trapped in the falling water I clung onto my paddles and was bounced shorewards again.

Geoff was now further out than me and struggling to hold his position. It really did not look as though we would be able to get out through the surf today. As I watched I saw him start up the face of a wave. The top of the wave was beginning to collapse and as Geoff piled into the breaking water he disappeared almost completely. Long moments later the point of his yellow deck launched skyward from the foam and he was flung backwards in a spectacular back loop. Then all was hidden again. It was a few minutes before I could see him again. He was clinging to the end of his upturned Vyneck, swimming it towards the shore. I manoevred close to check that he was all right but he was swimming strongly and was soon ashore. It did not take us long to decide to call it a day. The hut seemed even more inviting now. In the soft lamplight, a cup of chocolate in my hand and the roar of the surf now muffled I felt utterly contented.

The next morning I awoke to see Geoff disappearing through the door in a hurry. He returned with the news that our kayaks were full of wet sand and that the surf was still big. While we boiled up some porridge for breakfast, we checked the weather again. The wind seemed to be freshening from the south-west. By the time we were ready to change, the wind had definitely increased and we decided to stay where we were and busied ourselves with cleaning the hut.

Rather than waste the rest of the day I decided to follow the route marked on the wall chart and try to find a shop and buy some more food. Unfortunately the freeze-dried meals we had brought from home for this stretch of the coast had been chewed by mice while we waited for the ferry in the Faroe Islands, and we could get nothing similar here. Consequently the food we carried was more bulky and by now we had almost run out. Geoff was reluctant at first but finally agreed to come. We set off across the sand at about 1.30 p.m. following a line of poles from the hut. The area was bleak. The strong wind coming off the sea carried waves of dry sand past us, filling our trainers with sharp granules. Here and there the white bones of bleached driftwood, smooth from years of sanding, pointed gnarled fingers at the sky. We reached a few tufts of coarse grass which rose into huge hummocks, curving like the backs of green hairy mammoths twenty or thirty feet high. Still following the marker poles we emerged from the hairy hills onto the shoreline of what appeared to be an enormous lake, so wide that we could not see an end to it. Stretching into the distance across the lake was a single line of forty-gallon oil drums, painted red and yellow.

'Well!' said Geoff. 'Either it's pretty shallow water, or we're going to find that they've stacked up great piles of drums! I laughed, pulled off my shoes and socks and waded into a full half-inch of water.

'Not too deep here!' I commented cheerfully. Geoff rolled up his trouser legs and joined me and we splashed along barefoot for a couple of miles chatting idly, nowhere in water more than a few inches deep. Then we stopped and looked around. It appeared as though we were standing on the surface of a huge lake, with water stretching into the distance in all directions. There was just this line of well-spaced painted drums cutting the lake into two. The effect was bizarre. 'You could probably get an Arts Council grant to create something like this!' commented Geoff. 'Not that anyone would come all the way out here to see it.'

I didn't expect to have to wade for four hours, but as the water gradually deepened and reached our knees we felt we had walked so far that there was no point in turning back. The shadowy line of a distant bank appeared and we were desperately looking forward to finding something dry to stand on to warm our freezing feet. But we were disappointed. The bank was simply a waterlogged mass of moss and grass, cut by meandering sandy waterways. A solitary sheep stared at us with disdain as we squelched past, warily avoiding hidden hollows in the moss, into which we occasionally stumbled up to our thighs.

Eventually we reached a tiny house and knocked on the door to ask where the nearest shop was. It seemed the obvious thing to do at the time, but the horrified reaction of the elderly couple that lived there was quite understandable when we thought about it. After all, we were at a remote place, at the end of a long gravel road from the main road, without any transport and looking, no doubt, rather disreputable. If they had spoken English or we had spoken Icelandic, then they could have asked the obvious questions, 'Where have you come from? Where is your car? What do you want? Why are you here?' As it was, we could not understand the questions and they could not understand the answers. In the end the old lady, displaying a touch of genius, picked up the telephone and spoke to the operator. Then she handed the phone to Geoff. The girl at the other end of the line spoke English and acted as an interpreter, explaining to the old lady what was going on. With the explanation completed the old lady visibly relaxed. We were to wait for the postman to arrive and he would take us to the main road, where a local woman would come to collect us. In the meantime the old lady with typical Icelandic courtesy prepared coffee and cake for us.

We had only a few minutes to wait before the postman arrived and then we were away, rattling down the track which led through an ancient lava field, so old that the contorted shapes had become clothed in a grey-green fleece of lichen which hung down in shaggy folds. We were dropped at the road junction, and the van tore away to the east leaving a huge drifting cloud of dust to mark its progress. Minutes later we were in the company of a vivacious lady in a battered Sunbeam car. As she steered adroitly between the worst of the potholes and around the bigger boulders, smaller stones were kicked up by the wheels and smashed against the underneath of the car so violently that clouds of dust would explode from the floor around our feet. It was my first experience of Icelandic roads. This was the newly completed circular route around Iceland; the Icelandic M1 motorway! We were almost too late by the time we reached the shop. With the assistant counting the day's takings, we rushed around grabbing the essentials for our journey and passing by many inviting but expensive items. Then we were back on the dusty road again. Our driver insisted that we return with her for something to eat, assuring us that her son would drive us back to the coast in his Land-Rover. It was to be more than just a meal, however, as before we left she presented us each with a traditional Icelandic sweater, with the circular yoke pattern, and the soft warm wool that we had so often admired in the past. These works of art were knitted by her own skilful hands and became treasured possessions.

Her son did indeed drive us back, crossing the lagoons we had waded through as if in a boat. Geoff attempted to show our gratitude by presenting the lovely lady with a small bottle of brandy that he was carrying to celebrate the completion of our journey. We had little we could give, but she seemed delighted with the offering.

When we finally managed to leave the hut, we still had difficulty forcing our way through the surf onto the open sea, but then we sped along with renewed energy after our few days on land. It was great to be afloat and travelling again. It didn't last long, however. The wind swung round against us and Geoff reaffirmed his dislike of a headwind. So when in the early afternoon we spotted the square shape of what we took to be a refuge hut, we decided to land again. There was a nearby river outlet which helped to confirm our position, but there was no sign of the hut on our chart. The surf seemed much smaller here and we landed with no difficulty, carrying our kayaks well clear of the backwash. But there was no sign of the hut. 'It must be hidden by those sandbanks,' I suggested, so we strolled over to investigate. There was no hut. Instead, there was a massive bone, part of the skull of a whale, with the square upright piece facing out to sea. We burst out laughing. There had been nothing against which to gauge the size of the object, so we had assumed it was a hut because of its shape! We walked around it, scrambled over it and ran our hands over it, feeling the warm irregular smoothness. The square upright was about five feet high and stretching out in front of it were two long curving slabs of bone some eighteen feet long. We were fascinated. After satisfying our initial curiosity we returned to our kayaks for some food, and sat side by side on the comfortable 'settee', our legs stretched out on the horizontal bone and our backs, sheltered from the wind, leaning against the upright. Then, eating over, we unloaded the tent and dug it into the sand, pinning it down with the logs that were scattered along the shore. Then, with such an abundance of wood to hand we piled up a pyramid of small pieces and lit a fire.

After a number of nights spent in refuge huts, returning to the tent put us right back among the elements again. It was warm. The sun beat down on the black sand setting up dancing heat waves, and the tent flapped and flicked sand everywhere. Arriving by kayak seemed to give us an understanding of the true size of the area. To the north-east the skyline consisted of miles of dark mountains and glistening icecaps and glaciers, streaked here and there by showers of rain. Between us and them was the vast emptiness of the coastal plain. I strolled around slowly, looking at cartons and bottles from Europe, logs from Siberia or Norway and glass fishing floats that Geoff thought were from Portugal. I am a compulsive beachcomber, and although I seldom find anything of more value than a box to sit on or wood for a driftwood fire, I live in hope that I might find something of more interest or more value.

Here we were, miles from where we had started, in a completely different world, and with a long journey still ahead of us. In a few days the scenery would change. There would be thousands of seabirds again, and seals, and people. But for the moment I had nothing more important to do than to shuffle my bare feet in the sun-warmed sand and absorb that precious emptiness of the southern sands.

Our journey was a fascinating one. It was about nine and a half weeks before we reached our starting point again at Seydisfjordur, having paddled all the way around Iceland. Our arrival was not the magic moment that we anticipated. Instead it was tinged with sadness. Our reason for being there was gone. Our relaxed timeless existence was over. We could no longer look forward, only backwards to the treasured memories.

The Nile the Wrong Way by Marcus Bailie

One of the few advantages of being in jail is having time to reflect. As we sat in our Egyptian prison we did not have much else to do except wonder how we had got there. For over four months our main aim had been to reach the sea; now it was so close we could almost smell it. We were just 27 miles from the Mediterranean. But we were in custody, contemplating a jail sentence, and all we could do was wait, and reflect on the last few hours, few weeks, few months.

When my involvement in the expedition had started, less than a year earlier, I had not been very enthusiastic about going to the Nile. In my ignorance I had thought of it as a flat river and I was looking for some white water excitement. A few months later we were all still fairly ignorant and ill-informed but I was sufficiently intrigued by what we had learnt to go and see for myself.

Of the team members, I already knew Pete Vickers and Richard May; when they became involved with the Nile idea they invited me to join them. Mike Higginson was the leader and driving force behind the expedition, and he was the only one with any experience of really long river trips. Mike's Australian nationality was also the original justification for calling it The *International* Nile Canoe Expedition. Though thoroughly English, Bruce Tower's claim to internationalism was based on the fact that he was born in Sudan where much of our time would be spent. Dave Shell was introduced to me as 'the team's white water expert', though if even half of what we now heard about the river was true then *everyone* would need to be a white water expert.

We planned to do the trip using open Canadian canoes which are ideal for carrying loads. Suitably modified and with tight-fitting spray decks we hoped they would be able to cope with the long sections of rapids.

Slowly the team grew to eight—the intended size. We were lucky to get a paddling doctor, Tony Laxton, who had a special interest in tropical diseases. Kieren Lee was the last to join. He was not really a canoeist but he had just spent three and a half years cycling around the world and was itching for another adventure.

Sudan Airways agreed to sponsor us by flying us and our equipment out to Africa and P.G.L. Adventure Holidays had provided us with the canoes we would need. We also arranged to take along two lightweight one-man kayaks to act as scout boats on the difficult mountain section at the start of the trip.

With the help of Shirley McConnell who would also be our U.K. secretary while we were away, we had managed to get most of the gear we would need, had picked up a few letters of introduction, had a few radio interviews and even appeared briefly on television.

Mike, Dave and Bruce flew out to Sudan in the middle of September 1978 and the rest of us followed two weeks later. We landed in Khartoum, the capital, which rises uneasily and reluctantly from the desert, a mixture of concrete and mud. The city presented a picture of semi-completion, with a bizarre blend of the new and the old. Along the main streets there were lamp-posts and footpaths but if they were ever used for their intended purpose they certainly were no longer. Market stalls were laid out on the paving stones, and goats were now tethered to the redundant lamp-posts. This type of imaginative vitality pervaded every corner of the city, seeping through the whitewashed brickwork with an odour of excitement. Yet to this vitality we were blind, our eyes seeing only the poverty and our noses sensing only the filth.

A chance meeting with a British businessman, Chris Mortimer, provided us with an expedition base. When he casually started chatting to Bruce in the British Expatriot Club over a whisky and soda and offered him a bit of floor to sleep on, I don't believe he knew what he was taking on. Two weeks later, with eight people and half a ton of expedition equipment all over his flat he was still a bit stunned, and drinking noticeably more whisky.

Officialdom and bureaucracy do not work in the same way in Sudan as they do in Britain. Basically in Sudan they do not work at all. We required dozens of forms, hundreds of signatures and thousands of official stamps, all in a city where the system is incapable of issuing the necessary forms let alone processing them. Amidst this administrative chaos Mike, Dave and Bruce had already spent days on end in crowded offices, getting and showing the all-important letters of introduction, and waiting in stuffy ante-rooms for people who had either gone home or who simply did not want to see them.

Our stay in Khartoum was prolonged by a series of minor disasters which seemed to epitomise Sudan Airways and caused us to refer to them by their local nick-name of 'Inshallah Airways'—inshallah meaning 'if

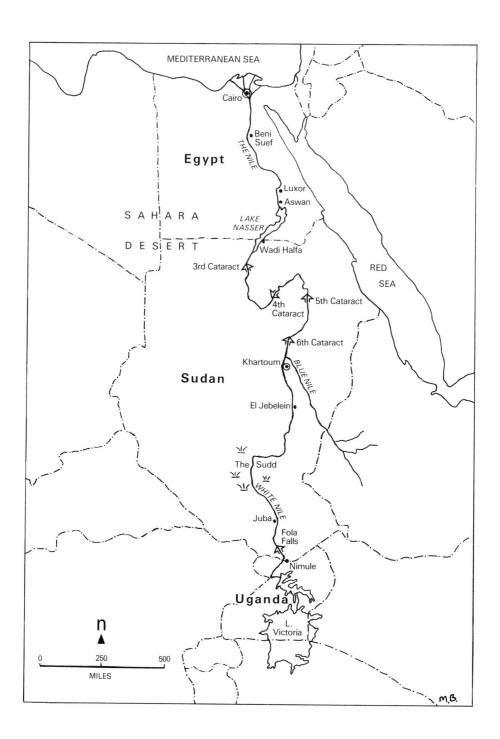

MEDITERRANEAN SEA

Cairo

Beni
Suef

Egypt

THE NILE

SAHARA

Luxor

Aswan

DESERT

LAKE
NASSER

Wadi Halfa

3rd Cataract

RED

SEA

4th
Cataract

5th Cataract

6th Cataract

Khartoum

BLUE NILE

Sudan

El Jebelein

The Sudd

WHITE NILE

Juba

Fola
Falls

Nimule

Uganda

L.
Victoria

n

0   250   500

MILES

M.B.

28

Allah wills it'. There seemed to be a way of life in Khartoum which could be described as cynical fatalism. No one seemed to get flustered by delays and if we were going to survive in this country then the best we could do was to learn to live with it.

Eventually we left the Arab world of Khartoum and deserts behind and headed south into the Black African world of jungle, swamp and bush. Southern Sudan is the poor relation of the North, and there is great friction between them. We bounced down onto the grass airstrips at Juba and passed through the shed which was their air terminal. Juba, the capital of Southern Sudan sprawls for miles over the African bush. Mostly mud huts and mud roads, it is little more than a collection of primitive African villages held together by a glimmer of hope and an inspired local administration. Poverty is a way of life in the south and even in Juba basic commodities like food and fuel are erratic luxuries.

As the last of the rains turned the rich red mud into an ocean of chaos we tried desperately to arrange transport for the final 150-mile road journey to Nimule, our starting point on the Nile. Our AA World Road Map clearly showed a road, and information in Khartoum assured us that trucks and buses used it regularly, so for several days we tried unsuccessfully to convince people in Juba of this. Our sanity was at risk and our resolve showed real signs of cracking. Mike was torn between trying to maintain unity and trying to get on the water. The trip was fast becoming an exercise in manipulating the unexpected and when we eventually found a truck driver prepared to take us to Nimule we hurriedly threw all the gear in the back and rattled out of Juba, still heading south.

The road was in a terrible condition and our ancient truck barely seemed up to the task. The rainy season had wreaked its annual havoc on the structure of the road and clearly our forty-year-old Bedford (still with its original tyres I suspect) had its work cut out. It took two days to reach Nimule during which time we broke down on four occasions, had two punctures, and lost count of the number of times we had to get out and push. Now all we had to do was to find the river and paddle 3,000 miles to the Mediterranean.

The border town of Nimule is where Sudan, Africa's biggest country meets Uganda at that time the continent's most violent. Indeed it was this very political turmoil and in particular President Idi Amin's disturbing habit of shooting unwanted visitors that prevented us from starting at the true source of the Nile in Lake Victoria. A number of small lakes and about 150 miles of river were thus denied us.

An early morning mist hung over the village and the surrounding jungle. We waited patiently inside the dilapidated wooden shack which was the customs post while the local police officer incorrectly copied our names from our passports into a massive register. In the village we were able to arrange for porters and a guide to help us get our small mountain of equipment the few miles to the river. Eventually we were left in a tiny clearing beside the river feeling very much alone with our disturbingly large pile of equipment. There were bags of food and bundles of paddles, cooking pots, ropes, waterproof containers of all shapes and sizes, and to add to the chaos everything was wet from the torrential rain during the truck journey. Through the tall reeds we could see the river steaming past, wide, fast, brown, and immensely powerful.

We had no idea whether we could fit everything into the canoes or not; we had never actually seen it all in one place before, let alone tried packing it. Sorting and drying, packing and repacking took until early afternoon, but at last the three large Canadian canoes and the two small kayaks were ready. There seemed no point in delaying any longer so we climbed aboard and pushed out through the reeds onto the fast-moving current.

We were amazed, then and later, by the speed and volume of this river. In our ignorance we had expected head waters; we found a massive torrent. It was the beginning of October, the end of the rainy season and the river was in maximum spate. For the first few miles we were swept along at great speed, each of us wondering what on earth we had let ourselves in for. We were all nervous, tense and shaky, both physically and mentally, and each of us watched the others to see if anyone had spotted the lack of control.

Inside Uganda the river is comparatively flat but from Nimule it plunges down through a steep valley and out of the mountains to Juba and the plains and swamps of Southern Sudan. The local villagers (and even the map) call the Nile in this area *Bahr-el-Jebel*—'River of the Mountains'. The map showed many rapids and falls, and the river had an awesome reputation. We had been assured that if the rapids did not get us then the hippopotamuses and crocodiles would!

After only a few miles, and before we had had a chance to settle down we arrived at our first major obstacle. Fola Falls proved to be more ferocious than even the rumours had suggested. From a width of over a hundred metres, the river narrows down to less than thirty before it plunges over the edge of an escarpment to crash some fifty feet below. Despite our bitter disappointment there was no question of running the falls, and we made our preparations for the long portage around it. Perhaps the rest of the rumours would be true as well; perhaps it was like this all the way to Juba. Suppose we came on the next one without warning? We had come hoping for big water and now it was too big. We trudged through the jungle in despair.

We saw our first hippopotamus as we struggled with our loads. He was on the far side of the river and only his head showed above the water. He looked enormous, yet despite his massive size he seemed at ease with the river, whereas we were struggling with it.

We found a suitable launching place near a small village and set up camp there. It was chaos. Our trappings of civilisation were strewn everywhere as we made a pitiful attempt at cooking a meal. A few of the local villagers looked on in amazement at our incompetence. Like the hippo, their lifestyle is simple and totally in tune with their environment. Once more, sophisticated and uninformed we were making a poor job of things.

We were in our usual state of confusion again next morning as bags and bundles refused to fit where they had fitted the day before. Once on the water the river was rougher and faster than it had been above Fola. The large waves and fast current were familiar features to us, although here the scale of things was bigger, but we were all largely unprepared for the enormous size of the boils and whirlpools to be found at the bottom of each rapid—a feature of big volume rivers.

Disaster struck at the very first rapid of any note, and Tony and Pete found themselves in the water holding onto their capsized canoe, victims not of the waves and rocks of the rapid but of the boils and whirlpools beneath, which had clawed and sucked at the canoe until it had capsized. Dave and I had seen the capsize from our kayaks positioned at the bottom of the rapid and between us we were able to tow the swamped canoe to the bank. With some difficulty we got the canoe emptied and the slightly shaken Pete and Tony back in. The whole incident had taken a little over two minutes.

We were very lucky; we hadn't been attacked by anything, we hadn't damaged the canoes, we hadn't lost anyone and nothing very serious was missing. At least we had proved that rescuing one of these heavy craft from the water was possible, but having had one capsize in the first hour on rough water I began to wonder how long we could survive.

The same pattern of rapids with whirlpools and boils continued for the rest of the morning, but we had no more swims. The rapids were frequent—every half-mile or so—with the turbulence below continuing for hundreds of metres. At most of the rapids the kayaks with their greater manoeuvrability could safely scout ahead, checking the line and looking for rocks, large stopper waves or boils. If the line looked reasonable we would signal to the others in the Canadians to follow.

On the harder sections of the river we had to try to find a route near the bank where we could sneak the heavy Canadians through in comparative safety. On some stretches we were even forced to lower the Canadians down the rapids using ropes or to portage along the bank if the thick jungle vegetation allowed. This cumbersome procedure of hauling and manoeuvring was both exhausting and time-consuming and we could spend an hour or more on a section of rapid which could have been run in seconds.

Exhaustion rather than time or distance signalled the end of each day's paddling. Erecting tents, lighting fires, collecting wood or pumping river water through the purification filters all seemed strangely relaxing after the long day on the water. We were relieved that it was over, but concerned about the next day. Each evening our camping routine became a little more organised, and our enjoyment of our surroundings more intense.

From time to time we saw hippopotamuses sink below the water far in front, or we would hear their whale-like blowing as they surfaced some distance behind. We had the occasional sighting of a crocodile, but like the hippos they only watched from a distance, seemingly as suspicious of our presence as we were of theirs.

In the first four days after leaving Nimule we covered only 25 miles. We had hoped to do 20 miles daily, and soon we would start to run out of supplies. Already our sugar, our main source of fast energy, was running low. On the fifth morning we encountered some of the biggest rapids so far, and the afternoon was not much better. Our nerves and our gear were at breaking point and the river showed no sign of relenting. That night as we sat around the fire with the jungle noises around us we agreed that we could not continue like this. To lose a boat now would be the end of the trip for two people before the journey had really begun. We had 3,000 miles to do; it was madness to waste everything on the first few, but none of us wanted to give in. There were disagreements, arguments, sullenness.

Reluctantly it was accepted that we must take the Canadians off the river at Shukoli, some miles downstream where our map showed a road, and somehow transport them back to Juba. We hoped that the kayaks would be able to continue to Juba by river in some sort of a lightweight dash but discussion on that would have to wait.

Ironically the river was better behaved the next morning, and we reached Shukoli without incident. However the large cotton plantation there had long since reverted to jungle and the nearest road we now discovered was eight miles away. We found a tiny scattering of huts a mile or so inland and using broken Arabic, attempts at the local dialect and sign language, we managed to hire porters for this unexpected carry.

In the end it was decided that Pete and I, and not Dave and I, would try the lightweight dash in the kayaks. We extracted just enough food and equipment to get us through to Juba, now some 80 miles away and as the others staggered off into the jungle, each canoe balanced on the heads of two porters, Pete and I slid out once more onto the river.

Lightly loaded, the kayaks moved easily over the water and we confidently tackled rapids larger than the Canadians could have safely handled. Huge waves fell on top of us but the little kayaks rode them well. It felt tremendous to be on our own on such an exciting river, with miles to cover and unknown hazards in front. Fear fell away and we felt freed, a part of the river. At last we were like the gazelles and the herons we saw, moving easily in an element we loved.

At the end of the first day we spotted a small village where if nothing else we hoped to find some company. A young girl carrying a water jar on her head screamed and fled; dogs barked and we entered a village in confusion. Despite our strange attire, we were welcomed unconditionally. Food was brought, fresh baked sweet potatoes and cassava, and as we sat around the fire watching our hosts watching us we felt safe for the first time in many days.

The village was no more than a handful of mud huts scattered randomly over a small clearing. Each hut was round and thatched and smoke percolated through the whole of the straw roof, rather than through any obvious hole. Dried fish and corn hung from the edges of the roofs; earthenware pots were stacked outside each hut and by each door the mud was beaten into a hollow by generations of bare feet. Next morning we parted from these people like old friends.

Gugi Rapids, Makedo, and Bedden came and went but they failed to live up to their reputations and we encountered nothing like Fola. Each time we were scared, anxious, ecstatic and finally relieved.

We spent a second night at a similar village to the first and received a similarly friendly and amazed welcome. On the third day the rapids tailed off and the final miles to Juba were flat and very hard work. Enthusiasm returned when we sighted the iron bridge at Juba; we would not see another for a thousand miles. Back in the sanctuary of Juba we gave way to our exhaustion and ate and slept for two days.

As it turned out the other six had encountered much greater problems than we had. The porters had gone on strike and it became necessary to do the carrying in shifts, which took a day each way for each load. In all it took them five days to reach the road and to arrange for a truck to take them back to Juba where the eight of us swapped stories and made preparations for the next stage of the journey.

The Sudd was our next major obstacle. Throughout the early exploration of the Nile the swamps of the Sudd, possibly the largest area of swampland in the world, had impeded travel up and down the river. For 600 miles there is nothing but papyrus, reeds and floating Sudd grass. Early travellers had either gone around the Sudd or in later times had tried the crossing in paddle steamers. No one had ever tried the crossing by

33

man-powered craft. The modern traveller now takes the steamer which plies a regular trade between Bor and Malakal, if anything in Sudan can be described as regular.

Time was becoming crucial for us so again we agreed to split. Four of the team took the steamer through to Malakal and started to paddle from there, thus ensuring the progress of the expedition towards Khartoum. The remaining four, Mike as the expedition leader, Tony as expedition doctor, game for anything, Pete and by a very close margin, myself, were to spend a few days in Juba trying to arrange for a guide to lead us through the Sudd. If we failed we too would go by steamer.

This time we struck some much-needed luck for Joseph Lagu was back in town. We had a letter of introduction to him from a retired Irish missionary who years earlier had been his teacher. Fortune had smiled on the young Joseph for he had risen to being Major General Joseph Lagu, President of the High Executive Council of Southern Sudan, and Vice-President of the whole country. Lagu was one of the Southern men of vision, struggling to keep his country out of famine and civil war. We were granted an audience.

While he talked secretaries prepared letters of introduction to the Commissioners of the various provinces we would pass through along the river. Everything for the Sudd crossing would be arranged for us in the small town of Bor, on its very edge, and some hundred miles downstream.

Within a couple of days we were on the river again. We had abandoned our kayaks in Juba; they had done their job well but now the entire team would be paddling the open two-man Canadian canoes. There were very few trees now and even fewer people. The villages that we did see were of the cattle-raising Dinka tribes, an immensely tall, friendly people who even towered over our 6ft 6in doctor. Their animals are raised for esteem and status within the tribe and never killed for food. In a bad year people and cattle perished together.

We camped each night on the increasingly rare patches of solid ground, worried by the number and size of the hippo tracks which seemed to cover the sites. At night we could hear them crashing through the reeds, frighteningly close. It was humid, and at night we were tormented by mosquitoes as we tossed and turned through sleepless hours often to the sound of distant Dinka drums. Yet despite the discomfort I was fully content. There was something compelling about what we had started.

At Bor we made contact as instructed with the local Inspector from the Department of Wildlife, Mr. Joseph. Everything had been delegated to poor Mr. Joseph, who clearly had no idea how he was going to find us a motorized launch to act as a support boat let alone the fuel which would be required to get it to Malakal. After a couple of days a launch was found. It was ideal; open-topped, 15ft long, shallow draught with an outboard engine. We stocked up on enough fresh food to last for two weeks and enough flour and dried dates to last a lifetime. Our guide, we were told, would meet us on the morning of our departure.

On the appointed day we assembled at the waterfront with our now familiar array of bags and bundles and met our guide. He grudgingly introduced himself with the one word 'John' and from the start it was clear that he intended to do nothing except guide. Presumably he disapproved strongly of our venture and in particular of his involvement in it. I say presumably for in all the time he was with us he made no attempt to communicate. He claimed to speak no English and found sign language beneath his dignity. Moreover he claimed to know nothing about engines and refused to drive the launch.

The four of us took turns at driving the launch while John sulked in the bow and the other two paddled one of the canoes. It was bit of a compromise but at least we were back on the water. We had no real idea whether one barrel of petrol was going to be enough for the 600-mile crossing; no idea of the terrain nor the speed of the current, and not a notion of where or how we would sleep during the coming days and weeks. There was, however, a clear channel to follow and a good current carried us along, so things started well. Giant reeds and exotic ferns rose twenty feet or more on either bank, and little floating hyacinths swirling along beside us vied with the multitude of birds for colour.

At night we slept in the bottom of the canoes with mosquito nets tucked round the rims of the cockpits to keep out the swarms of mosquitoes which appeared just before dark and stayed until just after sunrise. We tried tying up to the bank at night but great islands of floating grass ripped us from our moorings. In the end we just drifted and slept, hoping that a steamer would not squash us in the night. Of the many stupid things we did on that trip, drifting through the Sudd at night was certainly the most dangerous. We saw the steamer three times in all and each time it was during the day. A night-time encounter did not bear thinking about.

Space was limited and we had to cook with the primus stove on top of the 55-gallon barrel of petrol, thus adding death by fire to the growing list of dangers we were facing.

The current remained powerful and the channel was clear to follow as it weaved its way through the high reeds and swamp grasses. Working hard and eating well we could cover 50 miles a day with perhaps another 20 drifting at night. However, towards evening on the third day the launch's engine spluttered to a halt. It was not the first time but on this occasion changing the plugs did not help. The next morning we applied our collective ignorance to the problem, but without success.

We could not just abandon the launch for both cooking and sleeping would have been quite impossible without it. Besides without it there would have been nowhere for our grumbling guide to sit, though we even considered abandoning him as well! The only solution was to strap one canoe to each side of the launch and paddle the whole unwieldy contraption. It was slow but in the strong current we made progress.

As always a routine developed, a routine which became a way of life, and in the days that followed there was little to break it. At any one time two people were paddling, one in each canoe, another person was steering and the fourth eating or resting. Health was a problem as first one person then another picked up a touch of a fever, but somehow we managed to keep enough people active to operate the system. No one grumbled when they had to do someone else's share of the work. We worked hard when we were fit and did what we could when we were not.

We made progress steadily, day after day, until the winds came. Headwinds, sometimes very strong, would blow up during the morning and continue until late afternoon. It was very hard and sometimes impossible to paddle our cumbersome raft against it and at times we just tied up to a floating island and went with the current. Malakal was getting closer but at a very slow rate.

On our ninth day in the Sudd we sighted a tiny village. It was the first dry land we had seen in eight days and we celebrated by buying a chicken. By the eleventh day we were close to exhaustion. I don't believe I have ever thrown myself into anything with such force and anger. Our determination was almost tangible, but we were losing. We sighted another village and dejectedly pulled in. We must admit defeat, abandon out efforts to cross the Sudd, and wait for the next steamer. When the villagers told us that Malakal was only two miles away, however we collapsed with joy. We had made it after all. We had crossed the Sudd. We slept in the village that night relieved and exhausted and paddled the remaining two miles to Malakal the next morning.

On first impression Malakal was a wealthier town than anything we had seen south of the Sudd, though it was still built largely from corrugated iron and mud. It is a trading town, the main steamer port between Sudan's Arab north and its African south. There were white-robed Arab men in the streets with turbans and beards, and bejewelled women, colourfully dressed and beautiful. But there were naked children as well, half starved and begging; poverty existed here too.

Malakal did not provide the rest and hospitality we had hoped for. We arrived on the first day of a five-day Muslim holiday and everything was closed. John predictably disappeared and, exhausted though we were, we left the next day.

We had company on the river now. There was the occasional trading steamer en route to Kosti, and a growing number of the white-sailed Arab feluccas. The river was sluggish and at times many hundreds of metres wide. As we watched the feluccas move easily upstream, we had a growing suspicion that we were attempting the Nile the wrong way; perhaps we should be going upstream with the wind instead of downstream with the current.

After a few days of growing headwinds it became apparent even to our stubborn minds that our efforts were becoming futile. To add to the problem Pete's shoulder, wrenched on the final push to Malakal, was getting steadily worse. As a last attempt to beat the wind and to give Pete's shoulder a chance to heal we switched to a nocturnal system. The nights were quiet and perfectly still and so while three of us paddled, Pete was able to catch a few hour's sleep perched in the bow of one of the canoes. In the morning when both the sun and the wind came up quickly we would land and set up camp. Then while Pete set about the domestic chores Tony, Mike and I would collapse into an exhausted sleep.

This was another gruelling part of the trip. We had been on the river without a proper rest for six weeks and Nimule seemed a lifetime away. We sometimes paddled for thirteen hours a night, yet in the baking heat of the day we could barely get enough sleep to keep us going through the following night. We would wake still feeling exhausted, eat, clear up and be on the water by five in the evening.

Each night the sun would set, large and orange, at 5.30 p.m. It sank quickly, almost vertically, and by six o'clock it was quite dark. For an increasing period each night there would be no moon and we would see a wonderful and complete star-scape. Then, at first hardly distinguishable from the orange glows of distant fires, the moon would creep timidly into the eastern sky. Slipping from one auburn cloud to the next it gained courage and strength, casting its clear silver light over the water. We paddled often in silence, overwhelmed by the unfolding drama above. Slowly the stars would fade and the east would send out orange and crimson precursors of the dawn. The colours spread further across the sky until only a single star remained sentinel in the east, as though supervising the preparations for the entry of some great celestial queen. Only when all was ready, the greens and crimsons arranged in order, and the whole sky modulating from the silver grey of night to the silver blue of morning would she deign to enter the scene, defiant and strong. She quickly discarded her robes of banded red and orange, and rose higher to unashamed yellow and higher still to bright white solar light. The moon, caught unawares and each night further from the safety of the horizon, faded into transparency. Night after night we watched this procession, always magnificent, always different. It was the only world we knew now.

We passed the towns of El Renk, Geiga and later El Jebelein where twin peaks rise above the flat plains to mark the border between Northern and Southern Sudan. We hoped to catch the others at Kanana, the European-run sugar plantation near Kosti where they intended to stop for a few days, but as we grew closer the wind started to blow in the night as well. We grew irritable and lost our self-confidence as the wind debilitated us mentally and physically. Once more we were fading, but somehow we managed two weeks of night paddling until finally we reached Kanana in a state of extreme exhaustion.

Dave, Bruce, Kieren and Richard had been at Kanana for nearly a week when we arrived. They had had their own adventures and there were numerous stories to swap. There were letters and parcels from Britain, but mostly Kanana offered facilities for complete rest. We slept and ate for a couple of days before even thinking about our plans for moving on.

The advance group had waited for us at Kanana because there were important decisions to be made. We were well behind schedule and our deadline for being back in Britain was fast approaching. We had agreed to appear as one of the 'exhibits' at the annual Crystal Palace Canoe Exhibition in February to give our sponsors some publicity and return for their investment. Now we were divided between our loyalty to them and completing the trip. There was much talk of another split. A fast group would do as much of the river as they could in the time available whilst the others would, if at all possible, complete the whole journey. Exactly how the split would be made, or indeed whether it was necessary, would be decided finally at Khartoum, now only 200 miles away.

Back on the river everything was different. We were entering a new land, an inhabited land, a fully Arab land. Random towns and villages were scattered along the bank; flat-topped houses rising out of the dust and crumbling back to desert. There were palm trees and herds of goats. We joined cargo barges and paddle steamers moving up and down the river, and ancient metal and wooden ferries scuttling back and forth across it, precariously overloaded and brilliantly coloured. Our little group was different too. Each of us had been used to working in a team of four; now we were a team of eight. It was not a problem of personalities, just numbers. Camping, cooking, paddling, shopping, all were more cumbersome. There was often tension, sometimes over serious matters, sometimes over trivia, and there were arguments and bickering—something neither group had encountered on the trip so far.

By El Duem Pete's arm had worsened to the extent that he would have to come off the river. Richard, who was also weakening, felt that he should also come off. It was a difficult decision for both of them, as they set about looking for a truck to take them and their canoe on to Khartoum.

Our progress improved by degrees, but strong headwinds, the complete lack of current and finally the debilitating effects of a bout of amoebic dysentery began to devastate our good mileage. Our fiftieth day on the river came and went, as did Bruce's birthday, neither with much celebration. By the time we reached Khartoum nearly two weeks later we were down to an infuriating 15 miles a day.

We arrived bedraggled, bearded and sunburnt. Dressed partly in worn-out European clothes and partly in Arab or African dress we pulled our boats up on the bank in front of the Khartoum Hilton Hotel and rather timidly entered its grand portals.

Since our first visit to Khartoum we had learned a lot about the language, the people and the customs and we now felt relaxed in the streets and local markets, the souqs, of Khartoum. It was all more familiar than before, comforting, welcoming. We became absorbed in the whole teaming mass of activity, getting food and tiny gems of experience, pleasantly and at random.

Almost as a matter of course now the expedition agreed to split once more into two groups of four. The groups were formed by mutual consent. I found myself in the front group with Dave, Kieran and Tony. Our aim was to see how far we could get before flying home in time for the International Canoe Exhibition. The other group would follow at a slower pace and try to complete the river.

For 700 miles from Khartoum to Lake Nasser the Nile, swollen now by the added volume of the Blue Nile, threads it way through a number of barren and sun-baked mountain ranges which turn the temporarily placid river into a torrent again as it twists through narrow gorges and drops and plunges down to the plains of Egypt. The ancient Egyptians grouped long stretches of these rapids under the name of Cataracts, counting six in all, though some are 60 miles long. Our information about the Cataracts was minimal but it seemed that even the white-sailed feluccas did not sail there. To the best of our knowledge no one had ever tried to take anything as frail as a fibreglass canoe all the way through.

Within a few days of being back on the river our new team were working well. It was a strong team and I felt concerned because I was probably the weakest of the four. Dave was a pillar of strength, physically and mentally. Good hours on the water was the key to good miles and Dave was great at keeping things moving. Kieren was the gentle giant of the team, immensely powerful, quiet and good-natured. Most nights he would not bother with a tent but would sleep beside the fire or when he could find two suitably spaced palm trees he would rock happily in his cherished and much-travelled hammock. In the morning, the personal effects he could find before he sealed up his 'dry-bag' stayed dry and what he came across later got wet. Tony on the other hand was meticulous to a fault, and we joked mercilessly about his unwavering routine.

We had become a part of the river, and the river was our lives. We did not just travel on it now; we lived it day after full day. Ageless we moved together, and it was the river that grew older.

After several days we reached the first of the Cataracts, the Sabaloka Gorge, and known to the Egyptians as the Sixth Cataract since they count upstream. The gorge is 15 miles long and after a remarkably short time we shot out at the bottom of it, having had a very fast ride but with nothing more startling than a few large waves to contend with.

With Sabaloka we entered the mountains proper. There was less cultivation, fewer people, fewer towns. Our maps were inaccurate or at best vague and we travelled for days at a time without being sure where we were. Yet in this wilderness we met with the greatest kindness and the most unexpected hospitality. We would arrive on a deserted beach and sometimes within minutes a small group of people would appear, often timidly, for travellers are not common in this area. There would be warm words and gestures of welcome; frequently glasses of sweet tea would follow, prepared on fires or stoves in some hidden house. If we camped near a village we would be invited to eat with them, and to stay the night. They did not have much but what they had they gladly shared; it was *their* way of life.

The Fifth Cataract was much as we expected, almost the only thing on the entire trip which was. It was wide, perhaps a quarter of a mile across, with long rocky islands and shallow reefs which split and squeezed the river into channels of fast and turbulent water. The Canadians rode the big waves well, but heavily loaded as they were any tight manoeuvring was difficult.

The current remained strong and we managed 40 miles or so a day. On one of these days we passed the true halfway mark, 1550 miles completed. It was 20 December, ten days out of Khartoum and seventy-two out of Nimule. We had time to play such mental games with dates and numbers and in some way or another almost every day could be made significant; the 1,000-mile mark, three months since leaving London, or two million paddle strokes completed (approximately). I also worked out at arbitrary moments of arithmetic that by Cairo we would each have made approximately 5 million paddle strokes, that two canoes could support the weight of a fully grown hippopotamus, and that the River Nile was longer than I cared to think about. The mind turns to strange topics when it has hours to fill. It was all part of the time game.

For me another part of the time game was to play with words, to jumble lines, until I had a phrase, a story, a song. Singing as I paddled was another part of my time game.

> 'Lead me on to the sea, River run from the hills,
> Guide me out across the plains.
> Like a child at play
> I can not say where I go,
> Or if I will come again,
> So River lead me on,
> And lead me down to the sea.'

It would be many more years before I was in a place spectacular enough to inspire a second verse (see page 154).

At Abu Hamed the river turned to the south-west. The current steadily strengthened producing long and frequent rapids and the canyons deepened until we felt sure we were in the notorious Fourth Cataract. Again rocky islands divided and redivided the river. Here and there local villagers would explain which was the best channel, but for the most part we just guessed. One such rapid gave us our second capsize of the trip but with a calm pool several hundred yards below, and no hippopotamuses or crocodiles to worry about it was a very relaxed rescue compared to the time when Tony and Pete had taken a swim above Juba.

The Fourth Cataract continued for two days but when the rapids finally ended the strong current remained as the river threaded its way amongst the all but empty hills. Our campsite one evening, perched high on the bank above the river gave a long vista of hills, desert, and far away the thin ribbon of the river glittered in the fading light. It was one of those perfect moments, and we gazed long and thoughtfully to the horizon and beyond. The following day would be Christmas Eve.

The next evening we were taken in by yet another village, and an evening meal was produced. Neither the forces of Nature nor the Muslim people take much notice of Christian festivals, but we felt strongly the spirit of 'peace on earth, and goodwill to all men' as we ate and chatted and laughed with the men of that small village. We seldom saw the women; they were kept veiled, unmentioned, and at a distance. As a final gesture four rough wooden beds were produced and we slept in style beneath the palm trees. Next morning we were brought glasses of their wonderful sweet tea in bed, and we watched the sun creep above the horizon, heralding a most perfect Christmas morning.

We reached Karima early that day and by evening we were miles beyond. Camped as always by the river and that night we had our own Christmas celebrations with local Ariga (a brew distilled from dates), British Dewar's Whisky (kept for the occasion), cigars, beans, fish and sweets. Men from some hidden village joined us and they and their children took part in our singing and revelry. Afterwards we slept pretty much where we lay by the fire, with the roar of the river loud and close. It had been a Christmas unlike any I had ever experienced.

We now had a long haul to look forward to. Inevitably we looked ahead to the next major point on the route, but to look too far ahead was depressing and therefore dangerous. We had learnt not to grab at mental images until we were certain we could hang onto them. Christmas had been our previous focal point and the town of Dongollo was the next, but it was too far away to think about yet, nearly 300 miles. It would be a long haul.

There was no rota for the evening jobs. At some stage in the afternoon someone would volunteer to cook the evening meal and when we landed the rest would fall in to place. Since we cooked entirely on open fires, collecting wood was a high priority. Water for the next day had to be sterilized with iodine, tents had to be pitched, and a hundred other chores done. There was seldom much time to relax. As soon as the meal of lentils, fresh vegetables and rice was over we would put a pot of rice and a pot of beans onto the embers of the fire. By morning both would be cooked. The rice we heated up with powdered milk and sugar into a creamy pudding for breakfast while the beans were stored to be eaten cold with bread for lunch.

In the villages we bought bread when we could and flour to make it when we could not. We bought turbans to keep out the evening cold and Arab *jelebias* to replace our worn and meagre supply of clothes. If the village was far from the river we sometimes returned to the boats on the backs of camels. Without realizing it we were slowly becoming more Arab ourselves and as we grew closer to the country we were travelling through we found we enjoyed the company of its people and the solitude of its open spaces more and more.

It took over a week to reach Dongolla yet even then we stopped only long enough to stock up on rice, lentils, flour, dates, fresh vegetables and whatever else we could find to vary our diet a little.

On the last day of the year we found ourselves back in real Cataract country with the now familiar steep hills, cliffs and rocky islands. That night, New Year's Eve, we finished off the last of the 'festive whisky' and fell asleep to the sound of rapids yet to come. Next morning the distant rumble grew to a terrific roar and we beached the boats to find ourselves at the crux of the Third Cataract, a rapid different in character to anything we had attempted before.

A difficult rocky approach led to a narrow gap in an enormous stopper wave which reached far out into the river. In all, the run would be only 400 or 500 metres but it would be the most technically difficult rapid we had paddled and with extremely serious consequences if we made a mistake. Concentration returned like a fog and blotted out everything but the river. As we walked along the bank studying the line we spoke a few words to each other but did not listen to the answers.

As we paddled the rapid it proved extremely difficult to find our chosen line, let alone keep to it, as we dashed first one way then another across the current, dodging rocks and crashing through waves to the crucial gap in the last stopper. The waves below were so big that even heavily loaded the big Canadians were almost flipped over backwards. At the bottom we collapsed onto the beach laughing and shouting. According to local information this was the last of the major rapids.

As we continued through the last of the Cataract area the villages became fewer and poorer; just a few families trying to scratch a living from tenacious date palms, a small herd of goats, and fishing. The land was barren but hauntingly beautiful. Each day was a novelty; each village a delight; each offered a glass of tea and a brief but valuable insight into a culture we were coming to understand.

On one of these days the mountains grew as the hours passed and by evening we were encased in a deep still gorge with nowhere even to pitch a tent. We paddled on into the gloom with steep unbroken cliffs on either side. It was nearly dark when a final burst of current threw us towards a small village almost lost from sight amongst the rocks and palms. A few villagers came down to see us, and offered us a house for the night. It was a poor village, but they were determined to give us a good welcome. We were touched by their kindness and sincerity, and, poor though they were, they had killed a goat especially for the occasion and prepared not just a meal, but a banquet. It was bitterly cold outside, and a sand storm had blown up. These were wonderful people, and we wondered how we would have survived these harsh days without them. We were trying to survive in the same stern environment, and they could relate to that. We were all river people, one way or another. A couple of weeks more in this country and I might not have left.

Next morning we discovered that the final burst of current the night before had been the death throes of the Upper Nile and we were now on Lake Nasser. At first the lake was only the width of the river and for several days we threaded our way past forgotten hill forts and steep crags. At night we camped in the derelict villages, using fallen roof beams for firewood and giant earthenware pots as tables. In the darkness our fire lit up the walls and our laughter filled the houses for the first time in years.

Late one afternoon we were drawn into a promising looking bay by the sight of a radio mast somewhere between the horizon and our strained imaginations. There had been many such sightings during the previous few days but after an hour this one retained its reality and after a further hour Wadi Halfa appeared at its base. We had reached the end of Sudan.

The new town of Wadi Halfa replaces the old one which was submerged by the rising waters of the mighty Lake Nasser. It survives largely on the Chinese-run fish factory, the railway/steamer connection, and vast quantities of local tea.

The Chief of Immigration was helpful but said that our papers would take some time to process, so since there was nothing else we could do we retired to the Nile Hotel on his advice and joined the rest of the tea-drinking populace. The 'hotel' was more of a glorified eating house with a few rooms at the back which passed as bedrooms. Hire of a mattress to keep the sleeper off the floor was extra. Its main, indeed its only attraction, was that it sold scalding hot milky tea, *chi leban,* all day long and in the evenings was the only place in town, apart from the railway station, to have electric light. It was bitterly cold the whole time we were in Halfa and we took full advantage of the Nile Hotel.

After a couple of days, our exit visas were ready but we were told that our entry visas into Egypt would have to wait until we reached Aswan. This would technically mean entering Egypt illegally but we were assured this would present no problems. No one wanted to know about our request to paddle on the lake so we took that as tacit consent and made our plans accordingly.

The next place of interest would be the ancient temple of Abu Simbel, but even in Halfa no one was sure what we would find there, not even how far it was. Estimates varied from 60 to 120 miles. Our own 1:2 million scale map did not even show it, but then the whole 250-mile lake only took up $6^{1}/_{2}$ inches!

We followed the coast for a couple of days keeping to the more sheltered western side of the lake which had widened to about fifteen miles. Progress was slow and navigation far from easy amongst the numerous inlets and islands. During the day the lake was quite rough so we hugged the shelter, crossing small bays and inlets but keeping close to the shore when the waves were bigger. The wind dropped in the evenings and we would paddle on for a few hours on a perfectly calm lake; the only movement was our own . . .

> '. . . like paddles on ripples
> or waves on a lonely shore,
> or like a stone in water
> we generate waves around us.'

44

Our progress one morning was interrupted by a single rifle shot. On the distant shore we saw two men running from what we had thought was a fisherman's tent down to the water's edge where a third man was still holding a rifle. Fearing that he might have been shooting at us and that he might do the same again we played safe and paddled to the shore. You just don't argue with guns! The figures had looked like scruffy fishermen but they turned out to be Egyptian border guards, the tent the border post and we had just tried to sneak past it!

They may have been about to interrogate us or worse, but first they went through the normal Arab hospitalities. We were given glasses of tea and while we and the other soldiers drank, sitting in a circle on the floor of the tent, the soldier in charge stared blankly at our passports and letters of introduction. Arab fishermen and herdsmen arrived in droves and soon the tent was crowded with people laughing, shouting and offering cigarettes. The name Abu Simbel was mentioned a few times but no one seemed to know how far away it was. It became clear, however, that we were under arrest.

Eventually they decided to take us to Abu Simbel under armed guard and they seemed confident that if we used the canoes we would get there that evening. There was a lot of jostling and shouting as we rearranged our gear so that our 'armed guard', who characteristically forgot to take his rifle along, could travel with us.

We paddled for hours past endless headlands in the gathering gloom. It was well after dark when we reached the lights of the town and by then we were far too exhausted to explain anything to anyone. Our guard agreed and seemed only too pleased to settle instead for a glass of *chi leban*, from Idi, a fisherman friend of his who had a fishing tent pitched on the beach.

A space was cleared for us on the deck of a derelict steamer beached near by. Our guard bade us good night with a cheery 'See you in the morning' and went off to boast to his friends about his canoe ride. It was probably this which alerted the Chief of Police to our existence, for several hours later we were woken rudely by a police squad, some in uniform and some in plain clothes and whisked away in a jeep. We were taken to the police headquarters, a scruffy single-storeyed concrete building looking remarkably like a set from a Humphrey Bogart film. A smartly dressed but tired-looking officer read our passports and documents in silence.

Normally there would have been none of this fuss; indeed in most weeks the normal doziness of the town would have remained undisturbed by our arrival. However on this very week President Anwar Sadat of Egypt, President Jimmy Carter of America and the Shah of Iran were to make a state visit to the temples of Abu Simbel. All normal flights and steamers to this otherwise isolated town had been cancelled, and the town had been sealed off. The border guards it seemed had taken us for Israeli assassins and indeed it was some time before we could convince even the Lieutenant that we were not.

Even then our presence there remained a considerable embarrassment to him. The solution to his dilemma seemed to be to keep us quietly out of the way until after the visit. Eventually in an almost apologetic voice he offered to bring our remaining gear from the beach. 'You are not under arrest, you understand,' he assured us in an uncertain tone, 'but for reasons of security . . . ' And with that he led us to the cells.

It was rather like house arrest and we could move freely from cell to cell. The endless rounds of cards became tedious and each day, in spite of the elaborate and repeated threats of the frustrated Lieutenant, we would 'escape' to make secret visits to the impressive temples, to join Idi for a glass of tea and a chat on the beach, or just for the hell of it.

The approach of the state visit caused obvious turmoil within the police headquarters. The soldiers who were quartered in a single barrack room attached to the jail could be seen trying to smarten themselves up, a task which was hopelessly beyond them. We became great friends, sharing their meals and their jokes when the Lieutenant was not about and we wondered how such a bunch of half-wits ever became an army.

After the State Visit there was still great confusion as to what should be done with us, and the Lieutenant's dilemma deepened until he decided to be rid of us altogether and send us to Aswan. Four days after our arrival in Abu Simbel, therefore, we were taken down to the steamer with our canoes and all our gear to be shipped off to Aswan. As a last act of defiance we escaped once more by jumping overboard to say our farewells to our friend Idi.

Later, as the shore slipped past we realized that in all probability we were seeing it for the last time and as the hours turned to days we independently accepted it. The rest of Egypt was in front of us and it was this which now held our thoughts. After two days we reached Aswan and tied up alongside its famous High Dam. We were keen to continue immediately with our journey now and to put the delays and disappointments of Abu Simbel behind us; but it was not to be, for further detention awaited us. Here, however we were at least free during the day to wander in the town.

Aswan is a tourist town. There are road, rail and luxury steamer connections with Cairo, some 600 miles to the north, and hotels and expensive facilities for all those who make the pilgrimage to this, the furthest limit of tourist travel in Egypt. It could easily be taken for any large town in southern France. Grubby blocks of tenements on the outskirts are followed by roads and avenues with trees down the middle and shabby street-corner cafés where old men drink coffee and play dominoes and backgammon. On the river-front are expensive hotels and tourist shops.

We gravitated naturally to the souq. This at least was not European; it was old, it was Arab, it was friendly. We drank coffee and strolled around the stalls in the dust in the cool of the evening. During the day we visited the temples, or talked to other travellers about conditions in Egypt. We wrote letters and drank more coffee.

It was a low point; we were all tired, agitated, irritable. Even if we were not actually forced to end the trip here in Aswan, the enthusiasm had certainly gone out of it. We were promised travel permits to continue on the river but nothing came of it. We talked about hitch-hiking to Cairo, or going by bicycle. At least that way we would see some of Egypt.

In a small corner café I could watch the people pass by or play backgammon with an old Egyptian, interested enough to teach me the rules and polite enough to almost let me win.

'Another coffee, a kind of comfort to the lost,
a kind of warming to the past.
Scruffy in a tourist town.'

We eventually got our papers one evening and left the following morning.

We were keen to escape totally from the claustrophobic reminders of modern Egypt that first day back on the river and we paddled late into the evening. We arrived at the immense Temple of Kom Ombo as it was being struck by the last rays of the setting sun and it seemed an ideal spot to camp. But this was Egypt, not Sudan and we were moved on by an armed watchman. We slept instead on the beach which was cold, damp and smelt of oil and rotting vegetation, our memories of the warmth and friendliness of Sudan strong in our minds.

On subsequent nights we were joined at our camps by a variety of Arabs who would arrive by walking, rowing across the river or even from feluccas which sailed in out of the night. But these were not the friendly Arabs of Sudan, the givers of tea and cigarettes and hospitality. These were the takers, the wanters, the watchers. From ten feet away they would watch in silence as we unpacked our canoes and set up our camp and our fire. After a while they would ask for some small gift, a bowl, a cigarette, one of our plates or a knife.

The Lower Nile is a tethered river. The High Dam at Aswan ensures that it never rises to dangerous flood levels and much of the bank is faced with great alabaster stones to prevent erosion. The annual floods of Egypt which for 300 generations had brought rich silt to the fertile plains no longer happen. There were even barrages and lock systems on the river.

At Isna we stopped for a wander around the ancient town and temple, and to stock up on food. On the quayside we were challenged by soldiers and since we were not the normal sort of tourists there was much questioning and searching before they were satisfied. It was a procedure we were to go through many times in Egypt.

We found no enjoyment in these large towns. We were jostled by adults and stoned by small children. There was none of the rhythm of river life nor even the friendly smiles and hospitality of small villages. We stopped as little as possible now. Some phantom in our collective conscious was always nagging at us to be gone, to race blindly for Cairo and the sea. We were looking at Egypt with our eyes shut.

Old the river was now, getting on for 3,000 miles old, but it still pushed us along firmly and we could still make 35–40 miles in a hassle-free day. But the days were seldom hassle-free. Rowing boats would come out from the shore to pester us with an oppressive curiosity which we could not easily avoid. When we reached Luxor we stopped for a couple of days to give vent to our growing frustration. With its shops and tourist streets Luxor was another Aswan, but here too are the Valley of the Queens and the Valley of the Kings, resting place for a while for many of the Pharaohs. The Colossus of Memnon is here as is the Ramesseum and across the river near the modern town are the splendid Temples of Luxor and Karnak.

As expected we found in Luxor the world travellers, bejewelled, cashed and cashmered. Solemnly they followed the parade of splendour, guided from temple to tomb in horse-drawn carriages and everything, but everything, for a fee. We on the other hand played the tourist game by different rules. In four months we had degenerated from members of a serious expedition to a bunch of travelling bums. We argued amicably in Arabic with the traders and ate cheaply; we walked or hitch-hiked to the places of interest and at the temples and other sites we usually bluffed our way in free; and at night we slept beside the river. It was like a holiday and as we laughed and joked we could almost see the tension of the last few weeks evaporate.

As we got closer to Cairo the weather got steadily colder. Off the river there was seldom much to be found in the way of firewood on these much-scavenged shores and in the evenings we would huddle around the single primus stove until our meal was finished then retire immediately to bed.

Places to camp were difficult to find; the areas which were not towns were heavily cultivated and we had to make do as best we could. The night before we reached Cairo we failed completely to find any scrap of land to camp on and settled for sleeping on the oily deck of a moored cargo barge. It was the first time we had failed to find a spot to camp since the Sudd.

Our entry into Cairo went totally unnoticed. 'Hail the conquerors' was somehow lost in the early morning mist and smoke. Yet we felt excited as we paddled into the heart of this crowded famous city. In its long and colourful history we felt sure few people could have entered its walls as we now did having followed its lifeblood almost from source. Once more we enjoyed our anonymity.

Soon we were bobbing under bridges, past skyscrapers new and tottering tenements old. Venetian-style *vaporetto* river buses zipped past us unaware of us as the city unfolded and drew us in. Once more we pulled up in front of a magnificent and luxurious waterfront Hilton Hotel; a letter of introduction from the Khartoum Hilton should, we hoped, secure a welcome and an introduction to Cairo bureaucracy. We were a hundred miles from the sea and poised ready for the final push.

At first Cairo seemed too good to be true. The General Manager of the Cairo Hilton agreed to look after our gear while we were in Cairo, and arranged a press and television interview for us. Sudan Airways, our main sponsors, were pleased to see us and put us up in a hotel. It made a nice change from tents and prison cells. Soon however things began to collapse around us. Our hard-won permits from Aswan were only valid as far as Cairo, and try as we might the authorities refused to extend them to the coast, now only two or three days' paddling away. Egypt was still technically at war with Israel and the whole of the Nile Delta had been declared a military zone, even though it contained only a few small towns and a lot of fields.

We were not a serious military threat; everyone agreed with that, so the problem was largely administrative. Four months earlier we had started our venture with an interview with a Vice President. Since then we had moved steadily down the ladder of influence and in Cairo we fell off the bottom. Officialdom could do nothing for us so we chose once again the path of secret defiance. Early one morning, with our canoes lightly loaded, we slipped surreptitiously out of Cairo heading north towards the sea. We planned to paddle past the few remaining towns and bridges at night and if stopped we would just try to bluff our way through using our now invalid permits from Aswan, and our appearance as harmless idiots. Even so it was nerve-racking paddling where we knew we should not be. Memories of Abu Simbel were still fresh in our minds.

We returned to the river as someone confused and rejected returns to an old lover, for comfort and familiar thoughts. After a few miles a fatalistic kind of contentment settled over us all. It was raining but we barely noticed.

Just ten miles out of Cairo the Nile divides; one route goes to Damietta, the other to Rosetta. Just past the divide, on each branch, there is a river barrage and an army garrison. This we thought would be our 'make or break' point. We were challenged by the soldiers at the barrage and taken by them to their headquarters where we stormed from office to office, demanding attention, permission to continue, and an apology—in for a penny, we thought. To our astonishment the bluff worked and we returned quickly to the boats. In the afternoon heavy storm clouds built up into a blaze of thunder and lightning, heightening even further the feeling of drama.

The whole area was pleasantly rural and the few people we met were positively polite and helpful. Was this really still Egypt? Already we were pleased that we had attempted this final push; it was good that our last encounters with the local Egyptian people were pleasant ones.

That evening instead of getting ready for bed after our meal we got ready for night paddling, the sensible option now seemed to be to keep paddling until either we were stopped or we reached the sea. The first few miles in the dark were fun, reminiscent of earlier parts of the trip, but all too soon the weariness set in and our mind games had to be more urgent, more compelling to keep us from falling asleep as we paddled. Home thoughts. But I had been paddling the only home I had for as long as I could remember. The Nile was our life; we knew no other now. The end had come so close now we could almost touch it. This bend, the next. We were there, on the brink of the very last instant. But the bend went on for ever.

The bridges were the most frightening aspect of the night's paddling. They were guarded with machine guns and spotlights, but fortunately the lights were stationary and we did not hear the feared shout or shot which would have brought our efforts to an end, one way or another. Slowly the light of realization that we might succeed strengthened into a grey dawn. This would be our last day. A journey which was too vast to describe lest we destroy it; too long to really understand, was about to end.

We were all in need of a prolonged rest, not to mention breakfast, but we paddled well into the morning before spotting what looked like an excellent place on an island to stop. It was well hidden from view and there was even an old barn we could cook in. Inevitably a trickle of Arabs arrived and soon the barn was packed. From their information it seemed that we had paddled about 65 miles during the night, which meant that with the previous day's total we had paddled over 100 miles in 24 hours; no mean feat for a sluggish old Canadian canoe. Better still it seemed we were only 27 miles from the sea so breakfast was eaten in the midst of great excitement. It was then that the police arrived.

I think we all knew then that it was over, but we carried on with the bluff to the end. We went with the police to the town of El Mahmudiya, just across the river, and to the shabby police headquarters there. A long morning and afternoon of questions and answers followed, phone calls, bluffs and counter-bluffs, but all to no avail. We had paddled over 3,000 miles of one of the world's mightiest rivers and been denied the last 27! For us at least the International Nile Canoe Expedition was over. Maybe if we had waited until later for breakfast, or stopped earlier, or not at all. Maybe . . .

We were in jail again, waiting to find out what was going to happen to us. Yet one of the few advantages of being in jail is that you have time to reflect; on the last few hours, few weeks, few months . . .

There were no official charges, just a reprimand, and we were to be returned to Cairo. With the realization that it was over a kind of relief settled in. I smoked my last Egyptian cigarette on the back of the lorry which took us back to Cairo, and watched Egypt roll past. For the first time in over four months we could really relax and enjoy ourselves.

In Cairo Sudan Airways were tremendous, again providing us with a hotel and showing us the sights of Cairo in style. We were in just the right mood for some fun and so for three days we laughed, sang, let off balloons in the streets, and even climbed one of the pyramids. But for each of us, always in the back of our minds was 'maybe'. All we could do now was hope that the other four, who still had not reached Cairo, might somehow make it to the sea. For us it no longer mattered, we had found things of so much greater importance in the end than any sea could offer.

We flew back to London in a celebratory mood and as arranged set up our stand successfully at the Crystal Palace Canoe Exhibition. Two weeks later we received a telegram from Mike in Cairo and then even the failure disappeared. It read: REACHED MEDITERRANEAN 25th FEB STOP EGYPTIANS FURIOUS STOP I.N.C.E. FULFILLED ALL OB-JECTIVES STOP I.N.C.E. RULES STOP

MIKE.

We did not think they would even have tried once they had heard what had happened to us, and our failure, but somehow they had managed to paddle all the way to the sea. Only Lake Nasser had eluded them. We had left the Uganda border at the beginning of October and towards the end of February had reached the Mediterranean, having between us completed the longest-ever river trip by canoe or kayak.

The Call of the Bio Bio
by Terry Storry

'The Bio Bio[1] is the most dangerous river in the southern hemisphere.'[2]

'There is no way to do this trip unless you go as part of a fully organized and equipped expedition.'[3] So said two leading authorities on the Rio Bio Bio, Chile's largest river. Guaranteed to temper the enthusiasm of most people, these comments were to Jim Hargreaves, ex-head of canoeing at Plas y Brenin and now a bored petrol and canoe retailer, like red rags to a bull. To Jim, chasing unpaid bills and lost orders, the more exciting the challenge the easier it was to forget the view over the forecourt. Thus in the autumn of 1981 a trip down the Bio Bio grabbed Jim's imagination.

Jim and I were close friends. We had just finished writing a guidebook to North Wales,[4] and were paddling (and drinking) together a fair amount. He asked me if I was interested in going to Chile to paddle the river ('Well actually I've got to paint the . . . . did you say Chile?'), and did I know anyone else who would be interested. We thought a team of four would be best. I suggested Dee de Mengel, whom Jim and I had worked with two years previously at Plas y Brenin. He was now an electrician at the Blue Circle Cement factory in Hope, Derbyshire. In our prospectus for sponsorship, Dee described himself as married with no children and living in Hope. Dee brought in our fourth member, a Welshman, Alun Hughes, also an ex Plas y Brenin instructor and a long-time climbing partner of Dee's. We four were by no means top paddlers; but we were friends, and on a trip such as ours, that was more important. (Obviously friendship makes for an enjoyable time, but often it is also safer; because contrary to received wisdom, a team is not only, or even, as strong as its individual members. Rather it is as strong as the bonds between its members. The

---

[1] The Bio Bio is an onomatopoetic Mapuche Indian word for the song of a local forest bird.

[2] Sobek Rafting Company in a letter to Jim Hargreaves.

[3] Richard Bangs in *South American River Trips* (Bradt Enterprises).

[4] *North Wales White Water* by Terry Storry and Jim Hargreaves (Cascade Press, 1980).

S.A.S. have known this for a long time; it is the basis for their four-man squads.)

To begin with, Jim was very definitely the leader of the expedition. Not only did he have the shit to go with the bull, but he had the name. He was a member of the first British team to canoe the Grand Canyon of the Colorado River in 1971, and had been one of four to round Cape Horn in kayaks in 1979, unsupported by land or sea. By contrast we were mere nothings, and were just glad to be associated with the man. It is true that I was spending more and more time canoeing, but like Alun and Dee I was still basically a climber. So we let Jim lead, and were glad to do so. Without his fame in the canoeing world, and his organizational ability, we would never have left the country. In a matter of four months, he turned a hare-brained scheme into a practical proposition. His description of the process involved, written shortly after we returned, makes it seem deceptively straightforward.

'In September 1981, I set to work researching the river. I wrote to one of the first paddlers to do the river, Pete Skinner in the U.S.A. He wrote back with a little bit of information, but not a lot. The first rafting company to complete the river was a firm called Sobek, so I wrote to them. Their reply was calculated to put anyone off unless they were accompanied by a Sobek raft. I phoned Pete Skinner in the States, and asked him a little more about the river. Unfortunately I got the time difference a little wrong, and still half asleep he was pumped for information and bombarded with inane questions. He allayed some fears by saying that the river was nowhere harder than Grade IV. Later, much later, I remembered how good he was. In any event, all our information pointed to a river that was more than a little bit different.

'The descriptions I was given varied from ". . . the most dangerous river in the Southern Hemisphere" to ". . . a piece of duff". Satisfied that the truth lay somewhere in between, we decided to give it a go. For the next six weeks the phone became permanently engaged, and the typewriter developed verbal diarrhoea. Chris Bonington, hastily approached, agreed to be our Patron to assist with fundraising, and the B.C.U. gave us their approval. Our original plan was to go in the winter of 82/83, during the height of the Chilean summer, but plans soon changed as support for the trip snowballed.

Being, amongst other things, a petrol retailer, I approached National Benzole to see if they were interested in sponsoring us. Within a few days National put the trip quite firmly into the realms of reality by donating £2,000 towards our estimated £5,000 budget. We decided to bring the trip forward a year and go in early January 1982. Chris Hawkesworth of *Wild Water* gave us some of his excellent anoraks, buoyancy aids and Twinseal spray covers and a cheque for a further £200. With this encouragement and an application for a grant from the B.C.U. Expedition Fund in the pipeline, we borrowed the rest of the money from the listening bank—all the others were blind and dumb.'

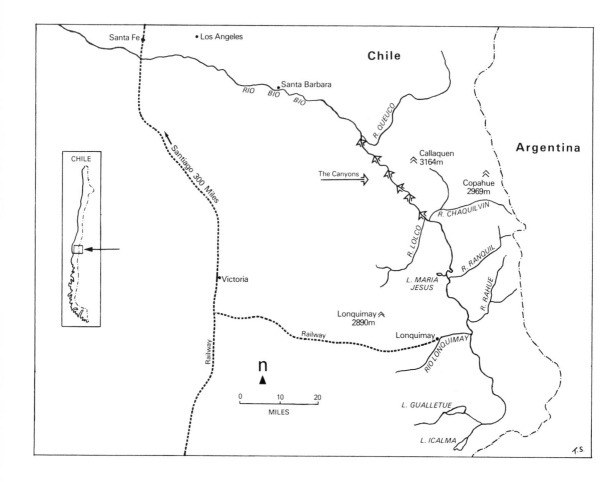

On the morning of 5 January 1982, the four of us drove to Uckfield in Sussex and collected our custom-built kayaks in National Benzole colours from Gaybo. They were strengthened Olymp IVs, a boat first produced by Gaybo for the 1972 Olympic Games in Germany, the only time when canoe slalom has been an event. The boat is designed with a high degree of rocker (saucer shape) on the hull to make it turn quickly. It is also, for a slalom canoe, a big volume boat, the inherent buoyancy of the large hull making it stable—this was seen to be a necessary characteristic to cope with the big turbulent water of the newly constructed Olympic slalom course at Augsburg. The Olymp IVs combination of manoeuvrability and stability made it ideal for the heavy technical water we expected on the Bio Bio. Moreover, with plenty of volume fore and aft, the boats would be able to cope with the extra weight of a week's supply of gear.

The major, and at that time unavoidable, problem with the kayaks was the material of their construction. Like almost all kayaks in the 60s and

70s, these were made out of glass fibre. Although an excellent material for the designer of competition boats, allowing a very precise hull shape, its tendency to crack or break on impact with rocks is a real worry for the expedition canoeist. Gaybo tried to counteract this problem by putting extra layers of glass fibre on our boats over and above normal specifications. They also used extra gelcoat to get the National Benzole colours right, and, they suggested, this would also make the boats a little stronger (and heavier—by 7lbs). On top of this we took a fairly substantial repair kit of chopped strand, and woven roving fibreglass mat, resin, catalyst, and lay-up tools. This fooled nobody. We all knew it would be virtually impossible to put a kayak back together again if it broached on a rock, even if—and this would be problematical—we could rescue the bits. So the possibility of breaking a canoe, when we had no raft or bank support, remained a major headache. The aspirin for later expeditions was the plastic canoe.

Plastic canoes also travel better than fibreglass ones, so we were like anxious parents sending their children off to their first day at school as, next day, we saw our kayaks onto the 747 at Heathrow airport. Getting them on the plane in the first place had been fun. Jim put his foot under the scales to make the luggage weigh less, and when it still weighed too much, baldly stated that Pan Am had given us a 'two pieces' limit irrespective of weight. This bit of bull worked, but we had to jam all our gear in the boats, and any that we couldn't, take as hand luggage.

Settling down for a pre-flight beer, we were surprised by the arrival of the National Benzole P.R. Representative, with a *London Evening News* reporter in tow, and a foot-high rubber Smurf doll in his hand. We had our pictures taken with this horrible little mascot. The P.R. man had given it to Jim, as leader of the expedition, and he was forced to save its life on more than one occasion.

'It's obviously going to be a "fun trip",' Alun wrote in his diary at this time; 'the interaction between us is excellent with Jim priming us, and U.P.I.s are flowing freely.' With less expedition experience than Alun, I did not realize that some trips were 'heavy' and serious. I thought the banal banter provoked by Jim's 'useless pieces of information' was normal. In any case, I was enjoying myself hugely. 'I am nervous and excited at the same time,' I wrote on the plane that night. 'I don't know what's going to happen, and I don't care much. I just know it's going to be fun, alive, and dangerous. I am surrounded by three experienced expeditioners, so all I have to do is look after myself. This is a big difference from all my previous climbing trips where I was the leader!'

We arrived in Santiago on 7 January, and the heat of the southern summer hit us like a hair dryer. We were to be met Jim told us, by the

President (no less) of the Chilean Canoe Federation. There was no sign of a welcoming committee, and we were a little disappointed to be shown to a battered Ford pick-up by a boy in cut-offs—the son of the President as it happened. Obviously we thought, the President is tied up by matters of weighty concern to international canoeing. On the drive to the hotel however, it transpired that the President and his son were the *only* canoeists in Chile, and they took it in turn to use the car. The Hotel Monte Carlo was still being built, but having no side to one of our rooms was a blessing in disguise in that heat. The summer of 1981/82 was particularly hot and dry in Chile reducing the Bio Bio to its lowest level in 31 years. Alun was trying out contact lenses for the first time, but the climate in the team helped counteract the effects of the weather: 'My eyes drying up a little, but constant hysterical laughter keeps them wetted. Pleasant evening out, enjoying the stay.'

One of Jim's theories about the expedition was that if he ate and drank enough over Christmas, the New Year, and in the days immediately prior to the expedition, the accumulated fat in his body would see him through the trip without the need to eat much. Paranoid about getting a food bug—he had suffered badly on his previous Chilean expedition round Cape Horn—he used this as an excuse to eat hugely in the days before we came out, and in the days we spent at the Monte Carlo, where he reckoned the food was safe. Unfortunately for Jim, this Whillans-style[1] theory of expedition troughing, which may work for Himalayan climbing or even for sea canoeing, where there is usually a long build-up before any gymnastic ability is called for, does not work for rivers, where the difficulty is usually greater nearer the beginning of the expedition than at the finish.

I doubt whether someone of Jim's experience really took this self-professed 'theory' at all seriously, but we knew for certain that his other 'theory' was a put-on: this was that we would live off the river. He had brought a fishing rod, and every evening after making camp beside the river, he would spend an hour or two casting into the emerald water. But he used a fly, instead of worms or maggots as the locals did. Jim only caught one fish during the entire trip, so it was lucky that we had bought other food in Santiago.

Expedition food has to be light, to keep well, and be easy to cook. It came down, as it usually does, to porridge, soya, rice, sugar, salt, chocolate and tea. I never did find the Spanish phrase for 'Have you any porridge oats, not this instant muck?' but Dee did manage to get pointed to a plastic

---

[1] Don Whillans, famous British climber of the post-war years, often began the walk-in to base camp on his Himalayan expeditions with a big beer belly.

bag shop, where he bought a job lot of 500 for waterproofing purposes. We also bought baseball hats and suntan cream to keep the sun off our faces. (The first time we applied the cream, we forgot to put it on using the back of our hands instead of our fingers, and the paddles behaved like well-greased axles swivelling in our palms.)

On the evening of our second day in Santiago, we boarded the south-bound express at Alameda Station, having sent the kayaks on ahead by goods train. Both Jim and I were into steam trains, and this, Chile's famous *nocturno,* revived some boyhood memories. Dee, on the other hand, with problems at home to forget about, was more into the wine, and spotted the buffet car faster than you could say 4-6-0. The buffet was rapidly reduced to a shambles by the four gringos, with the help of seven bottles of vino collapso. The waiter however, a Peter Sellers look-alike, still had a fixed grin on his face at two in the morning when, alone in the buffet car, we launched into our fourth thousand-peso note. But at 4,200 pesos Dee announced that he was getting sick of the South American grape, and promptly was: swift exit of party.

We changed trains at Victoria. Chile's equivalent of Thomas the Tank Engine, at one point driven by Jim and stoked by me, took us to Lonquimay, a small border town surrounded by Andean volcanoes. Incredibly the station was just a hundred metres from the Rio Lonquimay, the tributary which we would paddle to the Bio Bio.[1] At last we felt close to the river we had thought about for so long.

Lonquimay was a poor town, even by Chilean standards. The houses were made of wood, except for the odd government building of stone. There was a dusting of shops with empty shelves—one incongruously selling Rubik cubes—and just a scattering of cars, horses being the main mode of transport. But it had a certain feeling of self-importance. It was the local market centre, where the Indians (dark, descended from the original inhabitants of South America, forming the lower class in Chile) sold their goods, and the ranchers (pale, descended from the Spanish *conquistadors,* members of the middle and upper classes, sometimes given the generic name *gauchos*) bought their supplies. Being a border town, with the none-too-friendly neighbour of Argentina, Chilean soldiers and policemen were much in evidence.

Two American raft companies, Sobek and Nantahala, had made Lonquimay their base. The latter were in town when we arrived, preparing to take commercial clients down the Bio Bio, and they offered us much-appreciated hospitality and much-needed information. They plugged huge gaps in our knowledge of the river. It was from them that we

---

[1] This branch line to Victoria is now closed, leaving the alternatives of bus or taxi.

learnt about the three canyons, the hard rapids, and the best places to camp. Jotting down notes as the rafters talked, Jim later wrote a useful summary of the information.

'The upper Bio Bio from Lake Galletue runs north with no major difficulties. However, downstream of the Rio Lonquimay, the Bio Bio gradually increases in difficulty until, cutting west through the Andes, it forms a series of gorges and canyons. The character of the Bio Bio is that of a 'pool drop' river. This means basically that the fall in altitude from source to sea is achieved in a series of steps, each step followed by a calmer section of river, although this is rarely more than 100 metres long. With each drop the rapids increase in difficulty until the major rapids are reached in the main canyons: Nirreco, Quiet, and Royal Flush Canyon. The river then breaks out onto the central Chilean plain at Mountain Gates, flowing eventually into the Pacific at Concepcion. Below Santa Barbara it is of no further interest to the white water enthusiast.

In January and February, the best months for running the river, the average temperature in the middle of the day is between 90 and 100 degrees fahrenheit. There is very little rain although cloud-bursts are not unknown. In 1981 Nantahala were on the river as a freak summer flood brought the river higher than it had been for a hundred years—they managed to pull off when the river reached 30,000 cubic feet per second. We have 6,000 cfs for our run—6,000 to 10,000 cfs is normal.

The American parties have divided the river trip into a ten-day run, each day ending at the best camping spots along the way. There are Indian tracks all along the river which eventually lead to dirt roads. A number of primitive Indian settlements and farms are dotted along the riverside, where it may be possible to buy simple food such as eggs or freshly-baked bread. Although it is fairly easy to get off the river before the canyons, once these are entered the trap is sprung, and the only real way out is downstream.'

The Nantahala team, and in particular Les Bechdel, their boss, seemed to think that an unsupported kayak trip was too committing on the Bio Bio. Having packed the boats with food and gear for ten days, and tried them out, we were all worried about how sluggish they felt, particularly on the turn. We had never paddled a river with boats this heavy—85–90lb on the station luggage scales. The presence of the rafters seemed to hold out the option of accompanying them down the river, and paying them to take our gear—but should we use that option? It was a difficult decision as Alun's diary of those two days in Lonquimay makes clear.

'Jim is as busy as ever, sorting everything out; very fast on the uptake—good at Spanish already. Terry is cool and calculated, taking everything in his stride. Les Bechdel, the Yank boss, says the Bio Bio is twice as hard as the Colorado. No idea what to expect . . . Deciding how to do the Bio Bio—i.e. with or without raft support—is a problem at the moment. Sobek arrive tonight

58

(Sunday) but no rafts will set out until Wednesday. I would prefer kayaks empty. So would Terry and Jim. Dee wants to get going and be independent . . . Dee got drunk on wine with Jim and Les, and talked solid for two hours. I went down to the station with Terry and fitted the cockpit with karrimat. Returned and felt a little out of phase with things for the first time. We were hanging around the Yanks too much hoping for a lift with gear. Also Dee and Jim were drunk, and we weren't. We went out for a last peer at the Lonquimay. The others caught us up. All O.K. Decided to leave tomorrow and be independent. Nantahala rafts can't support us; they have 23 people to look after. Feels good to be independent.'

We left Lonquimay at 1.30 p.m. on Monday, 11 January 1982, five days after leaving London, and after a false start when Dee discovered he had left his passport in the rafters' house—we kept our passports and money in a zip compartment in our spraydecks, in case we became separated from our kayaks. We all felt good to be on the river at last.

The first four or five miles were flat, followed by some Grade II and III rapids. This gave us a chance to get used to the weight of the boats. In the early afternoon we came to the confluence with the Bio Bio. At 5 p.m. we camped a mile below the *balsadero* (an Indian ferry made of logs) at Rahue, and in the shelter of a twenty-foot cliff because it was so windy.

Although dinner was also a bit of a *balsadero*, the scenery around us more than made up for it. Grassy river terraces led away through brush-covered slopes to distant snow-capped volcanoes. Stands of Chilean pines (monkey puzzle trees) bordered the river. Cattle grazed nearby and in the distance there were ranch buildings. Some Indians came down to fish. They stood next to Jim peering occasionally at his slack rod and line as they pulled in trout after trout on worm-baited string wrapped round old tin cans. When Jim wasn't looking Dee bought a couple.

Prepared for the ferocious heat of the Chilean summer, we were not a little upset to be turfed out of our camp in the morning by a cool breeze and a shower of rain. Donning every available bit of clothing, including wetsuits, we caught sight of four mounted *gauchos* breaking the crest of a nearby hill, looking like extras from some spaghetti Western. If they carried rifles, they were keeping them hidden under their protective capes. After thirty minutes' paddling, the now superfluous suntan cream was being washed off our faces by the drips from our sun visors. Fortunately the rapids at Grade III were sufficiently continuous to keep our thoughts from either the 'English' weather or the hill-billy sequence in the film *Deliverance*. We were beginning to get our elbows wet, and Jim went for a dip, thus owing us a bottle of wine for the first Eskimo roll.

It rained again that night, and we spread the flysheet over our split paddles, making it wide enough for four. A grinning *gaucho* woke us the next morning when two steaming piles of horse dung forced us from our pits. The usual fire of driftwood was soon alight, burning well even after the night's soaking. Dee's socks burnt well too as the flames licked at the clothes line. Our food forage of the previous evening to Lago Maria y Jesus—a beautiful lake, high on the left bank, and well worth visiting (the spot approached by way of the large outflow coming into the Bio Bio 400 metres below Balsadero Boquimallin)—and the neighbouring *Casas* (farm) had resulted in neither fish nor eggs, so we breakfasted again on porridge.

Still that instant muck must have had some food value, for, apart from a chocolate stop, we paddled up to Grade IV continuously for five hours. At one point the paddling was so intense Jim and I wondered whether we had overshot our intended campsite and entered Nirreco Canyon. All but one of the rapids was canoed without prior inspection from the bank, and the difficulty of reading the water from the river led to mistakes. I led most of the way and had to roll. Dee swam, but nevertheless wrote in his diary, 'I have had one of the best day's paddling ever.'

Our only map was a photostat from the archives of the Royal Geographical Society. It was of course, in black and white, which meant the rivers, tracks and contours were difficult to distinguish. Moreover the relief was too general to be of use—contour interval 500 ft—and the scale (1:125,000) too small to plot our progress. In many ways it was worse than useless, because we wasted time trying to use it. Fortunately our information from the rafters was more accurate, and when we saw a large tributary entering from the left we could identify it as the Rio Lolco. Just past the confluence was a superb sandy beach, sheltered from the now raging sun by trees, and offering a view of Callaquen, the 10,000-ft active volcano which henceforward dominated the view from our camps. Alun and Dee spent the evening making plans to climb the mountain, but Alun was worried about what lay in store on the river, and about his friend.

'Arrived at river Lolco junction, very thirsty; pasta meal was appalling. Junction a busy place; many Indians crossing the river. Rio Lolco valley looks rich and fertile.

'Wondering whether to go up the volcano tomorrow. Also wondering what Jugbuster, our first named Grade V, will be like, if the rapids we have done already are not worth naming.

'Dee capsized in a small awkward rapid today. His mind is not on the river. I think he is thinking of Chez.'

It is difficult to know how much the break-up of Dee's marriage affected his paddling. During our drinking bouts he certainly showed himself more upset about it than I was about mine. But then, as a public schoolboy, I am not so good at expressing such feelings. Whatever the reason, Dee did make a bad mistake the next day.

This was day four, the day the Yanks had warned us the paddling would become very difficult. We managed to postpone our departure until midday, but soon after we left, and successfully negotiated a few Grade IV rapids, we sighted the footbridge above Jugbuster, the rapid which marked the start of Nirreco Canyon. This sheer-sided gorge accelerates the water over a series of drops, the river falling as much as 75 ft in one mile. The bridge carries the riverside track away up into the hills, making escape from the canyon virtually impossible. Here a broken boat would be a real problem, an injury unthinkable. At Jugbuster Dee must have wondered if his luck had run out:

> 'Jim sat and filmed while Terry ran it and made it look easy. Alun struggled a bit but made it. I blew it completely. Missed a break-out and couldn't get back on line for the main shoot. The hole ate me.'

Alun and I had already climbed out on the rocks below. Through half-closed eyes we watched the stopper grab Dee's stern, and loop him end over end. First the bow rose vertically then the stern. He was spun sideways and rolled horizontally. He dare not come out of his boat, lest after losing the buoyancy it gave him he was recirculated under the water. But in a stopper the downstream flow—the way out—is underneath, and the boat was keeping him on top. Dee was trapped.

Then as luck would have it, his boat, flung far out on one of its gyrations, landed beyond the surface backtow, and in the downstream current. With no air left, Dee was forced to bale out. Had he stayed in, he could have rolled in the pool below (instead we pulled him in with throw lines), but if he had come out of his boat earlier . . .? For Jim, who had watched the whole incident through the viewfinder of our cine camera, it was all too much, and he portaged. He also left the camera on the rocks beside the river to be retrieved later.

Two miles downstream we made an early camp to give Alun and Dee the chance to climb the now smoking giant of Callaquen. They left at 5 p.m. with rations for $1\frac{1}{2}$ days, saw sense, and returned for dinner at 7 p.m., bringing a loaf and five green eggs. 'All in all it's best not to go up the volcano,' Alun wrote that night; 'it's so far we'd probably need another day's rest after, so that would mean three days. Too long for the others to wait.'

Our warm-up in the morning was Milky Way, a Grade V rapid, difficult to read because of its chocolate colour (caused by Callaquen's glacial stream entering from the right) and hard to memorise because of its length—nearly half a kilometre, the longest on the river. I went first again, had to roll, and Jim portaged the middle section. Dee and Alun made it look easy.

The next rapid, signposted by a stupendous 200-ft waterfall falling from the canyon rim, we all portaged. Other parties had had trouble here as the name 'Lost Yak' suggests. Every line was blocked by huge boulders and stoppers, and our boats were too heavy for the necessary technical paddling. We, at least, could not afford to lose a kayak. Yet, despite these rationalizations, it was the first rapid all of us had portaged, and for an hour or two we were disconsolate, more especially since we also portaged the next rapid, Lava South.

Lava South was certainly possible. A straight run led through five-foot-high stoppers. But the mainstream ran under an overhung wall, and this blocked the way out of the stoppers. No one wanted to risk it. Perhaps if we had not been good friends before the trip, an element of competition would have raised the stakes. But we were more committed to the journey than our individual egos.

Lava South was named by the American rafters after the biggest rapid on the Grand Canyon of the Colorado River, Lava Falls. I paddled that rapid several years later, and was able to confirm Jim's opinion at the time that its southern namesake was harder. Alan Fox, a better paddler than either of us, tried to run the rapid on his trip down the Bio Bio in 1987. His team had lost their paddles in transit, and were using 'broom handles with fibreglass blades' bought from a shop in Santiago. Foxy takes up the story.

'So far the flimsy blades we had purchased had stood up quite well except for the occasional flutter in the turbulent water. Guy had already demonstrated a few rolls to increase our confidence in them. We camped that night above an infamous Grade V known to American rafters as Lava South, a rapid which had already claimed one life.

'The left-hand route ended in a huge stopper and protruding walls. The central route was blocked by a large hole, and the right-hand side ended in a drop. Only the right-hand side looked feasible with a little weaving at the end. So the following morning we prepared to ferry glide to the other side—a Grade IV ferry glide with Grade VI consequences if we didn't make it.

'Halfway across I put in a small support stroke to steady the boat; there was a sickening crack as the shaft of the flimsy paddle snapped by the blade. I watched the blade disappear as I slowly turned over into the blue-green, bubbling world of the river. I just couldn't believe it! But an attempted roll on a non-existent paddle blade confirmed it. I swung round to try and roll on the other blade, but the river didn't like that either, and from then on it seemed so natural just to eject from the kayak.

'There was no chance of making it to the bank, so I looped my arm under the rear deck line, took a deep breath, and expected the worst. I was swept down the central route; trying to relax was all I could do . . . I accelerated over the drop into the large central hole; there were a lot of bubbles down there. Fortunately I was swept straight through. The worst part was over, and I kicked my way through the last hundred yards of breaking waves to the bank.'[1]

The rest of Foxy's team, unimpressed by his antics on Lava South, portaged the rapid.

The next grade V in Nirreco Canyon is called Cyclops and I succeeded in putting the rest of the team off that. Dee was generous, or tongue-in-cheek, in his description.

'All but Terry portaged Cyclops' Eye. Top end Grade V with a small shoot through two horrible stoppers. He did it very well, backwards, but very well.'

We all paddled Last Laugh, a big dipper-type fun ride through dumping waves. It was the last Grade V in Nirreco Canyon, and we were relieved to find it such a soft touch.

Nirreco Canyon had been something of a shock to us, as Alun noted in his diary.

'The river is proving harder than expected, not the big helter skelter waves that we expected, but more technical rapids with difficult lines, many stoppers and large holes ragged, as the Yanks said. It's like a bigger Aberglaslyn Gorge all the way.'[2]

Jim in particular, as Alun recorded, was having a hard time.

'Terry is going well, Dee's and my confidence is building, but Jim has lost all his confidence.'

Jim had been away from hard paddling for too long, and physically and psychologically he was unable to cope with the hardest rapids. Looking back now I can understand his dilemma, but at the time I was surprised. Prior to the trip he had been the nearest thing I knew to God in canoeing terms. Now I felt cheated because the idol had fallen, and the first shadows of doubt crept into my mind.

---

[1] From 'The Lost Paddle' by Alan Fox, *Canoe Focus* No 51, August 1987.

[2] I describe the Aberglaslyn Gorge in my *Snowdonia White Water Sea and Surf* guide (Cicerone Press 1986), as 'one of the hardest bits of water in North Wales, and the scene of many epics'.

'Jim's comment on all these rapids is that, apart from Last Laugh, they were more difficult than anything on the Grand Canyon. I take this with a pinch of salt because of the extent to which he has psyched out.'

Years later, when I too had paddled the Grand Canyon of the Colorado, I realized that what Jim had said that day was true. The rapids on the Bio Bio, particularly in the excessively low water of that year, while not being 'twice as hard' as those on the Colorado, as Les had warned us, were certainly more technical. And while Jim did portage round a lot of rapids that he could have canoed, his response to the river was, in the end, probably more mature than my less experienced more pushy style. Thus he was the only one on the trip, who did not swim.

A huge pillar of rock in the centre of the river, called Heartbreak Hotel, marked the end of Nirreco Canyon, and three or four hundred metres below it on the right we stopped on a flat river terrace called Jose's Pasture. Camp that night was a fairly heartbreaking experience, as I noted in my diary.

'Horrendous night. Blowing a gale; then at 11p.m. it started raining. I put stones on the tent, although Dee protested that it would never blow down. A quarter of an hour later it did, with the flysheet ripping along the whole of one side. We had to repitch using stones and string. Using this makeshift shelter, the four of us slept the night half in and half out of the tent in gale force winds and torrential rain.'

In the morning, soggy and battered, our befuddled minds did not register the fact that the rain had completely altered the rapid below the camp, which we had inspected the night before. Breakfast Falls was now a much harder proposition, and none of us were quite prepared for it. Alun thought he saw the line.

'I went first taking a sneaky line on the right, and went over in the hole. I could not roll because I was pressed up against the rock, and felt myself going back into the hole. So I came out, and after a short desperate struggle, got the boat and paddle and myself out with Dee's help.'

I went next, and stayed a little further out from the bank. Just before entering the stopper I turned on the power; even so it nearly back looped me. The rapid however saved its worst for Dee.

'I had an epic on the first rapid of the day, after watching Terry struggle, and Alun take a swim. I saw a line further left than their route, but didn't see the rock in the big hole; it stopped me dead and gave me two sprained ankles. But I must not stress the epics. There were really no dangerous rapids in Quiet Canyon.'

Dee is nothing if not cool at times like this, but to us on the bank it looked bad. That night I wrote an account of what we had seen.

'Suddenly Dee realized he was heading for an enormous stopper. He accelerated with powerful forward strokes to try and punch the kayak through the hydraulic backtow. The nose of the Olymp IV dipped into the hole. And then the boat stopped. Not softly as it would in a cushion of water, but suddenly as it would against a wall of rock. Dee had hit a massive boulder doing perhaps twelve knots. The shock was transmitted through his footrest to his ankles. He rolled up yelling with pain, and for help, somehow struggled to the bank, and crawled out onto the boulders.'

Dee was badly hurt. He could put no weight on his ankles and we watched anxiously as they swelled to twice their normal size. Could he continue on the trip we wondered, or would two of us have to walk out of the canyon to get help? Astonishingly Dee, who could not walk even after we had bandaged both ankles, decided he *could* paddle, and crawled back to his kayak. For the rest of the day he stayed in his boat letting us inspect the rapids for him. Happily there were no portages, but we counted sixteen Grade IV rapids that day in the so-called Quiet Canyon. Every one must have tested Dee's pain threshold, as he pressed on the footrest to make a turn, or to draw the kayak sideways, or in one case, to roll. Yet we heard no word of complaint save for the occasional muttered curse. When at Camp 6, the bandages came off to reveal even more swelling, Dee just shrugged it off.[1]

---

[1] Dee's phlegmatic approach to epics is well illustrated in an account he wrote of his and Alun's sea canoeing expedition to Tierra del Fuego two years later. They had crossed the twelve miles of the Magellan Straits to that uninhabited land, and pitched their tent beside the Cockburn Channel, above what they thought to be the high tide mark. But . . . 'Beware the Magellan tidal enigma—twelve hours later we had a rude awakening. At 4 a.m. water came pouring into our tent; our sleeping bags were soaked, but worse the canoes containing all our food and most of the equipment had been left lower down the beach. We found them bobbing about in eighteen inches of water. The morning high tide in these parts is a good three feet higher than the afternoon high tide. Both the canoes had been afloat for some time, and the slightest wind would have blown them out to sea, leaving us marooned, with no hope of rescue.'

In a big wide river like the Bio Bio it is often difficult to spot souse holes or stoppers from a boat. One had crept up on us the day before, capsized all of us in turn, and forced me to swim. In Quiet Canyon only a few of the rapids had mean stoppers, so we could afford to do most 'on sight' from the river; on the few big Grade IVs—like Fang and Hermit South—Dee was happy to follow our lead. On the seventh day however, we entered Royal Flush Canyon, a stacked deck of Grade Vs each trying to undo the other in flushing the unwary canoeist from his boat. We had to inspect from the bank, and Dee felt he could not leave the decisions to us. So he used his paddle as a crutch and where he decided to portage let us carry his boat.

The first rapid, Ace, was sufficiently serious to frighten Alun off. None of us liked Suicide King and the twenty-yard portage was too easy to turn down. Queen, still Grade V, was fortunately not so suicidal, because it was the only rapid on the river that was impossible to portage. A climb of about 'Severe' was necessary even to inspect it, and Dee was forced to use 'aid'. Safely through that we arrived at One-Eyed Jack, a Grade VI, the most serious fall on the river after Lost Yak. One look at the four stoppers blocking the main channel, their far end closed off by the canyon wall, and we were all rushing to help Dee with his boat.

The last named rapid in Royal Flush Canyon, Ten, was a big bouncy Grade IV, and provided a good chance to do some filming. The movie camera was strapped to Jim's kayak, and the trigger extension was shoved into his mouth. This temporary gag made us realize the occasional flashes of silence could make his conversation sound quite brilliant.

The remaining rapids to Mountain Gates were highly enjoyable, as rushing to get to a flat beach, we paddled Grade IV after Grade IV on sight, stretching our nerves and our necks to the limit. At Mountain Gates the sides of the canyon dropped away, and the river doubled in breadth. The best and worst was over. Setting up camp thirty minutes later, we were feeling quite pleased with ourselves, until I discovered I had left our SLR camera at Ten. It took Alun and me five hours to get it back.

Seven hours' paddling the next day took us to our destination of Santa Barbara. We might have been tempted to break this last day in the beautiful Andean foothills, but jumbo flies, with bites to match, kept us going. So on to Santa Barbara with its one unpaved street, two hotels, a bed for the night, and a bus service in the morning. With kayaks strapped to the roof, the bus bounced us to the railroad stop at Santa Fé. The romance of the name however, belied the reality of that one-car hamlet, and having dumped the canoes, we took a taxi to the market town of Los Angeles for some R & R.

Returning to Santa Fé for the Santiago *nocturno* we were hard pushed to get on the train, for there was a religious festival taking place up the line. So we pushed hard, using our paddles as persuaders, and fused the buffet car lighting system. This worried the happy pilgrims even less than the drunken paddlers, and grinning *gringo, gaucho* and Indian, were soon rubbing shoulders in mutual hilarity at the frenzied efforts of the waiter turned electrician. But it was the waiter who had the last laugh. When the lights came on again he turned and said quite clearly in English 'So sorry, buffet car now closed.' We looked up and saw it was our old friend 'Peter Sellers' from the journey down.

Rio Balsas—River of Fire by Marcus Bailie

In the summer of 1986, with an Australian friend, Nick Collins, I joined a bunch of crazy Canadian kayakers to paddle the Grand Canyon of the Colorado. The Colorado is still seen as one of the world's biggest white water challenges for kayakers and rafters alike and so for fourteen event-filled days we bounced our way through such famous names as Horn Creek, Boulder and Granite Rapids, Crystal, and of course Lava Falls. With a local commercial rafting company from Arizona rowing the support rafts the trip was comparatively luxurious, for not only did the rafts carry all our gear and food but the rafting crew did all the cooking and washing up!

However, 5,000 miles is a long way to go to paddle just one river, even if it is the best river in the galaxy, and so while the Canadians returned home to find even bigger rapids to throw themselves into, Nick and I looked around for something else to paddle. Mexico was close and neither of us had ever been there before. We had a few road maps and a vague idea of some feasible rivers and besides, our rafting team seemed to think that Mexico was worth a visit. We hired a car, put the kayaks on the roof, and drove south through Arizona to Nogales on the Mexican border.

At Nogales we left the tranquillity of Arizona behind and entered a new world, one which was loud, brash, dusty and hot. The wide concrete streets were noisy with a jumble of ancient motor cars. Old men in ponchos and massive sombreros lounged in doorways, and plump women in bright dresses jostled with large baskets around the market stalls. By contrast the young men of the town were in denim jeans and cowboy hats and carried expensive transistor radios propped on one shoulder. The streets were alive with the excitement of their blaring music and their attractive giggling girlfriends with long black hair, and glaring neon signs advertised Dos Eques beer and Coca Cola.

A train seemed to be the best way of getting around Mexico so we set about looking for a railway station. We found one and were relieved to

68

discover that we could get ourselves and our kayaks onto a train to Guadalajara that afternoon.

Mexico is a profusion of foreign gifts which have never quite achieved harmony and so, though the country has many of the facilities of a modern state, it has neither the insight nor the inclination to maintain them. In particular it has an extensive railway system but no concept of keeping to a timetable, and so we bought our tickets and for several hours joined the gathering crowd on the platform until eventually a train arrived. We loaded our kayaks into the mail van and found ourselves places on the hard wooden benches which passed for seats.

The train bumped and rattled at a snail's pace up through the Sierra Madre, stopping at every tiny village en route through the twisting maze of river gorges and jungle ridges. The heat became sticky and the wooden seats harder until we found ourselves longing for the next station where at least we could get a cool drink and stretch our legs for half an hour. Each station was an adventure in itself. Before the train had even stopped a hoard of Mexicans young and old would besiege it, selling all manner 'of local foods and drinks, some appealing, some distinctly suspicious. They pushed and jostled for position, shouting unintelligible Spanish phrases as the passengers strained to get to a window to call for their desired dish.

Evening moved on to night and as we rumbled our way through the dark a cavalcade of flying insects poured through the open windows to devour us. Sleep was a short-lived luxury, and dawn a life-time away.

The early morning light revealed that we were not very far into Mexico. We checked our maps again and staring in disbelief at the scale written on the front realized that the journey to Guadalajara was over a thousand miles long. Fearing that we might simply die before we got there we decided to break the trip by stopping on the Pacific coast at Mazatlan where we thought we might get some good surf.

It was not to be. The Mexican Pacific Railway temporarily lost our kayaks, and most of the surfing area had been devastated by a recent hurricane. We slept on the beach that night and made an early start the next morning when we were woken by an unexpectedly early tide.

Another gruelling day on the train followed by another gruelling night finally landed us in Guadalajara station at 4 a.m. Our kayaks, we were told, would not be unloaded until daylight so we pitched our tent in a siding and collapsed.

Guadalajara held little for us. The railway company lost our kayaks again; the river we had hoped to paddle turned out to be fed largely by the city's sewage system and so we decided to give it a miss. Then, to add insult to injury, I had my passport, travellers' cheques and money stolen. Since this meant going to Mexico City to get a replacement passport we decided

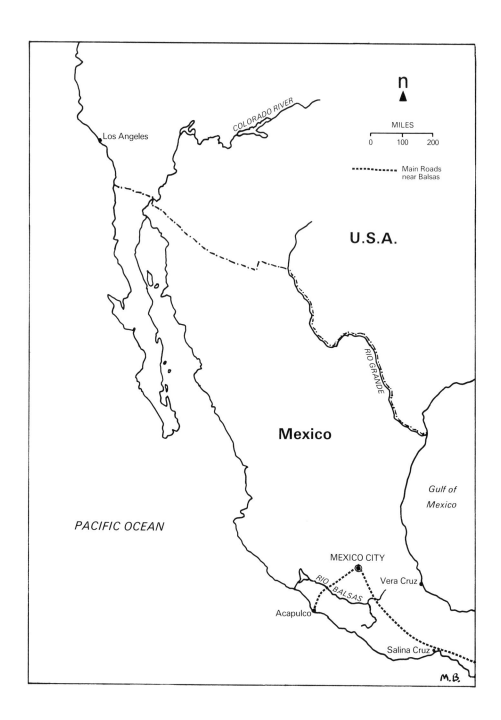

to hire a car and travel there in a bit more comfort. Besides, with the milometer disconnected the rate would be almost as cheap as the train. We risked death by firing squad by breaking into the warehouse where we suspected our kayaks were and succeeded in liberating them. Then hurriedly, lest injustice should prevail, we loaded up the hire car and headed south.

After a couple of pleasant days on the road we arrived in Mexico's bustling capital where we soon discovered that although dealing with Mexican bureaucracy requires persistance, patience is better.

After several fruitless days in Mexico City we got fed up waiting for my replacement passport and made plans for an attempt on the Rio Balsas. This is one of Mexico's longest rivers, but access to it is not easy. The headwaters rise in the remote southern Sierra Madre, where there are few villages and even fewer roads. The easiest approach seemed to be to start on the Rio Atayac where it crosses the main highway south to Oaxaca and Guatemala. We loaded up the hired car with boats and gear for the last time and drove south to our intended starting point. There was indeed a river there, but it did not look very big, more like a stream. We were getting impatient, however, and decided to give it a go.

There was a tiny village by the bridge, no more than a few mud houses scattered amongst the sparse trees and cactuses. Pigs and half-naked children played in the sun and old men sat in the shade of a solitary general store. We persuaded one of the villagers to store our kayaks and our gear for a couple of days while we took the hired car back to Mexico City, though after the theft in Guadalajara we were unsure what would be left when we returned. We reconnected the milometer to make the mileage look respectable and returned to Mexico City.

The return to the village by bus took four times as long as the car journey. This high mountainous area supported a poor population and the villages reflected this. There was none of the bustle of the city here, and life continued much as it had for centuries, indolent, amicable and vague.

Back at the village we were relieved to find that our kayaks were still secure. The man had temporarily evicted his wife and children to make space for them and so while they rebuilt the inside of their home Nick and I dragged our boats down to the river and set about packing.

In Mexico City we had tried to glean as much information as we could about the river but Mexican officialdom was as ignorant of what lay off the main highways as we were. Rumour and very dubious maps suggested that though there were no roads we would at least find a few villages. We expected to be on the water for anything between four and twelve days, and planned to carry four days' food at any one time, stopping to top this up as and when we could.

About 150 miles downstream the river was crossed by another road, the Acapulco Highway. Below that the river was supposed to be flat all the way to the sea, so we intended to get out there and get a bus back to Mexico City. What lay between us and that next bridge was anybody's guess. All we knew was that an uncertain number of years ago the Atayac had been rafted by an American woman, and that the Balsas was the course for the world's wildest and most disorganised white water power boat race.

It was so good to get back on the water that for a while we just basked in the delight of it. Life suddenly became superbly uncluttered, with success measured only by the ability to get through the day.

The Atayac was shallow and narrow, often only ten metres or so across, but it ran swiftly. It was September, the end of the Mexican rainy season and the steep valley sides were lush with vegetation. Close to the river it was a mixture of jungle creepers and desert cactus. Beyond was scrub grass and barren hills. All day the river dropped joyfully through deep valleys. Small rapids were common and so we just let the miles roll past. A fiery sun burned down on us and we basked in its heat.

In the late afternoon we spotted a fine-looking campsite and pulled in. There was a spacious grassy clearing, lots of firewood and even a few well-positioned bushes to hang our paddling gear on to dry. It was still warm and sunny and we decided not to use a tent. Our meal of rice, tinned fish, tomatoes and chilli cooked on an open fire, was soon prepared and eaten and as the light started to fade we built up the fire and settled down to drink a little local tequila and to smoke a few heady Mexican cigarettes.

Predictably we got peckish and in an act of total irresponsibility we demolished the remaining supply of packlunch goodies, and as sleep slowly crept over us we lay watching the pattern of clouds sweep and swirl and churn their way hurriedly across the sky.

'Clouds? Bloody hell—it's a STORM'.

We dashed around like ferrets, frantically trying to erect the tent before the cloudburst arrived. Seconds after we had thrown all the important things into the tent and dived in after them, great drops of water landed in the dust like tiny explosions, turning the earth into a bath of sloppy rust-coloured mud.

Next morning everything was the same rust-red colour; the river, our tent, our cooking pots where they lay by the fire and even our paddling clothes where they had been blown from the bushes. But the sun was out and steam rose from the ground in clouds. Soon everything was fresh and dry again and we could laugh about the antics of the night before. Once more the day was clear and hot and the river pleasantly cool. The sight of a few cattle coming down to the river suggested that the area was inhabited and when later in the afternoon we spotted a small village we stopped more out of curiosity than anything else. We left our canoes pulled up on the bank and as a token gesture towards security we fitted the spray decks tightly and rolled the boats upside down. There were about twenty houses in all, single-storeyed and mud-built, with thatched roofs and glassless windows. Cobs of corn hung everywhere to dry and pigs and chickens scurried away from us. As we walked we returned the stern looks of the villagers with warm albeit nervous smiles.

At what can best be described as a crossroads we found a tiny general store and entered. The shelves contained very little other than a few tins of fish, some boxes of matches, and a bundle of religious postcards. On the floor however, next to a bowl of eggs and a sack or tortilla flour was a bucket containing a dozen or so bottles of Coca Cola. In my best Spanish I ordered a couple of bottles and some eggs for the evening meal. We began to gather a crowd and soon the dimly-lit store was full of people. Hesitantly we made an attempt to chat and slowly the stern glares turned to friendly smiles. Soon everyone was laughing and shouting and when we eventually returned to the boats the entire population came to wave us off.

In the coming days the scene was repeated often. There was always the same style of mud and straw houses, and even the layout of the villages were often the same. Supplied only by mule trains the tiny general stores would always have tins of fish, bottles of Coca Cola and very little else. The people were always very friendly, often asking us to share a cigarette, a meal, or a glass of tequila. These people, dependent on the river, remain loyal only to the river and the things of it. In our own strange way Nick and I had arrived by the river and were received accordingly; always when we returned to our kayaks we found them exactly as we had left them.

After four days we reached the confluence with the Rio Balsas and with some excitement we poured out into its greater volume as it accelerated, brown and deep, towards the sea. There was a village at the confluence, larger than anything we had seen on the Atayac and when we arrived there, there was a festival in progress. We pulled our kayaks ashore to the sound of music, and headed in its general direction. There was presumably a road connection of some sort for a few old and ornate trucks and cars sat idle in the dust in various states of disrepair. The village had a Gothic-looking church towering above the houses and the low mud wall which surrounded it formed the town square.

Brightly coloured stalls had been erected around the edge of the square selling beads, material, cigarette lighters and a vast array of other fancy goods. By the door of the church an assortment of musicians were playing a mixture of lutes, guitars, trombones and tubas which produced a sound as lively as it was discordant and provided a beat for the bizarre dancers

73

who were acting out a strange ceremonial dance. In the turmoil we remained largely unnoticed for a while, the only outsiders at this amazing spectacle. The dancers were dressed in bright reds and yellows; headdresses and masks spoke of pagan, vaguely Aztec-inspired mythologies, and while some of the dancers carried long crucifixes others had totem poles with emblems of birds and animals. There seemed to be no conflict between Christianity and the older indigenous religions. Rather these people, older by far than either, had absorbed both into their own timeless culture, a bridge between the Spirit and Nature. When we left the village we did so aware that we had seen something very powerful, something very special.

The river was wider and the current stronger now, but as is often the case the new strength brought with it stretches of quieter water where the river ran deep and silent. At times high valley walls rose on either side giving an awesome atmosphere. At others the country would flatten out and cattle would wander down to the river or even wade across the shallows. We could sometimes see villages perched on distant slopes or terraces carved into the hillside but for the greater part the river was remote and we saw no one.

Days, like patches of time, fell from us as we became ever more absorbed in the river. Our goal was still the Acapulco Highway some unknown number of days away, but goals are only important if we enjoy the process of reaching them and so we relished each moment, each gift which the river gave us. The rapids were fun and although small by comparison to the rapids of the Colorado the remoteness made them every bit as challenging.

We remained sensitive to circumstances and when our arrival at a village coincided with our supply of food running short we would stop to stock up and to buy the inevitable Coca Cola. Then again we would stop to explore a side canyon, a rocky knoll or a cave as whim or opportunity dictated.

As our days on the Balsas turned to seven, then to eight then to nine and still there was no sign of the bridge, our buoyant sense of well-being began to fade. Allowing for village stops and other diversions we estimated that we were doing 25–30 miles a day. It was difficult to imagine what could have happened to the road, though common sense said that we must get there sooner or later.

When finally we did we beached our kayaks with relieved excitement and scrambled up to the road. There were a few houses, a general store, and a roadhouse with restaurant and bar. We ordered beers.

'Yes,' they said, 'this was the Acalpulco Highway.' And 'Yes, the bus to Mexico City will stop here. They run every two hours.' We ordered more beers.

Unpacking kayaks at the end of a trip takes a lot less time than initially packing them. Everything we no longer wanted, and since we now intended to fly back to Britain that meant almost everything, was piled in one great heap beside the river. Unused flour, rice, tins of fish, salt, chillis, potatoes all went on the pile as did cooking pots and old and worn-out clothes. The local children and animals would scavenge anything which was worth having, and the river would reclaim the rest. We had a final wash in the river, put on out last remaining clothes, and dragged our now almost empty kayaks up to the road.

The first bus was an express and the driver told us he could not carry our kayaks. When later buses arrived with the same story things began to look serious. We tried to hire a car or even a truck in the village but without success. Eventually we were informed that at the next town downstream, the town of Balsas, there was a rail link to Mexico City. There is a fishing industry on the lower river and they send their produce by rail to the city. Estimates as usual varied about how far away Balsas was—10 miles, 50 miles, one day, three.

'But it is very dangerous,' they added, and gesticulated.

'Grande oola!' My Spanish was getting better. Big waves, eh?

If we could not get a bus and there were indeed more rapids on the river then getting back on the water seemed the only option worth considering.

'OH HELL, OUR GEAR!' We dropped everything and ran back down to the river. Our elegant pile of discarded gear was now a scattered shambles. We chased away the last of the pigs and with the help of the bewildered children gathered up what we could. We replaced a few items at the general store, bundled everything into our boats and five hours after arriving we were away again.

We stopped early that evening in an attempt to return some semblance of order to our trampled gear, but it was a futile effort. Besides, there shouldn't be much further to go.

The next day was superb and we ran some of the biggest rapids we had seen on the river so far. Big waves there were indeed, and we crashed and dodged our way through the morning in a frenzy of excitement. We easily made it to the town of Balsas that day and reluctant to make the same mistake again we left our boats fully loaded by the river and went off to investigate the possibilities of a train. We located the station and made enquiries inside the dilapidated station office. 'Every morning, six o'clock'.

With some relief we eventually checked our kayaks in with a very surprised station master and with nothing but a small rucksack, we wandered off to explore the sights and tastes of the town. Over our shoulders the huge orb of the sun was turning the waves of the Rio Balsas into little flames; just sun and river, fire and water.

The Grand Canyon of the Colorado River by Terry Storry

Despite being the most researched and documented river gorge in the world, it is difficult to write about the Grand Canyon. There is so much of it, that to try and put it on paper makes it smaller than it should be. It is not just or even mainly the white water, although this is often what attracts river runners in the first place. Here are the biggest rapids in the world, but they are dwarfed by the thousands of vertical and overhanging cliffs. Even the great sweeps of redwall limestone, the diabase and basalt buttes, and the gorges of granite shist and gneiss, seem insignificant set in the totality of the mile-high and mile-wide Canyon. And the Canyon itself is dominated by the Arizona and Nevada deserts which surround and flow down into it, threatening life in all its forms.

To adequately describe what it is like to be in there was impossible, even at the time. Scribbled notes in a diary have helped me to remember rapids and people, moments of stress and laughter, but most of the sights, sounds and smells of the Canyon are lost to that fortnight five years ago. The 1.7 billion years of geological history which the Colorado has exposed in forty million years of erosion, stuns the ego and individuality into submission, even if you are not a geologist, which I am not. The effect this had was to make our efforts to survive on and off the water seem far less heroic than they 'should', because nothing that happened seemed to be of significance in the huge and immensely old silence of the place. Feelings of self-importance and immortality cannot survive in the Canyon, and on many evenings the big 'I' had nothing to record in his diary. After all is said and written, I still feel that is the truest perspective. But then we return to 'civilization' . . .

Now, trying to remember over the span of five years, what it was like, it is as though the river has been swirling through my mind, like water over an ink painting, making the definition blurred but the impact stronger. It is true that, to begin with, the detail was never as firmly imprinted as on other trips, because Arizona Raft Adventures were in charge, taking care of all the details. But I note that writers with experience of solo and unsupported trips, far more serious undertakings than the one I joined, also relate to something in the Canyon which is far more than just the river:

'As is the summit of Mount Everest, or as is the South Pole, the Grand Canyon is one of the definite end points of the earth. Nowhere else is like it, it is surely the ultimate whitewater boating experience . . . and at least 90% of the lure of the Canyon is off the river.'[1]

When I was researching this chapter I came across an interesting statistic. Although there are more than 160 rapids in the 226 miles between Lees Ferry and Diamond Creek, they account for only 9 per cent of the total distance. Thus, although the Colorado falls an average of eight feet per mile (from an elevation of 3,000 feet at Lees Ferry to 900 feet above sea level at our take-out on Diamond Creek), it is mostly flat. And we are talking flat; there are no continuous sections of difficulty, or even intermediate riffles. Almost all the rapids have been produced by flash flooding from the side canyons, the outwash damming the river and producing sudden drop-offs of twenty or thirty feet. It is no wonder that boaters are turned on to the geology of the place, for it is the stuff which fills their senses for 90 per cent of the time.

Water and rock are the overwhelming features of the Canyon (the one eroding the other at roughly one inch per century), and with an inhospitable desert surrounding these elements any human intrusion is bound to threaten the fragile ecology of the place. More than 20,000 people traverse the Canyon every year (before 1950 fewer than 150 had been down the river), but to their eternal credit the Park Service and commercial river guides have adopted, and religiously practise the motto: 'take only pictures, leave only footprints'. So while in summer some of the river beaches are camped on every night, there is little or no evidence of this. Gathering firewood is prohibited, and all ash, trash, and human waste is carried out. The only permanent human settlement is at Phantom Ranch on Mile 88 (miles given are from Lees Ferry) where the Park Service maintains a campground and ranger station. Since this takes a day to reach from either the North or South Rim, and there is no vehicle access, it detracts only a little from the commitment and isolation of the river trip. The desert has ensured that the Canyon has less habitation

---

[1] Fletcher Anderson and Ann Hopkinson in *Rivers of the Southwest* (Pruett Publishing Company, Boulder, Colorado, 1982).

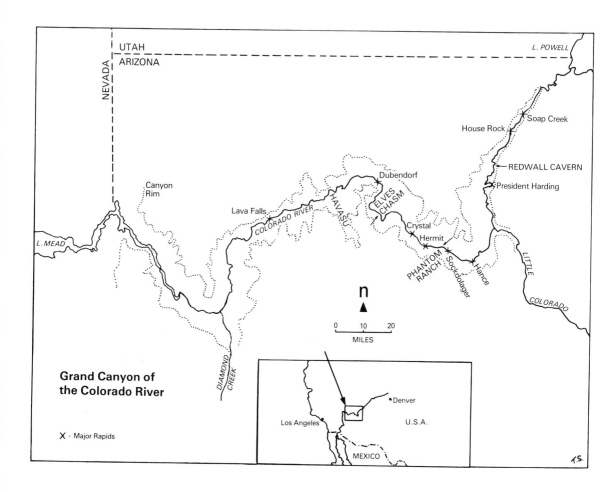

Grand Canyon of the Colorado River

X - Major Rapids

than almost any other river gorge in the world, and despite the numbers taking the ride it remains untamed and uncivilized.

Transient humans can and do insulate themselves from this barren and lonely place. In a raft full of people, pills, Pepsi and peperoni sausage, beer, batteries, water filters, sleeping bags, tents, tobacco, and tortilla chips, it is as though there is a hospital and restaurant round every bend. In a canoe you are more alone, more open to the Canyon, but if you have raft support, as we did, you can still build those illusory shells of security and comfort in the evening. Until, that is, you have been capsized by a wave, or you have been dragged out of the raft by a hole, or you have seen or heard these things happen, and you experience, or imagine, that gasping for breath, that intensity of cold and noise, that loss of all control in monstrous hills of icy water. It is good that the rapids are there to extract the respect which the Canyon deserves.

In 1983 the Colorado had been extracting a lot of respect, as the Comfort Inn receptionist in Flagstaff, Arizona took great pleasure in telling me, shortly after I arrived from the U.K to paddle the Grand Canyon.

'Boy, are you'se goin' down the Canyun? I'd rather go t'bed with a polecat myself. She's bin mean this year awlright . . . People bin fried, squashed, and drowned; they had'a stop running them trips . . .'

My girlfriend, Julie, was going to ride in one of four support rafts while I joined fourteen canoeists from Nantahala Outdoor Centre on a commercially organized trip. For the sake of Julie's nerves and my credibility this war story needed checking out. I found our trip leader, Gordon Grant,[1] in the back yard patching a massive rent in one of the rafts. He gave us a less colourful version of that unusual year in the Colorado's history.[2]

The Colorado had indeed been running at record levels that year—a peak of 92,000 cubic feet per second was recorded in the summer of 1983 compared to a norm of around 30,000 cfs—and five rafts had flipped on the river, one folding in half crushing a passenger to death. This accident, together with a number of rescues of passengers stranded in desert side canyons, persuaded the Park to close the river for a time. By September however, the river had returned to a more acceptable level (29,000 cfs). This was still high by autumn standards—the Colorado is fed mainly by spring snow melt—but we were not, Gordon assured us, likely to be 'fried, squashed, or drowned'. Relieved by his confident assertiveness we returned to our rooms to pack for the next day's departure, quite forgetting to ask him how his eighteen-foot raft had been ripped bow to stern; not by a polecat that was for sure!

In the two hours it took our team to drive from Flagstaff to the put-in at Lees Ferry[3] the bus's air conditioning system changed from warming us to

---

[1] Gordon was from Nantahala Centre in North Carolina. Nantahala had organised this trip down the Canyon with Arizona Raft Adventures. The latter were among twenty or so commercial companies that had 80% of the Grand Canyon river permits. To go with them was expensive (£500–£600 in 1983), but avoided the ten-year waiting list for private expeditions.

[2] In 1983 such was the quantity of snowfall in the Rockies that by July all of the Colorado River's reservoirs were full to overflowing. Hoover and Parker Dams spilled water into the inhabited areas of the Lower Colorado River Basin and the Colorado River flowed freely to the Gulf of California for only the second time in forty years.

[3] John D. Lee, a Mormon polygamist, operated a ferry service here in the 1870s, and was one of a number of his religion who used the Canyon to get away from it all. In 1929 the ferry was replaced by Navajo Bridge four miles downstream. Fifteen miles upstream of Lees Ferry is Glen Canyon Dam (and Lake Powell) constructed to provide irrigation, to prevent flooding, and to generate electricity.

cooling us, such is the effect of the sun in the desert between six and eight in the morning. Stiff-legged and bleary-eyed we emerged to find two other raft trips, as well as ours, packing, stashing, and lashing their loads. The river glided past massive, cold and flat.[1] I sensed its power as I struggled with the footrest in my borrowed kayak. I silently cursed my lack of training as, leaning over to shove buoyancy into the back of the boat, I felt my back go again, product of a last-minute surfing session off the North Wales Coast.[2] Was I ready for this silent moving ocean? I tried to off-load some of my fears into my diary.

'My back still kills, and the kayak I am borrowing doesn't help. It is smaller than the Olymp IV I usually paddle. I can't get in with my jayboots on, so I will try paddling barefoot—I just hope I don't have to inspect too many rapids. There are two C1s and two C2s[3] on the trip. The rest of the paddlers (9) are in kayaks. They look a strong bunch to me; I wonder if I will be able to keep up? Perhaps I will have to ride a raft some of the way? There are four rafts, two of 22ft rowed by Sharon and Dwight, and two of 18ft rowed by Gary and Laurie.'[4]

Fortunately for my nerves the first short day on the water went smoothly enough. We covered just eight miles, taking a leisurely lunch below Navajo Bridge, and stopping on the outwash beach of Jackass Creek (Mile 8) to camp for the night. After a meal of steak and salad, I jotted down some notes on our environmental potty training given by Dwight the Arizona Raft Adventures (AZRA) team leader.

'We are to use a porta-loo hidden behind a convenient boulder at every campsite. Its position will be marked by a large arrow painted on an ammo

---

[1] Upstream of Lees Ferry, even before the creation of Lake Powell, there had been little of interest to the white water enthusiast. In Glen Canyon the 2.8 foot per mile gradient precluded the formation of any rapids, and it was possible to paddle up as well as down it. Still, the dam submerged a beautiful and tranquil place, and there are many who regret its passing. Another effect of Glen Canyon Dam has been to lower the temperature of the water in the Grand Canyon, since the downstream release now emerges from the unnatural depths of Lake Powell.

[2] Like shoulder dislocations, lower back problems are common amongst canoeists. Mine bothered me for three years until, aggravated by further paddling, I was forced to bed for a week, to a physiotherapist for six weeks, and to R & R for three months. The problem, in this case, was a trapped sciatic nerve.

[3] C stands for Canadian Canoe, 1 is a single and 2 is a double.

[4] All the rafts were oar-powered—no motorized rigs were allowed on the river between 18 September and 15 December. Gary's raft was converted to a paddle raft halfway down the river at Phantom Ranch. AZRA was the only company to offer this option.

box (used for storing perishables on the rafts because they are waterproof). The raft guides (on a strict rota) empty the porta-loo into ammo boxes from which the previous day's food has emerged. Sherm, a doctor from Salt Lake City and a fellow kayaker leant across to me, at the end of Dwight's little speech, and said, "Like we say to our patients, if you don't eat you don't shit, and if you don't shit you die." '

Ripples of laughter on full bellies and the feel of soft sand under moonlit canyon walls dispelled any lingering doubts that Julie or I might have had, that we were in the right place or in the right company.

The next morning as I crept nervously out across the green swells of Badger Creek Rapid I felt far less at home. This rapid was only Grade 4 on scale of 10[1] and yet I had to pluck up courage to do a couple of crosses. I sneaked off downstream hoping no one had noticed.

The kayaks were first to Soap Creek (Mile 11, Grade 7), being faster on the flat intervening three miles than the rafts. I followed Gordon down the rapid as best I could. Most of the time he was blocked from view by fifteen-foot waves. Nothing in Britain, or the Alps, or South America, had prepared me for this. There was nothing technically difficult about it, no rocks to avoid, no holding stoppers, no dramatic twists or turns in the river, but the waves were so big that you had to paddle up them lest they surf you backwards, and every now and then a crest would collapse like a beach breaker for which you had better be prepared. And then as you kissed goodbye to that fabulous and terrifying roller-coaster, feeling that you could relax in the calm pools below, you hit the boils. Such is the depth of the Colorado that where the outwash of the rapids meets the calmer water below, the water sucks and surges in whirlpools and eruptions four or five feet up and down, twenty or thirty feet across. I was left wobbling on these glutinous swirls bracing this way and that, until Soap Creek felt it had had enough.

House Rock Rapid (Mile 17, Grade 7) was not so kind. Again I relaxed too early, and was left sitting on a boil. Alternately supporting with my paddles on one side and then the other I swirled round in circles. I wanted out, and tried paddling towards the shore. But you can't support on forward strokes, and sometimes you can't roll when you are out of your depth. So it was the big swim, small certainly to the nearest canoe, but big in my mind, because I was still of the opinion in those days that 'a good

---

[1] The Grand Canyon Rapid Rating System is individual to that river, 1 being the easiest and 10 the hardest grade.

paddler never swims'.[1] Fortunately a day or two more in the Canyon restored things to their proper perspective.

A further dent to my pride that day came in the form of Gordon Grant. We stopped at North Canyon (Mile 20$^1/_2$) for lunch and went bouldering on its smooth walls.

'Of course I have been training mainly for climbing this summer,' I said after my swim, 'and I do much more climbing than canoeing in my work at Plas y Brenin.'

'You'll like North Canyon then,' was all that Gordon said. Now as we smeared across the off-vertical sandstone it was quite apparent he was enjoying it a lot more than me. Sliding out of control like a bike on ice I was quickly up to my waist in the siltstone pool. I desperately tried to think of some come-back. 'May all your sperm be negative' was probably too radical for our new friendship, and 'I'll just have to go back to university again' was perhaps too subtle to have any impact. Thank goodness my mouth was too full of water to try either and the moment passed, for it emerged later that his wife was pregnant and he was doing a Masters degree by correspondence course.

After lunch on the second day came the Roaring Twenties. Its entrance is guarded by a large rock in Boulder Narrows (Mile 19). Driftwood from the 1957 floods was still visible on top of the rock fifty feet above our heads. Prior to the completion of Glen Canyon Dam in 1964 floods of over 100,000 cfs were a fairly regular occurrence in the Grand Canyon.[2] Now the river fluctuates on a daily cycle with only minor seasonal fluctuations.[3] The water is tamed, but the appearance of redwall limestone three miles later was to remind us that the Canyon is still a serious place to boat.

---

[1] This is similar to saying that a 'good rock climber never falls off'. Those who don't swim or don't fall off are in reality always climbing within their limits, a sensible and safe approach, but one in which improvement may be too slow for the impatient. Many of the best climbers and canoeists have, and are, surviving falls and swims; some have not. In point of fact the Grand Canyon is not a particularly dangerous place to swim as most of us found out at one time or another.

[2] The regulated flow of river introduced by the dam has made river running a more predictable business. It has also encouraged plant and bird life. No longer do annual floods scour the river corridor so that perennial plants have been able to colonize the ecologically stable beach habitat. Birds now have more to eat and the number of different species has grown considerably. On the other hand the lowering of the water temperature has endangered all the native species of fish. Furthermore the elimination of floods has meant there is little recharging of beach sediments, and beach erosion is now a major problem.

[3] The peak release of 92,000 cfs in 1983 was quite exceptional. The normal annual variation is between 2,000 cfs and 30,000 cfs. The daily fluctuation is caused by a peaking of electricity demand at midday and a fall-off at night. Thus there is a daily tide down the Grand Canyon. This often leaves rafts high and dry overnight.

The walls of crumbly red rock dropped sheer into the river making landing difficult and camping impossible. Apart from a small beach just above Tiger Wash (Mile 26$^1/_2$) where we slept, there is nowhere for a big team to stop between North Canyon (Mile 20$^1/_2$) and South Canyon (Mile 30$^1/_2$). Getting someone through the Roaring Twenties who is injured, hypothermic, or simply cold and psyched out, can therefore be a worrying business.

Bob and Colleen were paddling an old fashioned high volume end cockpit C2. It was a good boat for haystacks and stoppers riding high and stable on the water, but it was difficult to control in whirlpools and boils because the paddlers were at either end of a long boat often needing to lean opposite ways at the same time. Had they been in a more modern centre cockpit slalom C2 the stronger paddler, Bob, might have been able to override Colleen's mistakes. He might also have been able to roll the boat himself when they capsized in Tanner Wash (Grade 5, Mile 24$^1/_2$). But they failed to roll, and were washed out of their boat down into the notorious Hansborough-Richards rapid[1] (Grade 6, Mile 25) before any of us could reach them.

Following them down I emerged at the bottom of Hansborough-Richards to find Colleen swimming for the bank, Bob hanging grimly onto a paddle and the upturned boat, and Jim, another kayaker, trying to nudge the waterlogged C2 across the swirling eddies. Colleen crawled onto an outcrop of rock, and, pointing downstream, started shouting at us 'There's the other one', or 'there's another one?' I thought she had seen the other paddle, but then I realised she was warning us about Cave Springs Rapid (Grade 6, Mile 25$^1/_2$). Bob had seen it too now, and, trying to crawl onto Jim's deck, started muttering to himself, 'So cold, so cold, can't feel my hands, so cold.' I attached a tow line to the C2 and with the help of an upstream eddy we reunited Bob, Colleen, and the boat. With the spare paddle unstrapped from the deck they climbed back in, and, shivering, stroked back into the current.

Paddling a short way behind them towards Cave Springs I heard Colleen blaming Bob for deciding not to wear wetsuits that morning. His reply was inaudible in the roar of the approaching white water. They

---

[1] Major John Wesley Powell who was the first man to explore the Canyon in any scientific way, and who named many of the rapids and side canyons, portaged and lined his boats round this rapid in 1869. Twenty years later, on the second ill-fated and unsuccessful attempt to descend the Canyon, Peter Hansborough and Henry Richards from the Brown-Stanton Expedition were upset and drowned here. Another member of this expedition—Frank Brown—had been washed out his boat and drowned at Soap Creek. None of them wore lifejackets and they were in cheap lightweight boats with little freeboard. In 1949 veteran river runner Bert Loper is thought to have upset here and drowned while making a solo run at the age of 79.

capsized again in the rapid, and Colleen was now so cold that she had to be pulled onto the back of Gordon's kayak. Two other kayakers chased Bob and the boat. Here there was nowhere to land, not even a rocky shelf, and they had to lean across the C2 while Bob levered himself out of the water and into the rear cockpit. Colleen was too cold to paddle further, and when the rafts caught us up, she went with them. Gordon took her place in the front of the C2, his kayak jammed like driftwood across the back of a raft.

We made camp early, a mile down from Cave Springs. It was a couple of hours before the food and dry clothing began to flush the chill from our bones.

'We need a better buddy system,' Gordon said, beginning the post-mortem that night. 'Everyone was strung out, and we had a real problem getting Bob and Colleen in because there were so few of us there.'

'When I swam further up,' Don Sorensen (paddling C1) joined in, 'there was no one else around to help. I was lucky that it was flat, and there was a beach right there.'

Colleen, hands cupped around a mug of chocolate, was nodding vigorously. 'Yes and in some parts there aren't any· beaches and you just can't survive or do anything in water of that temperature for very long. Someone could get into real trouble, left behind by the rafts, or getting way out in front.'

We agreed to have a back marker and an informal buddy system, and to try and stay in touch with the rafts. Next morning, I noticed everyone was wearing wetsuits. My buddy was Herb Silverman, a fifty-year-old real estate developer from Houston, Texas, who had three children by a previous marriage, and a green parrot that sat on his shoulder and preened his hair when he came home from work. He had left his parrot in the pet shop, but his new wife was with him, becoming good friends with Julie in the snout raft. Herb was having a terrible trip, swimming during the day and dreaming of a white death every night. Kathy was calm in equal measure to Herb's nervousness, and mentally massaged him down the river. He needed more comforting cuddles after I had paddled with him three years later in the Colorado Mountains, but that is another story.

Fortunately for the morale of the canoeing and kayaking team, our third day in the Grand Canyon was fairly laid back. Only one rapid, President Harding (Grade 5, Mile 44), was of any consequence, and, coming at the end of the day, we were well prepared for it. Sherm was the only one to swim, splutterng oaths that Harding was a disastrous President anyway. We stayed with the rafts all day, like babies clinging to their mothers, and benefited from their knowledge of interesting places to stop. I was able to retrieve my diary from its ammo box during one lay-up.

'Five miles downstream of our camp was Stanton's cave, used by and named after Robert Brewster Stanton who attempted the second descent of the river in 1889 and 1890. Our raft guides tell us that split twig animal figurines were found here and carbon dated back to 2,000 B.C. Spent half an hour here, and also a mile further down at Vasey's Paradise, named by Powell after the botanist G. W. Vasey. We fill our bottles with the fresh water bubbling through poison ivy. We won't have to spend an hour pumping river water through the filter tonight! I lie back in the kayak close to a fan of watercress and watch a red-tailed hawk return to his nest. He has something in his beak. A fine spray from the spring forms a momentary rainbow across the cliff that's his home. A good place to live!'

Redwall Cavern, two miles further on, is in the crook of a bend. The river here has carved a cave so large that no architect would have the nerve to design it. Big enough to seat all the spectators at a Wembley Cup Final, its gigantic roof is unsupported for 500 feet in either direction, with a cliff a mile high resting on it. The weight of all that geological history seemed to oppress us, and I felt relieved when we were gone.

Our fourth and fifth days on the Canyon merge together in my memory; rock, sand, flat water, white water, a narrow sky, and an ever-growing feeling of distance from the other world. Of course we still had 'it' with us in the watches and walkmans, books and beer. Rob was drinking heavily, seeming to reject the Canyon at every opportunity. After one boozy day in the raft, he was having trouble getting his wetsuit off and asked his son Bob to help. Pulling and tugging at the neoprene Bob did not mince his words.

'I've skinned rattlesnakes and I've skinned rabbits, but shit I've never skinned my own pa before. You should go into hibernation Dad, then you could shed a skin or two.'

At the other extreme was Dwight, our raft leader. Every morning he would sit cross-legged in the cliff shadows and meditate. 'Otherwise I would get jaded,' he explained one day, 'to the beauty of the Canyon and to the danger of the water. I've been doing these trips back-to-back all summer, but you never know what may happen next time around. I saw a buckeye butterfly yesterday, and I've never seen one before. Yeah, the river can give, but it can also take away. If I start thinking I can cruise Crystal, or even a President Harding, then that's when I am going to wrap.'

As if to prove his point a violent storm hit us on our fourth evening.[1] Everything was wet by the time we had pitched the tent, and the effort of

---

[1] The Grand Canyon has about five inches of rain a year. We had two of the five on our trip. In common with most other desert areas evaporation substantially exceeds precipitation making permanent human settlement very unattractive.

writing my diary was too much. It was lunchtime the next day before I made an entry.

> 'Yesterday at Mile 61 a major tributary, the Little Colorado, entered from our left. It was warm and brown with desert sand, a strong contrast to the cold clear blue water of the main river. For hundreds of yards the two rivers ran parallel, flirting with each other along the blue-brown boundary, each trying to dominate the other in colour and form. It was no contest really. The silt swirled round by a small rapid, saturated the river until even the white water was brown. The lack of differentiation between broken and solid water makes the rapids hard to read.
>
> Today we are having lunch where Indians used to live 1,000 years ago—an Anasazi village at Unkar Creek (Mile 72). There must have been more rainfall then, because now it is just desert.'[1]

Below Unkar Creek we hit some big rapids. Unkar itself (Grade 6, Mile 72$^1/_2$) was straightforward but Hance (Grade 8, Mile 76) was the most serious rapid we had encountered so far, with holes blocking every straight line down the hundred yards of white water. We inspected from the bank and Colleen decided to walk. Bob, ever the extrovert, placed Garbo, a lifesize blow-up clown that the rafters had brought along, into the front cockpit of the C2 and paddled it alone. Colleen was not amused, but Bob did well, as I recorded that night.

> 'Hance was a big one. The river was wide, perhaps seventy or eighty metres across, the right-hand side a wall of rock, the left an open boulder beach. For canoeists the rapid was best run from right to left, whilst the rafts unable to manoeuvre, took a line close to the cliff on the right. Sharon misjudged her line and ploughed straight into a hole. Her partner had to throw himself onto the bow pontoon to prevent the rearing raft from flipping, gripping the bow pontoon, like a cowboy. In small boats we could dodge the nasties, but being lower in the water it was also harder to see them. Bob was further handicapped by the vast bulk of Garbo, and ran foul of a pour-over. He capsized. We ran for our boats. Then he reappeared from the trough right way up. He had rolled the C2 by himself and Garbo was still there, grinning from ear to ear!'

Below Hance the Colorado enters the first of its granite gorges, the sheer sides making it impossible to portage the rapids or find many campsites. The biggest drop rejoiced in the name Sockdolager (Grade 6, Mile 79), although Grapevine (Grade 8, Mile 82), above whose mighty roar we camped on that, our fifth night, was classed harder. In fact both

---

[1] Anasazi Indians lived in Nankoweap Canyon, the Unkar Delta, and Bright Angel Creek over various periods between 900 and 1140 A.D. They are the only people to have lived in the Canyon for more than a generation, and even their settlement was brief and unhappy. When precipitation declined between 1140 and 1150, the Indians were unable to grow their crops and left. It is possible that the Colorado itself dried up during this period.

86

Sockdolager and Grapevine—whose boulders Powell had thought looked like 'piles of grapes'—were flattened out by the high flow of that autumn. The boulders in the river may have been hidden by water, but in the boulders on the beach lay another unexpected danger.

I was crunching empty beer cans, the sound drowned by the thunder of Grapevine, when I heard, as if from a great distance, Julie scream. I turned, ran and tripped over. She was only a stone's throw away, but by the time I had reached her the hairy tarantula[1] was retreating underneath a pile of boulders. I grabbed her. 'Have you been bitten?' She yelled again and then hobbled away shaking her head. She had been unharmed until I had knocked the boulder she was moving out of her hands, and onto her foot!

It is possible to walk into or out of the Canyon at seven or eight points along its course, but Phantom Ranch (Mile 87) is by far the most popular hiker's route, because here the Park Service have installed a ranger station, campground, and small shop. We picked up three more raft passengers at Phantom on our sixth day, and at our lunch stop, a couple of miles further down, the AZRA team converted one of the oar rigs into a paddle raft. The three from Phantom Ranch and two other volunteers—Julie was one—were going to paddle the raft down the rest—and hardest part—of the Canyon. Gary sat at the back trying to keep some sort of order. The food and gear from his boat went into the other oar rigs. He had a more difficult cargo now.

The paddle raft had a baptism of white water in Horn Creek (Grade 8, Mile 90), Granite (Grade 7, Mile 93) and Hermit (Grade 8, Mile 95), and its occupants were somewhat subdued when we stopped early for the night at Mile 96. Gary however, was well pleased with their reactions under fire, and most of the canoeists were now relaxing in the big water. We needed to feel confident because tomorrow was Crystal,[2] our first Grade 9, and if all the war stories told that evening were half true, this one was mean. Herb had a bad night.

---

[1] Tarantulas are quite rare in the Canyon, and like most invertebrates are generally nocturnal. Scorpions are more often found, the most common being the straw coloured bark scorpion and the giant hairy scorpion. Despite the latter's prodigious size and formidable appearance, the former is more venomous. Red harvester ants also give a nasty sting. Black widow spiders are common in cliff faces, but like tarantulas normally come out at night. Wasps, bluebottles, moths, butterflies, and water striders are more pleasant rare sights seen in the Canyon during the day. And no one, of course, will forget seeing a rattlesnake or Californian king snake coiled like a spring in the shade of a cactus or poison ivy.

[2] Like most of the Grand Canyon rapids Crystal was formed by the outwash from a side canyon, in this case very recently. The largest flood in a thousand years crashed down Crystal Creek on 8 December 1966 washing immense boulders into the river channel and turning a minor rapid into an awesome cataract overnight.

The next day we stopped above Crystal (Mile 98) on the right bank. The raft guides, usually so cool about inspecting rapids, often staying on their rigs while we first-timers plotted our line, huddled in a group on the shore discussing the best route. I walked back with Dwight to his snout boat. He was talking to himself, as much as to me, reaffirming his ability to run the rapid.

'We do that mother every fortnight or so. Twelve or fourteen days on the river, two days off, and then back on. Man I worry about it. It's worse for us than the motor rigs. They can power outa trouble. See that boy?' Dwight pointed, claiming masculinity for the rocks in a turbulent female current. 'I've got to snick that boy with my rig, and he'll turn me right. That way I'm facing away from the hole before I get there, and I can run across the stream away from it. It's difficult to get it right. Last time I hit him too hard, and he kicked the snout back into the mainstream. I was in the souse hole before you could say rattlesnake piss. I was lucky—it didn't break back. I've never flipped, but if I do it'll be in that mother.' It was quite a speech for the normally meditative hippie rafter. He squatted facing Crystal, chin cupped in his hands, centring his thoughts.

All the oar rigs cruised Crystal this time. The paddle raft steamed past the outside of the hole too, the six oarsmen and women chanting like Haitians. Of the canoes and kayaks the C1s had the hardest time. They could not paddle and be ready to support on both sides, so they faced across the river leading with their strong side. Lacking forward momentum Pat and Chuck could not escape the big hole. They were eaten alive. Trying and failing to roll, the river took them for its own to be washed up as and when it fancied. Gasping and retching on the bank a mile downstream Pat looked as though she would never paddle again. But she did, subdued but not beaten, even at fifty-five years young.

Below Crystal is a narrow gorge (Middle Granite Gorge) the closing canyon walls combining with the side creeks to produce many rapids, including Tuna (Grade 6, Mile 99), Sapphire (Grade 7, Mile 101) and Waltenberg (Grade 6, Mile 112).[1] Between Crystal and our seventh camp at Mile 114, I counted eighteen major rapids all of them warranting a British Grade IV. We had two swimmers, and I had to practise my rolling again, twice in big water, and once when I was run over by a C2. This was a really good stretch of fun white water. The sheer walls of zoroaster granite

---

[1] Many of the rapids in the Canyon vary in difficulty according to the water level. Waltenberg for instance, is Grade 9 in low water conditions. All the grades given in this chapter are for the rapids as we found them, in other words for high water. The best guide to consult for rapid grading at different water levels, and probably the best overall guide to the Canyon, is by Larry Stevens: *The Colorado River in Grand Canyon* (Red Lake Books, Flagstaff, Arizona, 1983).

added to the excitement of the rapids. In the quiet stretches, amazing Cambrian rock formations, huge buttes and temples high above the gorge, formed a spectacular backdrop. It was as though we had been set on a stage carved for our enjoyment. It was one of the best of times.

'As we set up camp tonight the high talus slopes of bright angel shale glow in the sun. We lost it two hours ago. Five bigham sheep came down to the opposite shore to drink, their ears pricking nervously to strange sounds from across the oily calm water. Still warm enough for shorts. I have just tensioned the drying line from my paddle shaft, the other end stretched to a sandstone boulder, and shaken out the sleeping bags.

Julie and I seem close tonight. Perhaps she has as much adrenalin breaking down in her system as I have, now that she is in the paddle raft. I don't think I'll tell her about the gecko in her sleeping bag.'

No one was in a hurry to get up in the morning, so lunch on our eighth day was just two miles downstream at Elves Chasm. Here a continuous fresh water spring gurgles its way through caves and over mossy boulders, the walls of the ravine covered with a lush growth of maidenhair ferns. I lollygagged around with the raft guides on the beach. I did not have time to kick sand in the afternoon however, as my diary recalls.

'We paddled sixteen miles after lunch, a long way, and there were two big rapids towards the end, Bedrock (Grade 7, Mile 130) and Dubendorff (Grade 7, Mile 132).[1] Bedrock, with a huge rock slam bam in the mainstream, was difficult for the rafts. Sharon, her boat weighed down with the extra gear from the Phantom Ranch change-around, could not pull it clear to the right. She bounced off the rock snapping an oar in the process. Most of us went left, by a channel too narrow for the rafts.'

'For us Dubendorff was more difficult. Here were big, big, waves, probably the biggest on the Canyon. There were no stoppers, but plenty of fourteen-foot haystacks that broke back at the top, the distinction between the two feeling a little fine at the time. There were a dozen canoes in the rapid, but I only ever saw one or two others when we peaked on top of our white-crested mountains at the same time. In the valleys the river tried to turn us beam-on, and from the summits to surf us bow or stern first into the neighbouring trough. My shoulders feel as though they have been carrying a yoke of water all day!

Day 9 was declared a rest day by Dwight. We stopped, just a mile downstream from our overnight camp, at Tapeats Creek (Mile 133$\frac{1}{2}$). Here a trail climbs 1,000 feet up the creek bed, then heads west to meet

---

[1] This rapid was named after the upset of Seymour Dubendorff in 1909.

another ascending from Deer Creek (Mile 136). A crossover walk was arranged along this so-called 'Surprise Trail', but Julie and I felt there would be more surprises in walking alone.

The two of us continued to Deer Creek in a raft, and reached the high desert talus slopes in an hour. Walking at random amongst the frost-cracked bass limestone, I stepped gingerly round the sleepy form of a rattlesnake and backed into a barrel cactus. I let out a great shout, which woke the creature. It slithered towards Julie, who was trying to identify a Mojave prickly pear cactus, and there was a squeal of trainers as she set off on a 100-metre dash that Carl Lewis would have been hard pressed to beat.

The heat forced us back down to the beach after a couple of hours. We swam in pools below the majestic Deer Creek Falls, stared at the sky, and relaxed to the sound of falling water. Down by the river we waited for the others.

The next two days followed a similar relaxing pattern. The rapids were few and far between, and we spent time off the river. We knew in reality however, that it was the quiet before the storm, because the biggest rapid was still to come, Lava Falls (Grade 10, Mile 179). An underlying feeling of tension remained. Some tried to work it off by bouldering in Matkatamiba Canyon (Mile 148), and others sought solace in the Japanese-style gardens of Havasu Canyon (Mile 157).[1] It didn't take much however, to make us jump and start. I fell asleep in Havasu, to be woken by Laurie holding a Californian king snake. I moved like a herd of startled gazelles. So did the snake.

Our twelfth day on the river marked the end of the little holiday. We paddled fifteen miles before lunch in cold and windy weather. It was a miserable affair, this hurried break for food, and the scrabbling for extra clothes. Back on the water Vulcan's Anvil, a flat-topped pinnacle of lava, warned us that the Falls were waiting. Gary hurled a quarter onto the rock as we went past, and the more superstitious amongst us sent with it our hopes for a safe passage.[2]

A low ominous roar thundered up the valley towards us. The Canyon walls hereabouts are a mile back on either side of the river, the close banks low-angled, so there was no echo to magnify or distort the sound. It embraced and surrounded us as we approached the falls, until we were

---

[1] A turquoise stream runs down Havasu all the year round. Plants abound, and little waterfalls form where the calcium-rich water has precipitated into ledges and dikes. These travertine dams, forming pools one on top of the other, are natural beds for sedges, cattails, and bullrushes.

[2] Some years previously a boatman, defying the gods, climbed the pinnacle and took all the money on it. He subsequently flipped in Lava Falls.

immersed in noise. Storm surf can give off this sort of sound, but no other runnable rapid I have ever heard. I was as though the river was dropping over some great cliff, like Niagara or Victoria Falls.

The canoeists climbed high on the left bank to take their first look at Lava Falls. A raft from White Water Expeditions was just beginning its run. The thirty-five-foot raft, big by comparison to ours, disappeared from sight in the first waves. The snout reappeared shedding water like a lifeboat in heavy seas, and then buried itself in the next lump. Swamped, it shuddered its way down the rapid, a crazy uncontrollable motion which did nothing to inspire us.

Our rafts were now coming through and we scrambled down for a closer look. Like a nineteenth-century battle fleet they came on astern, Laurie's little raft leading, followed by Sharon's, Dwight's snout boat, and finally the paddle raft. A Boadicea in her chariot, Laurie was standing on the thwarts, leading the charge, trying to pick a line. All her manoeuvering had to be done in the calm waters above the rapid, for to change direction in those giant waves would be impossible. Satisfied with her choice she strained against the oars to gain an extra knot of forward speed, and swept down the green tongue of water into the Falls.

The raft hit a hydraulic high in the rapid and for a moment all horizontal movement was changed into vertical. Zeiss, her partner in the raft, threw himself across the bow as it lifted skywards. Frustrated in this direction, the water tried to lift the stern. Zeiss stood up, heaving on the bow strap to lift the front. It was an act of balancing both delicate and aggressive, that had to be repeated three or four times down the rapid. Preoccupied thus they never saw the rock. An oar snapped and Laurie was left on one side rowing with a pole. She was down the rapid but drifting. Craning our necks from the highest boulders we scanned the lower reaches, cheering as we saw her hands go up in triumph in an eddy.

Sharon and Dwight with the greater momentum of their heavier rafts to help, cruised Lava Falls. Finally the paddle raft entered the fray. Being the lightest of all the rafts, power at the right moments would be crucial; only acceleration could see it through the stoppers and standing waves. Hitting one of these awkwardly the paddlers were thrown against each other. One let go his paddle and grabbed the side strap, another stroked air rather than water. Losing speed the raft turned broadside and broached on a rock. 'Top side,' Gary yelled already onto the pontoon that was lifting against the rock. The rest of the crew, trained for this eventuality over the past few days followed suit, their combined weight preventing a flip and allowing the raft to be carried off. It was five seconds before they were all paddling again, but the luck of Vulcan kept them away from any more rocks until they were back on course, clear to the bottom of the rapid.

Seeing the rafts go through successfully boosted my confidence in one sense. There were obviously no waves that had real holding power. Clearly however, it was going to be difficult keeping upright in water turbulent enough to flip a raft, and once upside down, even if I rolled, it would be impossible to keep a good line.

I tried to tell myself that I could do it. Mental preparation however, has never been my strong point and anxiety adversely affects physical performance, which I am sure is why I felt out of control in Lava Falls. That night I tried to put into words how it felt.

'I picked up my marker, which was a curling green wave, and rushed into the first haystack. Then I was bracing left and right. There seemed no pattern to the waves. I could only react. A curling breaker caught the back of the kayak and threw it sideways across the current. Water piled high onto the deck threatening to capsize me. I leant on the paddle and flicked back upright. I couldn't see above the water to where I was, or where I wanted to go. A wave hit me in the middle of a reverse stroke. Too slowly I turned the blade onto its back and pushed up and away from the water under my armpit. I was into a stopper before I had time for a forward stroke. Like a pinball, I was bounced from wave to haystack to stopper, getting more tired of the game all the time.

'A blob of yellow in the corner of my eye turned into a kayak as I took my eyes off the water for a split second. It seemed possible I could get to the eddy it occupied. A final spurt of adrenalin took me there, and I gave a weak smile to Joel bobbing up and down on the three-foot swell next to me. Not having the strength to get out I slumped in the boat, the blood thundering through my ears with a noise almost as great as the roar of Lava Falls.'

We awoke on our thirteenth and last full day in the Canyon with fuzzy heads from the night before. Lava was only five miles upstream, but, after the first few beers and joints, it might as well have been on another planet for all the truth there was in our war stories of killer boulders and boat-gobbling holes. We canoed thirty miles, falling asleep at lunchtime, coasting in the quiet sections, and trying to summon up enthusiasm for the unnamed but big rapids at Miles 205 and 209. Camp at Mile 215 was a quiet place.

It was just ten miles to our take-out at Diamond Creek. Fourteen days on the river meant we were accustomed to a slow pace of living. The hustle and bustle on the Diamond Creek road, deflating rafts and packing lorries with other raft teams behind us, was a swift and unpleasant return to the real world. (Just nine miles more of moving water lie between Diamond Creek and Lake Mead, and the first roadhead in that vast expanse of boring flatness is forty-five miles away at Pierce Ferry, so the Diamond Creek road is the most popular place to end Grand Canyon river trips.) The Hualapai Indians have discovered that controlling the use of this U.S.

government-built and maintained road is a lucrative proposition, and white America's continuing guilty conscience about the reservations allows the Indians to charge £50 per person at the take-out (no cheques accepted).

Jolted back to reality by the rutted gravel of Diamond Creek—which had flash flooded the day before—a little worm of resentment at the amount of money Julie and I had had to pay for the trip, crawled around in the back of my mind. There is no doubt that the raft companies over-monopolise the river. Non-commercial river running is severely restricted by the Park authorities—to about 20 per cent of river use—so that most people who want to raft or kayak the river are forced to turn to the raft companies—unless they are prepared to wait ten years for a private permit (or can somehow jump that queue). The Park Service prefer dealing with commercial organizations because they are easier to regulate, a not unreasonable point of view considering the fragile ecosystem in the Canyon. Perhaps the Park Service itself should monopolise Canyon use, and organize a river running service that would be fair to the environment, *and* to all the people who want to be in there. Such a solution however, is probably too radical for the free-enterprise system that is America.

Fortunately my memory of the Canyon is unsullied by these commercial considerations. No doubt this is what the raft companies rely on when they make money out of the experience. Even being part of a giant shuttle service—there were over a hundred people getting out at Diamond Creek on our last day—does not seem to matter. Of course it would be good to explore the Canyon as Powell or Stanton did, knowing that few had been there before, or even to have run the river before the war, when less than a hundred people had been down it. But in the end it is the Canyon itself that matters, not its history, or the temporary arrangements of its human visitors, for in all the world there is only one Grand Canyon.

New Zealand—The Favoured Isles by Terry Storry

'People die, are killed, migrate, disappear; not so the land, which remains for ever.' The Maoris did not know about nuclear fission when they passed this aphorism down to their sons and daughters. Nor indeed could they guess that someday white men would come to conquer their land, and change it beyond all recognition. Yet despite the great cities and factories, the harbours and paved roads, the invaders and their successors also revere the land they settled. Partly this is because farming was the backbone of their early existence—there are still twenty times more sheep than people in New Zealand. Partly it is because there were so few of them—there are still only three million people in a country bigger than Britain, a population density of just 28 people per square mile. And partly it is because of the land's incredible diversity, a variety of form and vegetation which is my most striking and lasting impression of New Zealand. So although Maori and white argue about many things, they agree on one. There are no nuclear power stations or nuclear weapons in New Zealand.

Living in and off this land, it is natural that New Zealanders, with increased leisure time, have taken to the outdoors. And because of the country's diversity—although the land is narrow and nowhere is more than 130 miles from the sea, a chain of mountains running down it's long spine makes the east as different from the west as the north is from the south—there is something for everyone. A person may dive in the clear waters of the Coromandel Peninsula or, in the same season, do some snow and ice climbing in the Southern Alps. He or she may orienteer in the half million acres of conifers that form the Kaingaroa forest, or tramp across the still-frozen steppe of Mackenzie sheep country. They may fight through rain forest in unexplored Fiordland, clamber up vine-and-tree-fern-strangled ravines in Wellington, or climb pumice and ash on the active volcanoes of the North Island. You can surf late winter storm swells off Christchurch, or, at the same time of year, heli-ski on Mount Cook,

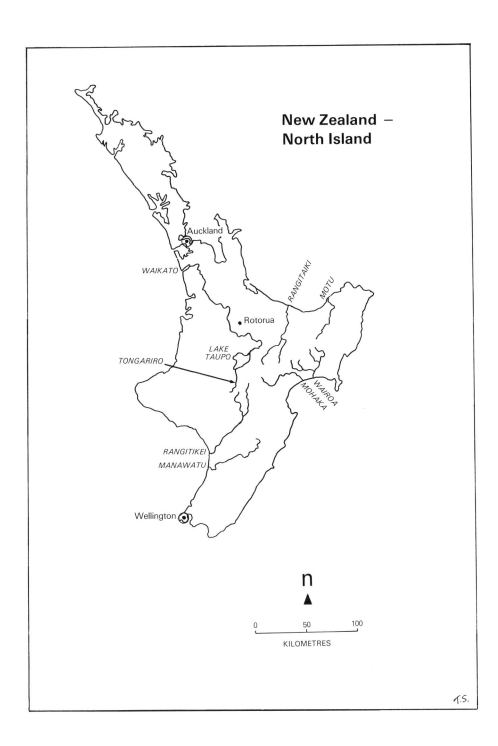

New Zealand –
North Island

Auckland

WAIKATO

RANGITAIKI

MOTU

• Rotorua

LAKE
TAUPO

TONGARIRO

WAIROA
MOHAKA

RANGITIKEI
MANAWATU

Wellington

n
▲

0   50   100
KILOMETRES

T.S.

water-ski in the Bay of Plenty, or sunbathe in the subtropical Bay of Islands.

Like the land through which they flow, the rivers of New Zealand are incredibly varied. In the north, central, and western regions of the North Island, steep small streams feed quickly into larger flatter rivers flowing through muddy valleys choked with willows. The eastern and southern hill country of the North Island provides better white water canoeing, notable rivers being the Rangitikei, Rangitaiki, Motu, Mohaka, Tongariro, and Wairoa. Characteristically these rivers have steep rocky gorges where they flow from the volcanic uplands into the plains.

In the South Island most of the rivers flow east and west from the Main Divide. In the west the rivers flow fast and steep through dense bush, before reaching a narrow coastal plain. The Buller and the Grey are the best canoeing rivers in Westland, being exceptional in the length of their gorges. Further south there are also some good rivers (the Waiatoto and Arawata for instance) but they are generally more difficult of access.

By contrast most of the rivers flowing east through Canterbury and Otago have roads leading close to their catchment areas. One reason is the greater population in the flatter drier land of the east. Another is the damming of rivers like the Rangitata, Clutha and Kawarau, which necessitated the building of access roads. Hydro schemes, of course, are a mixed blessing, making the water-flow predictable (by phone), but less plentiful, the rivers more accessible, but less wild. Most of the east coast rivers are glacier-fed, so the peak run-off and the highest dam releases are in the spring and early summer. At that time of the year conditions resemble the European Alps, the water cold but the air warm.

Finally there are the two strongly contrasting tips of the South Island. Nelson and Marlborough in the north have many small rivers, canoeable only after heavy rain, the one notable exception being the Clarence which offers a medium grade trip of three or four days. In Fiordland, at the other end of the island, heavy rainfall is the norm, making for many canoeable torrents. Here, getting to them is the problem, since much of this area remains a wilderness even to mountaineers.

I knew little of all this before I went in January 1985, but I had discovered enough to guess that New Zealand would be a white water paradise. A geologically young country such as this—volcanic activity is an everyday source of heating and power in the North Island—with an upthrusting landmass, must have many steep and irregular rivers. Throw in a maritime climate, producing high annual precipitation, and the rivers will frequently be canoeable. Add the seasoning of few people and an absence of feudal property rights, making for openly accessible rivers, and the recipe was

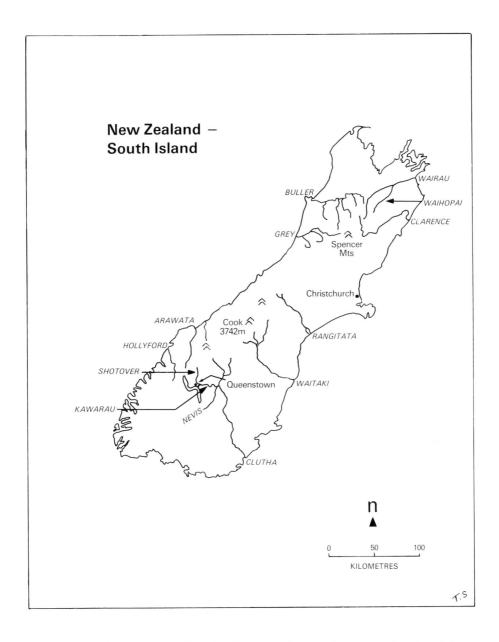

**New Zealand –
South Island**

WAIRAU

BULLER

WAIHOPAI

CLARENCE

GREY

Spencer
Mts

Christchurch

ARAWATA

Cook ⋀
3742m

RANGITATA

HOLLYFORD

SHOTOVER

Queenstown

WAITAKI

KAWARAU

NEVIS

CLUTHA

n
▲

| 0 | 50 | 100 |

KILOMETRES

T.S

irresistible. The only question, having saved enough money for the airfare, was how to get a kayak on the plane.

Julie and I approached the British Airways counter at Gatwick Airport carrying the vast red bulk of my Prijon Taiphun kayak between us. The scantily clad queue bound for California (we were to change planes in Los Angeles) stared at 'the Beast' and at my vast sweating bulk—in an effort to save on excess baggage. I was wearing two sweaters, a canoe bag and a buoyancy aid. 'Just playing it safe eh!' a porter said, nodding at my personal flotation while lifting the bags onto the scales. I grinned weakly, having heard the joke twice before that day, and stuck my foot under the scales.

'That's light,' the check-in clerk smiled.

'Good,' I grunted with the effort of holding ten kilograms on my toes, 'because we are taking that as well.' I pointed at the Beast.

'I am afraid I will have to charge that at the excess baggage rate,' she said reaching for a green form.

I drew in a deep breath. 'But I checked with British Airways and they said I could take it as normal luggage.'

'I am afraid we always charge for more than two pieces.' She copied the name from my passport onto the form.

'In that case I will pack all my luggage into the canoe.' The Beast did not let me down. Tent, rucksack, stove, sleeping bag, even the paddle, disappeared into its voluminous depths. I dragged the eighty-pound monster back to the counter leaving a red smear of plastic on the floor tiles. Miss Townshend—a tag on her uniform introduced her as such—gave an 'Ah yes' when my turn came, and reached to one side for my passport. I noticed there was now a pink form slipped inside it. She looked at me over her spectacles. 'Boats are oversize loads and we will have to charge you as such.' The new form was brought out with an ill-disguised flourish. 'How long is it?' The pen was poised; my name was already filled in.

'I took canoes to Chile four years ago, and we were never charged extra then.' She must have sensed victory from the whine in my voice, for she relaxed into the classic bureaucratic ploy.

'I am sorry, but I don't make the rules.'

They do say that all is fair in love and war, but I did something then that I promised myself I would never do. Infuriated by her Nuremberg excuse[1] I turned to Julie for support. The effect was frightening.

'We wouldn't have brought the bloody thing to the airport if we hadn't been promised it would go on the plane as normal luggage. Why don't you check with your supervisor. Don't you keep records on this sort of thing? We could hire a canoe out in New Zealand cheaper than the price you are going to charge us for taking it there.' Julie stood on a fellow passenger's suitcase to raise her five foot nothing over the counter; a small crowd gathered behind. Miss Townshend, who was vigorously prodding her

---

[1] A defence used by a number of Germany's war criminals at the Nuremberg War Crimes Trial was that they had simply been following orders, as soldiers must. The defence was not allowed.

glasses back up her nose, had been joined by a man with gold stripes on his cuffs. 'I have travelled twice before by Air New Zealand,' Julie continued, 'and bicycles and windsurfers were going on the plane at no extra charge. Yet here is British Airways suggesting carrying something no bigger, and far less breakable, for more money. You are living in the dark ages . . .'

The mauling would have gone on, but a wave from Gold Cuffs ended the unequal contest. Two luggage handlers weightlifted the Beast onto a trolley, and wheeled it away towards the loading doors and the waiting plane. Miss Townshend took a well-earned tea break, and Gold Cuffs gave us our boarding passes. A light smattering of applause followed Julie as she set off for the duty free shop, and, after wiping her footprints off the pigskin suitcase, I followed in her majestical wake.

We were greeted in New Zealand by airport workers with aerosol cans spraying us with fungicide, and customs officials in shorts saying 'good day' out of the sides of their mouths, 'gudaye'. The heat radiated off the tarmac and down our faces. It was good to get out of Auckland and onto the only piece of dual carriageway in the country, a cooling wind rattling the windows of our rented wreck. Our first stop was Rotorua and the Immigration Department. Julie renewed her residence permit (having previously worked in the country), and I found the offices of New Zealand River Runners, a raft company whose brochure I had picked up at the airport. They were running a trip on the Rangitaiki river the next day, and agreed to give me a lift, after Julie had paid to go in the raft.

The forty-seater coach bounced us along the Kaingaroa forest dirt roads to the put-in at the confluence with the Wheo. The rafts and their guides had already arrived and I watched with some interest as the tourists—New Zealanders, Australians, Americans, and one Briton—were given a land drill. There was another trip to be run that afternoon, so the punters were quickly squeezed into, or swamped by, an assortment of ill-fitting wetsuits, helmets, and lifejackets, told how to paddle forwards, backwards and sideways, and given advice on what to do if thrown into the water—'don't panic'. Without further ado they, and I, launched, and we were rapidly into a Grade IV rapid, 'Jeff's Joy'.

Jeff's Joy is the most notable rapid on the Rangitaiki (apart from Aniwhenua Falls, a one-shot wonder, which I canoed just before leaving New Zealand[1]) and is certainly the hardest on this section of river (from

---

[1] Aniwhenua Falls, a 30 ft waterfall, is the last drop on the Rangitaiki before it flows, via Matahina Lake and Dam, into the Bay of Plenty. Originally considered uncanoeable, a dam constructed in 1980 diverted all but a small stream of water round the fall. Its height of course, is unaffected, but there is now no vicious stopper to greet the canoeist below, and no difficult approach rapids to contend with above. I still found it a big deal!

the Wheo confluence to Murapara). The name suggests a certain lack of seriousness—Jeff was a logger who used to ride the rapid in a rubber tube in his lunch hour—but it is awesome to look at and the guidebook, at least, is unequivocal about its difficulty.

> 'Jeff's Joy is potentially very dangerous. Two of the country's top slalomists will not go near it, having had almost terminal swims there. The danger exists in the precision needed to avoid the waterfall on the right-hand side of the chute . . . It is about a three- or four-metre drop into a severe backwash.'[1]

Imagine yourself, on your holidays in New Zealand, more than likely with no closer experience of white water than the surf on some sandy beach, pounding down Jeff's Joy after just a couple of minutes in a rubber raft with people who had been strangers an hour before, and with a raft guide bellowing instructions in your ear that you first learnt five minutes before. There is not a lot of paddling going on!

The rest of this section of the Rangitaiki is easier, but nevertheless provides some excellent play waves for canoes, and some tight manoeuvres for rafts. Having extracted themselves from the floor of the raft, and their paddles from the river, the punters may now be able to contribute to its progress. If the raft guide has done *his* job, they will think, by the time they are tucking into their barbecue snack, that *they* have done it all.

Two more trips on the Rangitaiki on successive days sent me to sleep on the drive over the Ahimanawa Hills to Lake Taupo. Waking to a dull roar and a gentle drizzle out of clear blue skies my first thought was, 'surf's up'. Then, as I was undoing the roofrack straps, Julie said, 'The lads at New Zealand River Runners thought you might like to have a go at this rapid,' and I thought, 'Leave the boat *on*'.

The Waikato River which drains Lake Taupo is the biggest river in the North Island of New Zealand, and the longest (435 kms) in the country. It is heavily dammed and largely flat, but in two places, Aratiatia and here at Huka, there are big drops. Huka Falls is a long rapid ending in a 12-metre drop. The massive stopper which forms at the bottom of the fall has been known to recirculate floating objects for more than three minutes. This is discouraging for river runners.

Nevertheless Huka Falls has been attempted four times. The first was by a fisherman who, surprised by rising water released from the dam upstream, was swamped in his waders and carried off down the rapid. He emerged from the stopper alive. A suicide attempt followed; twice a local

---

[1] G.D. and J.H. Egarr in *Hawke Bay, East Cape, Bay of Plenty Canoeist's Guide.* (N.Z. Canoeing Association, 1978).

woman jumped into the Waikato from the bridge upstream of Huka, surfacing both times still breathing. She turned to religion. The third attempt was by two canoeists, and was intentional. They were still in their boats when the washing machine spat them out after a short thirty-second cycle. However, they had smoked so much hash prior to the run that neither had the faintest idea what it had been like to be in the stopper for that long.

I certainly did not want to find out, preferring a modest Grade V as my next major trip. Like the Rangitaiki, the Rangitikei flows out of the Kaimanawa Mountains, but whereas the former flows north into the Bay of Plenty, the Rangitikei heads south emerging eventually into the Tasman Sea. Most of it is flat and of little interest to the white water addict, but there is a gorge between the Matawhero road bridge and Pukeohahau, which is famous throughout New Zealand for its rapids. The authors of the guidebook have certainly done nothing to diminish its reputation.

> 'The notable rapids . . . none of which are really portagable without long and difficult detours . . . are Max's Drop, Foaming Rapid, Fulcrum and See Through . . . needing extreme care and caution to run and a readiness to roll quickly before being caught and swept into the next cataract or bluffs . . . At higher than normal flows, rapids such as Fulcrum would be Grade 5–6. Do not attempt this trip after a week of heavy rain.'[1]

Fortunately there were others, at the Outdoor Pursuits Centre of New Zealand where we were staying, who were interested in this trip. It did not sound like a good river to do alone—unlike the friendly Tongariro on which I had been messing about for the past two days.[2] After reading the description, a part of each of us was hoping that Brian Sage, who owned the private road at the Pukeohahu take-out, would tell us that the river was too high, when we phoned for permission to cross his land. The Rangitikei Gorge was in flood he told us, but it was canoeable. That excuse ruined, a couple of us mysteriously lost key items of equipment, like helmet and paddle, only to be loaned them by O.P.C. staff who were working that day. Then, having happily got lost driving through the steep papa gorges on the approach to the river, we were put right by an unfuriatingly helpful local, arriving with just enough time to run the river.

---

[1] G.D. & J.H. Egarr in *Manawatu, Wellington & Wairarapa Canoeist's Guide.* (N.Z. Canoeing Association, 1978). The same authors were responsible for the description of Jeff's Joy. Perhaps the Egarrs were briefed by the N.Z.C.A. to keep numbers down on wild water rivers, by psyching out paddlers.
[2] Sections 10, 13, and 14, all Grade III-IV. They are described in the *Hawke Bay, East Cape, Bay of Plenty Canoeist's Guide.*

Beneath the bridge the river was flat, and so it was for the first kilometre. We were carried over shingle banks and past open grassland by a fast muddy current. Gradually the valley sides steepened. Bedrock began to protrude from the scrubby hillsides until finally there was nothing but rock all around us. The rapids became increasingly difficult, and the friendly banter of our run-in died away as we each concentrated on our canoeing.

In Max's Drop, the first Grade V, I made a mistake. A momentary lapse of concentration and the Beast was sliding sideways along a diagonal curling stopper. At the end, where it met the main current, I was flipped over. This was not a good place to swim, since I would be swept into the other rapids before anyone could reach me. I had to roll, I had to get up, but the very urgency of the demand forced another mistake. I screwed my paddle round on the surface and pulled down. The kayak started to right itself, but I lifted my head before it was past the point of no return. I got a breath which I needed, a look downstream which I didn't, and crucially altered the centre of gravity way out to one side, so that I capsized again.

'Calm down,' I told myself. 'Set the paddle on the surface, unwind, hip flick, lie back, and . . . yes you're up.' I was immediately into the next rapid. 'Come on Storry you can do it; draw and . . . and . . . watch that hole, go, go, full power, right and left . . . look, there's a break-out . . . missed it, there's another, sweep, sweep, into the slack water on the lean, brace and . . . rest.' Dropping my head and arms I gulped great draughts of air, and let the eddies of Foaming Rapid lap over my hands.

The others made it look easy, but then there was Fulcrum, impossible to portage and impossible to inspect, a long rapid of considerable technical difficulty. Marty was third man down and third man unlucky. He angled his boat across a chute that had a hidden stopper at its base. Dropping sideways into the hole, he could not escape its clutches. He stayed upright bracing on the wave, but was going nowhere.

Those of us who remained upstream could not see Marty's predicament. We only knew that his boat had not reappeared, so either he was stuck in it, or he was swimming and we had missed him. I got out on the bank, preparing to throw him a line if he was stuck. I was in time to see Chris, who had continued downstream, hit Marty at full tilt.

Somehow Chris stayed upright, and the momentum of his charge carried them both out of the hole. Marty however, was upside down and apparently hurt for he neither rolled nor came out of his boat. I could do nothing as I was marooned on a small beach ending in a vertical cliff. Eventually Marty's head appeared beside the upturned boat. Chris could not do much to help Marty either, as he was concentrating on paddling in the difficult water. Marty let the boat go and half swam, half floated to the rocky shore. He pulled himself painfully onto a small peninsula of land.

The bank was still sheer hereabouts, so Marty was committed to finishing the trip. Moreover since the cliffs prevented us getting to him, he was forced to jump back into Foaming Rapid (after trying every rock climbing alternative) and swim down to where we had dragged his boat to the shore. Stiff, battered, but unbowed, he paddled all but the last big rapid.

The safest route down See Through was an almost vertical drop the height of a canoe. Even the Beast, by far the most voluminous kayak, was completely submerged in the pool below. The other kayaks disappeared for seconds at a time, surfacing ten metres downstream, their spray decks imploded, and their passengers exploding like whales coming up for air.

Jabbering like fools in the release of tension we frolicked in the last few rapids. We spotted Brian Sage and his raft boys high on a bluff overlooking the gorge. Some of us waved; but others gave a dismissive gesture as if to say, 'Yeah, we know you thought there was going to be trouble because the water was high, but we did it, so you can go now, back to your homes, without that story you were making up about "dum kayakers, should have known better" And isn't it the same for men (or is it boys) the world over, this 'us against them', this male bonding in fight or flight, and don't we just love it. Still, better the playground than the battlefield, I thought, wrestling Chris to the ground in the long grass beside the car. We were still punching and slapping in the back seat, as Julie, casting the occasional motherly smile in our direction, drove us home.

The Cook Strait was as calm as this wild stretch of sea can be, on our crossing from North to South Island. Then shortly after we landed, the spinning edge of a vicious Pacific cyclone brought wind and rain enough to force us from our tent into a caravan. It also meant however, that we could sample one of Marlborough's rivers, the Waihopai,[1] which is normally only canoeable in the wetter winter months. Julie was not impressed with her borrowed gear, or with the backlash and strong eddies around the rocky walls of the narrow ravine, but in the process of retrieving her and her boat we made friends with Annette Richards, a companion on my next river.

---

[1] The Waihopai provides very good canoeing in the short gorge below the power station. The gorge extends for about 7 kilometres, is Grade III when the dam is spilling water, and Grade IV in full flood. It was interesting to note that the formerly deep reservoir behind the dam is now completely silted up into braided shingle flats, a process which will affect every hydro project eventually. Now the flow of the river must be diverted round the dam and into the power house by a concrete spillway.

The Buller is famous in New Zealand because it provides one of the longest, canoe, or raft (or rubber tyre!) trips in the country. Its headwaters are in the St Armand and Spencer Mountains, but Lake Rotoitu, with its feeder the Traverse River, is the source of the main stream. From the lake the Buller collects water from a host of tributaries, many of them—like the Gowan, Hope, Howard, Mangles, Matakitaki, Matiri, and Maruia (the influence of different patterns of settlement apparent in their names)—canoeable in their own right. It then drops steeply through two gorges below Murchison. The upper gorge contains the famous rapids of Whale Creek, Jet Boat and Ariki, while the lower gorge is quiet-flowing, a noted tourist attraction. The last sixty or so kilometres to Westport are also reported to be very scenic, and, as with the rest of the river (as I was to find out), best seen from the water due to the dense bush that covers the banks.

Having warmed up on the big and bouncy Granity Creek Rapid,[1] Annette and I moved down to the upper gorge below O'Sullivan's Bridge. The rapids between here and Newton Flat Gravel Pit contain the best white water on the Buller, and although they were washed out to a modest Grade IV at the time we were on the river, they still contained the odd doubtful stopper and enough weird boiling eddies to command a good deal of respect.

Annette watched me paddle Ariki, the biggest rapid of them all—like a stretch of sea between two rocky cliffs—and decided to walk. In my egoism (well I didn't have to roll) I expected her to follow, and, when she didn't appear, I got out to see if she was in trouble. Getting out (and getting back in) however, was easier said than done. I had to rock climb with a line attached from my chest harness to the bow toggle of my boat. Bobbing up and down in the boiling eddy, it threatened all the time to break out from its little harbour and drag me backwards into the water. At the top I hauled the Beast up, and set off into the bush.

Jungle is actually a better way to describe New Zealand bush, since the only way through it is with a machete. I tried heading for the road just 50 metres away but could make no progress. I tried scrambling along the rocky cliff, but it was too steep. I had abandoned the boat long ago, but did not realize, until I could no longer remember the way that I had come, that my cagoule had been torn from around my waist. The Beast was bigger, so I eventually found it again, launching precariously from the cliff back into the Buller. This manoeuvre may be good for going off ice flows, but seals (it is called a 'seal launch') do not have spraydecks to fit, or paddles to grab as they over-balance, and it was with some relief that I

---

[1] Granity Creek (Grade III) comes towards the end of an excellent stretch of 13 kilometres between the Gowen and Owen Rivers.

emerged from the 20 ft slide in a dry boat, paddle in hand. Annette met me at the take-out, looked me over—the missing cagoule, the ripped wetsuit, the scratched face, the wild eyed stare—and said 'Boy, am I glad I didn't run *that* rapid.

Flowing out of the Southern Alps into the dry east coast Canterbury Plains are a number of big snow- and glacier-fed rivers. Famed amongst river runners is the Rangitata. The Gorge of the Rangitata, our host in Christchurch, Mick Hopkinson, said, contained one of the most frightening rapids in the country—The Pinch with Harry's Hole. Indeed Mick, star of the first descent of the Dudh Kosi (the river of Everest) admitted, after a few glasses of wine, and with a shudder that shook his black curly hair, that he had swum in there—'Ooooh, horrible'.

To try and calm my nerves I spent an afternoon surfing on Christchurch beach, and then we took in *Ghost Busters* at the cinema. On the moonlit drive south to Peel Forest and the Rangitata I thought about what the lads from N.Z. River Runners had said about the river: 'A wild water paradise. The rapids are unsurpassed anywhere for sheer heart-thumping excitement. You can only safely run this river between specific upper and lower levels. We decide in the morning whether we are going to run it.'

Arriving at Waikiri Hills Station in the early morning mist we found that N.Z. River Runners had cancelled all their trips down the gorge; the river was too high. Another raft company however, Value Tours, were going ahead with their plans, and although Julie would not take the ride, I decided, after a number of visits to the toilet, to join these dinosaurs (long necks and no brains!). Holding my kayak precariously balanced on top of two rafts, we were bounced across the tussock paddocks of Whiterock Sheep Station, and down to the river. Anxious to inspect the rapids before the rafts arrived, I changed while the punters were given their briefing. The familiar smell of my gear, redolent with sweat, sea water, adrenalin, and jet engine fuel, calmed me somewhat. I warmed up with some crosses. The kayak felt responsive to my feet, knees and thighs, the paddle light in my hands. I set off downriver leaving the raft crew pumping up their pontoons.

Tim, Value Tours' leader had briefed me on what to expect. There were three big ones, Pencil Sharpener, Rooster Tail, and The Pinch. These I should inspect. I paddled over a number of fast shingle rapids. The rapids increased in size as the gradient steepened and the river narrowed. I powered through a couple of meaty cataracts with 6 ft standing waves, and arrived at a flat section before an obvious drop in the river bed. I got out to have a look.

At the top of the rapid where the water dipped like a ditch across its full width, there was a huge isolated rock (which I thought, mistakenly, was the 'pencil sharpener'), sending up a plume of water (this was, in fact, the 'rooster tail') and splitting the stopper which formed behind the 'ditch'. This weakness in the stopper, two tongues of green water splitting the white wave, offered a route through, but there were the Sycilla of the rock and the Charybdis of the stopper to punish any mistake.

I was clumsy with nerves and could not get my spray deck back on. The Beast wallowed in the swell. Setting off I realised I was paddling with the blades the wrong way round. I fled back to the eddy, and held on to a rock. A tiny spider made its way across the wave-washed basalt. Legs tensed every time the river surged, it ran when the water dropped. For a few moments I watched its progress.

The Rooster Tail was obscured from me by the ditch, but I had picked up a little curling green wave as my marker. Paddling into the main stream again, it took me three or four powerful strokes before I was over the lip. I was slightly off line, and felt the powerful eddy running up to the rock draw me in. Then I was past and through the stopper at its weak point, Bobbing, bouncing, and beaming in the haystacks below, I felt elated with success. Paddling solo seemed to heighten every emotion.

Still thinking I had just passed Pencil Sharpener, I was walking down the bank looking for Rooster Tail when one of the rafts steamed past. A novice guide had stopped on the opposite bank from me, also wanting to inspect what was below. I paddled across to his stationary raft, but, before I had time to walk down the bank, he rushed back, nervous, and absolutely tight-lipped beyond telling me that the river narrowed considerably and I should keep to the centre. I suppose he and I were both hyped up, not having been on the river before, and he was afraid of losing contact with his leader. Anyway I decided if I needed a closer look I would get out again further down.

By the time I realized that I would not be able to climb the sheer banks above the narrowing it was too late. The eddy in which I had finally stopped was going up and down on a 5 ft confused and choppy swell. There was no way I could get out without capsizing, and there were no further eddies before the river funnelled into the narrows. I had no option but to run the rapid blind.

Breaking into the current I was immediately into green mounds of white-crested water. Backed up by the 20-ft narrowing the waves peaked higher and higher as 10,000 cubic feet per second struggled to get through. Suddenly I realized my mistake. Somewhere I had missed a rapid. What I had thought was Pencil Sharpener, was Rooster Tail, and here, what I had believed to be Rooster Tail, must be The Pinch. And this, I grimaced, gliding down the face of a huge hydraulic, must be Harry's Hole.

Paddling hard I broke through the stopper, whooped with relief, and relaxed for a split second. It was a split second too long. As my speed died, I slid down the front of a second even bigger hole, also blocking the full width of the river. Had Mick told me there were two holes? I could not remember. In any case it was too late now. Straining my back into the paddle I hardly made any impression on the real Harry's Hole. The world turned white, then green, then blue. It was like plunging into a swimming pool from the top board. Everything was fast and free until suddenly a solid mass of water hit me. The kayak stood on end, stern in the water, bow to the sky. I hung onto the paddle as if the blades flapping uselessly in the air could somehow control this crazy gyroscope. The stopper flipped the boat up and around so that it landed plum on top of the wave facing upstream. It was sheer luck. I was in the perfect position for a 'pop-out', a technique practised endlessly in the surf. Blood pounding in my ears blocked the approaching roar of the hole as it drew me in. I leaned forward dipping the bow and increasing my forward speed. The boat dived deep, until its bouyancy overcame its momentum and it was hurled back the way it had come, like an airtight ball released from the bottom of the bath. Airborne six inches off the water, the Beast cleared the stopper wave and dropped me clear of the backtow.

'Gudaye . . . I thought you was a gonner there mate.' The raft leader was perched on a rock like a garden gnome, camera in hand. 'Did you get any shots?' I managed, before collapsing on the comfortable buoyancy of his raft. Later I wondered about this obsession, so often voiced and felt, with pictures. Is it that extreme wild water is more enjoyable in the telling than in the doing? Or is it that it is so good, yet so ephemeral, that we want pictures to unlock the memory of it, like snaps of the children? Maybe we want to show our history to other people as a short cut to establishing our *bona fides*—this is what I have done, these are my children. I don't know the answer, but for some reason I was glad when he said, 'Sorry mate, I just forgot about the camera when you started looping the loop.'

Queenstown is famous for two beautiful rivers, the Kawarau and its tributary the Shotover. The latter is thought of as being New Zealand's 'wild river' by the public and the press, and although canoeists know better, the combination of its gold mining history and exciting white water make it an unforgettable experience. The river begins near Mount Aspiring and flows in a general southerly direction over shingle flats and through a lengthy gorge known as Skipper's Canyon. Dunedin Canoe Club have named Skipper's rapids; they are, in order of descent, Rock Graden, Boulder, Mother (a shortened version of the original), Pinball, Jaws and The Tunnel.

The last is just what it says, a 100-metre tunnel.

It was dug by gold miners to divert the river away from some rich seams. Unfortunately for the gold diggers, they misjudged the level of the Shotover, so water continued to flow down the original channel. Recently this channel has been blocked by a rock fall, creating an alternative rapid to the tunnel—Mother-in-Law, a dangerous fall of razor-sharp blocks only possible in high water. At normal levels however, The Tunnel remains the best and most spectacular finish to any wild water trip that I know.[1]

Again I hitched a ride with my nerveless friends from the Rangitata, Value Tours.

I was ahead of the rafts at Mother, and stopped to take pictures. Seen through the viewfinder of my camera the scenes were bizarre. SNAP—a legless torso surrounded by white water; SNAP—the torso gains legs, straddling a pontoon of rubber, steering a wild crew; SNAP—tangles of arms and grimacing faces in a raft, a paddle floating vertically behind, a burst of spray covering the front; SNAP—a cauldron of white and green framed by a bend in the gorge, grotesque buttes of rock leering into the river, a floating head amputated by the yellow collar of its lifejacket; SNAP—white flecks obscure the lens, like the rain on some end-of-pier viewing booth capable of the most extraordinary feats of projection.

The rafts retrieved their passengers from the various rapids, and we stopped above The Tunnel and Mother-in-Law to decide which route to take. There was just enough room between water and roof for the rafts to go down the tunnel. Julie describes her hysterical trip into that deep night.

'The Tunnel is only just wide enough to take an 18 ft Avon, and at the level we did it, only just high enough. In order to prevent us jamming and then folding in The Tunnel, the guide gave us instructions on how to pry (push away) and draw (pull towards) with the paddle. I remember a little of this from the Rangitaiki, and the Colorado, but none of the others had held a paddle in their hands before Deadman's Creek.'[2] Shortly after entering the tunnel we dropped through a small rapid and the guide started shouting "pry left", "draw back right" and so on. No one knew, or could see, what to do, and the raft bounced from one wall to the other in the darkness. Seeing nothing we heard everything and I can still remember the sounds of that tunnel.
"Pry Gary, just push off that . . ."—GRRRIPP—"quick . .
."—CRRRUNCH—"watch the roof it's . . . oooof . . ."—SPLASH—"my

---

[1] Canoeists might well wish to canoe the Shotover below Skippers, but this is not possible because jet boats run tourists upriver as far as The Tunnel (Arthur's Point). A jet boat travels at fifty miles an hour, and would, no doubt, come off best in any encounter with a canoe or kayak.

[2] Deadman's Creek is the put-in used by the raft companies for Skippers Canyon.

paddle . . . We must get further right, ouch, now left, only 50 metres to . . ."—BANG, HISSSSS—"The side's gone . . . aaaaahr, get off my . . . oooof . . . We'll make it, there's the . . ."—GRRRUMFF—"Help"—"quick pull her in, we've . . ." The tunnel ends in a Grade IV rapid, which we did with one of our chambers flat and someone hanging off the side. Rafting is good fun, but I've never been since.'

Kayaking the tunnel was easy by comparison, although still an absolutely unique sensory experience. Having paddled it twice I went over to have a look at the alternative, Mother-in-Law. As far as I could find out from the raft guides, who were inspecting the rapid at the same time, it had never been canoed. This was because of the sharp-edged boulders in the river bed which all the local canoeists and raft guides had seen at one time or another, and which, apparently, threatened to rearrange the features of anyone stupid enough to be upside down in that chute. But I had never seen it in low water, and ignorance is bliss.

I asked a couple of the raft guides to stand on a boulder which I guessed might pin me, and after walking up and down the bank for ten minutes I convinced myself that I could do it. I had to roll near the bottom, but my head hit nothing. I was through clean. A tremendous feeling of exhilaration swept over me, a feeling which stayed with me for the rest of the day. Adrenalin however, is a drug, and I needed another injection of excitement if it was to last much longer. I was sitting on top of a wall, but like Humpty Dumpty I was to have a big fall.

Two options appealed to me, the Lower Kawarau and The Nevis. First I paddled the rapids of Smith's, Twin Bridges, Doolittle, and Chinese Dogleg on the Upper Kawarau. Even Humpty was impressed by the immense weight of water in this river (20,000 cfs), and it seemed foolish, despite the known exaggeration of the Egarrs' guidebook writing style, to contemplate Nevis Bluff (not to be confused with the Nevis River)—'the most horrific set of rapids in the country'—or Roaring Meg Power Station—'impossible to run this rapid'—or even Sargood's Weir—'never successfully run by canoe'[1]—which all lay on the Lower Kawarau. The Nevis, on the other hand, had been run it seemed by Kawarau Raft Expeditions (KRE), even if not, according to Egarr, by canoe.

I had picked up the KRE brochure in the Queensland Tourist Office and was immediately hooked.

'The Nevis River is only one and a half hours from Queenstown, lies in an isolated valley behind the Remarkable Mountains, and is surrounded by the

---

[1] G.D. and J.H. Egarr in *Otago, Southland Canoeist's Guide* (N.Z. Canoeing Association 1978).

most spectacular scenery. The river, the narrowest and most spectacular in New Zealand, contains over fifty waterfalls and has continuous white water for 20 miles.'

I rang the tour operator ('Hi, I'm Bill') to see if I could hitch a ride, but there were no raft trips planned. Nevertheless, he put me in touch with Edgar, one of his guides ('You'd better not go alone on that river'), and offered to run Edgar and me up there if we decided to go for it.

Driving over Dulfer's Saddle a thousand feet above sea level, Bill had to put his jeep into four wheel drive to cope with the dirt road. A sense of isolation, such as I had felt on no other New Zealand river, crept over me.[1] This feeling of commitment was strengthened when Bill, dropping down through the abandoned gold digs of the Carrick Range, admitted that he had never actually rafted the river commercially, considering it too dangerous except for 'special' customers. Furthermore the only time he had run the river (with 'a bunch of friends') he had lined the rafts down many sections, and portaged others. Edgar seemed unaffected by this news, continuing to peer placidly out of the window at the bleak landscape. He told me later he hadn't been surprised: 'Bill never lets truth get in the way of good publicity.'

The river began pleasantly enough, but the land round Nevis Crossing was wild and inhospitable. The rocky earth was barren, quite useless for crops, and there was no evidence of permanent human settlement or even animal grazing. A short gorge a kilometre below the put-in took our minds off the lonely tundra (in winter snow blocks the road and covers the land, barring all access), and a 6 ft fall at the end forced us both to roll. Looking back upstream I recognized the drop; it was the brochure picture of the Nevis. I had a brief and all too forlorn hope that it was the measure of things to come.

Half a kilometre further down we rounded a bend and arrived at the lip of the valley. The river dropped away downhill, tumbling over waterfall after waterfall, while on either side the banks steepened sprouting rock bluffs and monstrous boulders. Through and over these we carried our canoes past impossibly dangerous drops, slides and chokes, occasionally able to paddle a short section only to be stopped again by another cascade. The portaging was so difficult that it was quicker taking the boats between us, one on either end. This meant we traversed that hideous terrain three times for every carry. Where the bank was too steep we were forced up into the maquis, a Corsican-style mixture of scrub, dwarf trees and bush. It was

---

[1] There are of course, many committing multi-day trips to be done in New Zealand—the Mohaka, Motu, Clarence and Landsborough to name only the most famous—but I had neither the time nor the money to get to them.

just too high to carry the canoes above, and we had to drag them on the sandy soil beneath, stepping over or through it ourselves. On one such occasion, Edgar turned to me, stripped to the waist, batting the flies from his sweat-soaked face, and said, 'Now I know what happens to canoeists when they go to hell.'

Finally the portaging got to me; I ignored the 'worst possible eventuality' rule. This goes something like this: 'If I capsize and swim, what is the worst that could happen to me, and am I prepared to accept the consequences?' We were about halfway down a waterfall gorge. A difficult chicane of white water led to a 10-ft drop. A pool of flat water followed, perhaps 20 metres long, fast-moving in the centre, but with eddies on either side. There was then another bigger waterfall which, you would not want to go down for any amount of money. I knew that I had enough time either to roll in the pool or swim to the bank. What I failed to think through was, what if I tried and then failed to roll.

Edgar continued carrying his boat down the bank, and then waited beside the pool with his throw line. I tried to control the bucking and bouncing boat down the chicane, conscious all the time of getting a clean line over the drop. It seemed to be right, but the stopper at the bottom flipped me over quicker than I could catch breath. Then my paddle was ripped out of one hand as I sat up for the roll. Screamingly conscious of the limited time available, I kicked out of my boat, and made for the bank. Edgar missed with the line, but I made it, just.

By some fluke my boat was pushed into an eddy on the opposite bank, but my paddles were gone. I yelled to Edgar to get my boat which was bobbing around upside down in slack water, undecided about whether to enter the mainstream again. He jumped in his boat, nearly capsized in the strong back eddy on the far side and grabbed the Beast's bow toggle. Grinning he gave a thumbs up ('The splits are still in it'[1]), and I started the long hike back up the river to where I could swim across and join him.

It was 3 p.m. and we were still only a third of the way down the river. Waterfall succeeded waterfall—in one stood my paddles, jammed vertically, a blade clear pulsing to and fro above the boulder choke, a monument to my stupidity. The portages started eating into our hours of daylight. We had to take risks again.

One cascade blocked the entrance to a sheer-sided gorge which would have taken an hour to portage. We waded across the river part of the way and balanced the kayaks above the steepest-looking pool. I made Edgar

---

[1] Splits, short for split paddles, a spare set of blades that Edgar had fortunately brought along, and which I carried in the bigger boat. Split to enable stowage, they pushed together to form a replacement for my lost paddles.

an offer he couldn't refuse. 'You go first; I'll hold your boat while you get in.' Very noble this, except that we did not know if there were rocks hidden just below the surface in the plunge pool. There was no sudden jarring impact. Now me; no one to push me off, so I toppled sideways upside down into the pool. 'I'll go first next time, Edgar.'

We paddled across the top of horrendous rapids to see if the opposite bank looked easier to carry. We jumped rather than climbed boulder to boulder, boats balanced on our backs (lighter now without the splits, the food—in our stomachs—and the spare clothes—on our backs in the cool of the evening), using the paddles as crutches in our hurried and precarious balancing acts.

Eventually the Nevis let us go. It eased from Grade VI to Grade V—where most things were canoeable after inspection—and then to Grade IV—where we could paddle rapids on sight. It was dark when we reached the junction with the Kawarau. Bill had left a two-way radio there. We called out a crackly message to KRE, and lay back under the stars.

'Do you know the similarity between a canoeist and a goldfish,' I said rolling over onto my side. 'One mucks about in fountains, and the other f . . .'

'No, no, the similarity iiiis,' Edgar sounded drunk, 'they've both got such small brains, that they've already forgotten where they've been when they reach the other side of the pond.' We started giggling, laughing, roaring, out of control, heads thrown back, doing little jigs, staggering arms round each other, dancing in the lights of the passing trucks.

It was probably just the exhaustion, the lack of food, and the relief; but I like to imagine, looking back, that some connections were made on that river, in those simple acts of survival, that made us friends enough in a day, to feel as though we had been together for a year. One fine January morning, long after we had returned from New Zealand, Edgar appeared on our doorstep in Wales. He helped me paint my son's room. From the top of the ladder he turned, and grinned, 'Do you remember . . .'

Oh yes, I do, I do.

A quiet moment on the Bio Bio framed by the volcano Callaquen.

Above: **The author taking a sideways look at the 'Ace' on the Bio Bio in Chile.**

Left: **Cruising 'Queen' in Royal Flush Gorge on the Bio Bio.**

Entrance to The Tunnel
(river right) on the
Shotover River, South
Island, New Zealand.

The author in
Mother-in-Law rapid –
the alternative to The
Tunnel on the Shotover
River!

The Tunnel exit,
Shotover River.

The smaller kayaks
scouting for the
heavily laden canoes
on the Nile.

A meeting with Arab
feluccas beside the
Nile.

Sleeping while the
wind blows the
'wrong' way down the
Nile.

The Tama Kosi River,
Eastern Nepal.

The 'night before the
storm'; camping
beside the Sun Kosi
near Harkapur, Nepal.

The team at journey's
end, Sun Kosi, Nepal.

Pat strokes her C1 through redwall limestone in the Grand Canyon of the Colorado River, U.S.A.

Entering Lava Falls in the Grand Canyon.

Pat approaching the big hole in Crystal Rapid upside down! A rescue boat is in the foreground.

The ice cliffs of the
Lowell Glacier on the
Alsek.

Wild water on the Alsek
River, Southern Alaska.

Camping beside the
Alsek.

Above: **A Vyneck's eye view of Baffin Island north of the Hudson Strait.**

Left: **Confronting an iceberg near Baffin Island, Canada.**

The Alsek—River of Ice
by Marcus Bailie

Once before, my travels had taken me to this part of the border between Canada and Alaska. Wandering alone on that occasion I got only the slightest glimpse of what this huge area held. The Saint Elias mountains rise straight from the Gulf of Alaska to heights of almost 20,000 ft in places. On the Canadian side is the Kluane (pronounced clue-ann-ee) National Park; it is the size of Switzerland and contains some of Canada's last unexplored places as well as North America's most extensive icefield and glacier systems.

Three years later in 1983, Pete Knowles, better known to many by his manufacturing name 'Greenslime', phoned me up to ask if I was interested in joining him on a kayaking trip to the river Alsek which flowed right through Kluane and on into Alaska. I was overjoyed at the prospect of returning to the area and agreed instantly. By July of the following year Pete had got all the details and logistics sorted out. We had sponsors; there were reports in the canoeing press; we had headed paper and expedition grants. We were a real expedition.

There were to be four of us on the trip. Pete's experience of this type of trip, particularly in Canada, made him the natural leader. Besides, he had done all the work so far. Mike Hewlett who, like Peter, worked in computing, was an extremely strong paddler and his knowledge of big water and his relaxed and laid back attitude were a great asset to the team. This would be the first major expedition for Phil Bibby, although he and I had been on many trips before, in North Wales where we both lived, in Scotland and in the Alps. It was a small team, an ideal number for this sort of paddling.

We arrived in Vancouver on the west coast of Canada in August and were met by Klaus Streckman, a professional rafter and a friend of Pete's. Klaus knows the rivers of Western Canada and Alaska better than almost anyone alive and he is one of only seven people to have paddled the full length of the Alsek. For a training trip Klaus suggested the Babine River, a five-day wilderness river trip with big water. Klaus provided the raft support and arranged transport and within a few days we were bouncing up into the heart of British Columbia in Klaus' truck.

The Babine was indeed a great river and with Klaus carrying all the gear on the raft we could enjoy it to its full. We played on its thunderous rapids, sunbathed on its banks in the middle of the day and savoured the solitude of these great northern forests as we sat around a roaring fire in the evenings sipping cans of beer.

At the end of the run on the Babine Klaus drove us to Prince Rupert and dropped us at the ferry terminal before he made the long drive back to Vancouver.

It takes the ferry three days to get from Prince Rupert to Haines, following what is still the easiest route into Alaska. High mountain peaks and tumbling glaciers form much of the mainland scenery while the many islands are covered with lush forest. As yet we had no idea how we would get from the town of Haines the 200 miles over the mountains to Haines Junction on the Canadian side of the border. All we knew was that there was a road.

Our ferry also carried cars and so we spent much of the three-day journey trying to arrange a lift for ourselves and our four kayaks. Alaskans love a challenge and by the time we arrived in Haines we already had the kayaks tied onto the roof of a pick-up truck which was en route to Anchorage.

Alaska is hot in summer, and the journey over the mountains took us through dry baked Scandinavian-style forest and up onto open moorland with snow-capped peaks high above us. Dropping back down into Canada the forest was sparse and dwarfed; a vegetation we were to come to know well over the next few weeks.

Canada's Yukon Territory is about the size of Britain, has a population of approximately 25,000 and has about six roads. Two of these meet at Haines Junction, the Alaska Highway and the Haines Highway, both dirt roads and largely impassable in winter. The meeting of the roads has produced a town which boasts a population of 350, which makes it one of the territory's larger centres of population!

We set up our expedition headquarters outside the weigh-station on the edge of town a hundred yards or so from the river. We had a lot of sorting, packing and repacking to do trying to make our large amount of food and camping gear fit into the four small kayaks. In keeping with the traditions of expedition paddling we had not had the forethought to try this while still in Vancouver!

Attempts to paddle the Alsek are rare and in the course of the afternoon probably everyone in town learnt about our venture and many came to

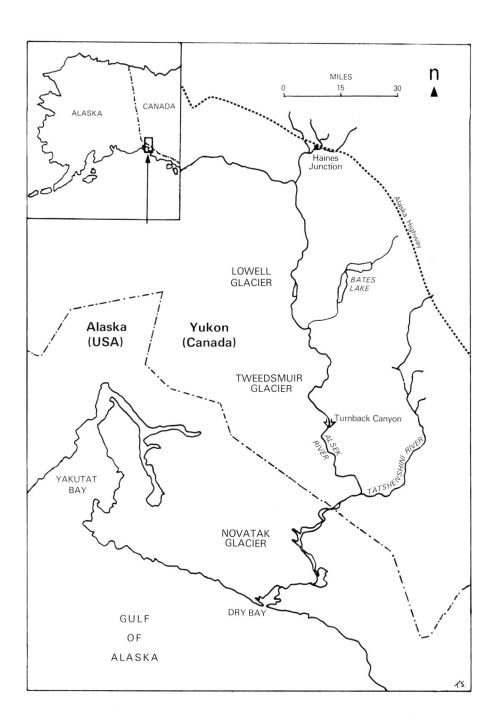

chat. One of these amiable spectators introduced himself as George Mobley from National Geographic magazine. He was, he said, doing a story on the Kluane National Park and he might drop in to see us on the river in a few days' time if that was all right. He left and we wondered just how he was going to do that!

Previous travel and exploration along the Alsek has been at best sporadic. The coastal Tlingit Indians hunted and fished on the lower Alsek but generally only travelled a short distance inland from the sea. In 1898, when gold was found on the Klondike River in the Yukon hundreds of would-be miners tried to use the Alsek as a way into the interior but most either gave up or died in the attempt. Turnback Canyon's name dates from this period. After the gold-rush the ongoing struggle between the river and the glaciers was left largely undisturbed, watched only by a few exploratory surveying parties and of course the grizzly bears and dall sheep which still roam freely.

The first known descent of the river was not until 1961. Two Americans paddled it in canvas kayaks but portaged around the major rapids and spent two days clambering over the ice of Tweedsmuir as they carried around Turnback Canyon. Turnback was not run until 1971 when the river was attempted for the fourth time. In an amazing solo run, one of North America's most experienced paddlers, Dr Walt Blackadar, paddled the entire river including the canyon. Of the subsequent five attempts on the river by kayak, only two groups, including one of Klaus', succeeded in paddling Turnback, and a third group had a fatality trying.

We had been well instructed by Klaus; it would all depend on the water level. His advice left us feeling uncommitted, open to circumstances, ready to enjoy what the river offered us rather than pining for what it had offered to others. Such feelings proved to be significant for as it turned out we were not to run Turnback either.

The Kluane Park Service were very helpful. They knew the country well, but warned us that the river was abnormally high, swollen as it was by freak summer floods inland. It took a couple of days to make final preparations and adjustments and when we eventually paddled away from Haines Junction it was with mixed feelings of relief and trepidation. With the first few miles of the river however our last-minute fears fell away and we settled into a rhythm as the country opened out before us.

The landscape of the Alsek is raw and new. Immense glaciers, rivers of ice, the most powerful sculpturing force in nature, pour into the river valley from both sides. Tweedsmuir, Lowell, Alsek and the Grand Plateau each wreak havoc on this most empty country. Periodically within living memory they have surged, blocking the river and backing up lakes hundreds of feet deep and dozens of miles long. Floods have swept the

116

valley of the Alsek when the ice dams have collapsed and there are scour marks hundreds of feet above the existing river.

In its early miles the Alsek flows shallow, green and braided through beaver country. On distant slopes above the river we could see the remains of flood beaches, wave-cut and littered with ancient driftwood; a reminder of recent ice dams. There were waterfowl, stunted trees, willows and alder bushes.

Later in the day the river grew in speed and volume when the Kaskawulsh river swept in from the right, and the intensely cold glacier melt water added even more complexity to the lattice of interwoven channels and islands. Paddling the braided sections of the river was at times more taxing than the rapids, for as the river divided and subdivided, reaching a width of half a mile or more, it became impossible to guess which was the most reliable channel.

As we came to the end of that first day the mile-wide valley steadily closed in and the diverse channels at last flowed together. We found a sheltered campsite amongst the alder bushes and took up residence. We pitched our tents, got a fire going and a meal on, and just lay back in the last of the warm sun and relaxed.

Next morning, and indeed every morning, after breakfast we began the tedious task of sealing all our food and gear into waterproof 'dry-bags', stowing them carefully into the boats then taking them all out again because either they wouldn't fit or we had forgotten to pack something. As we ate more the packing should have become easier but it didn't seem to work that way. When everything was packed we would struggle into wetsuits, fibre-pile jackets and nylon cagoules in readiness for the chill of the wind over the river and the iciness of the water itself. A final check around the site completed the clear-up; an overlooked mug or bag of dried milk left hiding in the grass could not be replaced. Nothing was superfluous.

More rivers joined us and the Alsek grew in strength. There were frequent rapids now, though none which gave too much trouble, even with heavily loaded boats, and none which needed to be inspected from the bank before running them. In sympathy with the river the valley walls were moulded into contorted shapes, giant red cliffs carved by the water, and dun-coloured sand-dunes blown by the wind. Where the valley widened a little there would be an emptiness filled only by alder bushes and a few gangly spruce trees.

The sighting of our first grizzly was fairly awe-inspiring. We were in mid-current at the time and the bear was high above the river on the bank. He reared up on his hind legs, partly for a better look, partly for a better smell of us, and partly to show us how big and strong he was. He was immense; there was no need for him to impress us with his 8 ft and 300 lbs, for even on all fours he was daunting. Finally he dropped down again, satisfied that there was no threat, and shuffled off into the bushes.

We meanwhile had been fumbling with our waterproof cameras feeling quite safe as long as we were out on the water. Months later we discovered that grizzlies are extremely good swimmers and that he could have outpaced us as easily in the water as on shore. At the time though, as on many other occasions, we remained confident in our ignorance.

The Lowell Glacier came into view early one afternoon. Even from a distance it looked threatening as it swept down to the water. Within an hour we were at the top of the long and quite difficult rapid which tumbled down to the narrow lake which was formed between the towering ice cliffs of the glacier itself on the right, and the jumble of glacial rubble which formed the left bank. Huge pillars of ice, certainly 200 and perhaps 300 ft high stood poised ready to topple into the lake which was filled with the floating ice debris of those which already had. The lake was several miles long but barely a couple of hundred metres across in places. In recent years it has varied in width from four miles to barely a raft width as the glacier has advanced and retreated.

To cross the lake would involve passing dangerously close to the cliffs and since late afternoon was the most likely time for ice fall we decided to stop for the night, set up our camp, and run it the next morning.

With the tents half-pitched and the first pot of water not quite boiled we heard the deep throb of a helicopter. It flew low down the valley, hovered briefly above us, then landed close by. A few moments later we were greeted warmly by George Mobley, the photographer we had met in Haines junction from National Geographic magazine.

'How was the run?' he asked as we shook hands and were introduced to his pilot. George was more relaxed than he had been in Haines Junction, more vivacious, more natural as if he felt more at home in the wilderness than in towns. He was also very persuasive! As a result, in spite of our fears of ice fall from the glacier, we agreed to run the rapid that afternoon and to paddle across the lake while George took photographs from the air. 'The light is perfect,' he grinned. 'Just stay away from the ice cliffs and the seracs won't hit you.' No problem was insurmountable. 'You don't even have to pack up your camp. We'll fly you back up here afterwards with the kayaks hooked underneath. That way you can run it again tomorrow,' and he grinned again.

With George taking photographs from the helicopter hovering just above us we ran the rapid closely together. The waves were bigger than we had expected and Phil was flipped over by the sheer force of the water. 'Show-off,' we grunted with considerable relief as he rolled back up. The lake itself was amazing, and of course we had no intention of staying away from the ice cliffs. Seen from directly below they were spectacular, rising quite vertically from the water with the tops twisted and grotesque spires of ice. Where there had been a recent fall the ice was a deep radiant blue, almost turquoise, while elsewhere it was snow white and glistening, as George had said, in the perfect light.

As we played with the floating icebergs, landing on them and even trying to push them over, we did wonder what it was going to be like sharing the rapids on the rest of the river with these great ice cubes. We moved along the lake and ducked in close to where there had obviously been a recent fall and nudged our way amongst the pulverized debris and bigger bergs. Then from behind us we heard a tearing, grating noise and swung round to see a column of ice the size of an office block topple and crash into the water, exploding into a million pieces not fifty yards behind us. Our first reaction was to duck, for the fragments were landing in the water all around us. Our second reaction was to paddle like mad for after the explosion there followed an enormous tidal wave, several feet high and breaking at its crest. As the wave rolled safely underneath us the breaking crest subsided, and we decided to give the ice cliffs a miss and head for the safety of the shore.

George had missed the ice fall but got some stunning shots. He was as good as his word, and we and our kayaks were ferried back to the comparative safety of our campsite by helicopter. George seemed well pleased with his shots; his efforts and the expense were well rewarded. 'At last,' he said, 'I've got something which gives the ice cliffs some scale.' One of these photographs later became a double-page spread in National Geographic.

We took a rest from paddling the next day and climbed for hours up on to the comparatively small mountain behind us. It faced the Lowell Glacier and gave a breathtaking view along its 45-mile length. In every direction we could see range after range of mountains with great glaciers sweeping between them. In the far distance, Mt Hubbard rose to over 15,000 ft and beyond was Mt Vancouver, nearly 16,000 ft.

The following morning we again paddled across the lake past the ice cliffs, this time being careful to keep our distance from them. We encountered some of the biggest rapids of the trip that day. At Sam's Rapid the river widened to about 200 metres as it tumbled and jostled steeply over boulders and small drops for a mile or so. There was no best line, just a vaguely defined optimistic guess. Even this was difficult to decide on from the bank though we spent quite some time trying. The sighting of a distant grizzly on the same bank added to the tension of the moment.

Once in the rapid the excitement continued for it was desperately difficult to know just where we were. There were holes and stoppers, enormous waves and pour-overs, all jumbled up together. Altogether it was an amazing run. We were getting more used to the heavy boats now; more relaxed about running rapids on sight, more capable of dealing with them when things went wrong, and more prepared to play the big stoppers which were increasing in number as the river gained in volume. It was now twenty times the volume it was when we started only a few days before.

Bill's Sneak, the second of the day's major rapids, and as imaginatively named as the first, took us somewhat by surprise and we found ourselves in the middle of some enormous waves. Escape to either bank was always possible so we just ran on and on, through bigger and bigger waves, having more and more fun. By the time we realized that this must be Bill's Sneak it was almost over, and we piled into a massive break-out at the bottom of the rapid, exhausted, laughing and spluttering. Pete was annoyed that we had spread out so much on the rapid; Phil was overwhelmed with the scale of the river; Mike was in his element and loving every minute of it. And me? Well I just hoped there would be more rapids like Bill's Sneak. This was the stuff we had come to paddle.

That night there was some rain mixed in with the wind and we erected our thin nylon tarpaulin over the cooking area to provide some shelter. As always our cooking fire was 20 or 30 metres from where we put the tents, so that at night any prowling bears would be drawn to there and not to us as we slept. On shore our thoughts and actions always took bears into account, worried that they may be tempted to include us in the natural food chain. Any spilt food or scraps were cleared up immediately and burnt and we went to elaborate length to pack everything back into its watertight and therefore airtight containers. At night out first line of defence against animals would be our own scent. Most animals, we were assured, would be drawn to the smell of food scraps but would generally be put off by the smell of other animals, especially unfamiliar ones. Our final task then, before going to bed, was to drink as much tea as we could, then wander around the perimeter of the camp, stopping occasionally and squeezing out every last drop of liquid scent!

Late the next day we reached Turnback Canyon and found a campsite on the left bank. It had been a splendid day with good rapids and ever-changing scenery. The river flowed in a deep, steep valley, twisting its way through the mountains before spilling out onto a huge dry lake bed above the Tweedsmuir Glacier. All day rivers and streams poured down off glaciers until the river was nearly twice the size it had been in the morning. It flowed with an air of seriousness and we responded with excitement and anticipation.

120

From our camp we clambered along the left bank as far as we could for our first good view of Turnback Canyon, but sheer cliffs on that side soon blocked our progress. All we could see was the river narrowing down until it disappeared out of sight between vertical rock walls. It was a cold, soulless camp. There was little in the way of shelter, and less in the way of firewood. The river was clearly very high, but was it too high? Could the Canyon be run at this level? We were anxious, tired, scared, cold.

Next morning we packed up and took everything with us across the river. From there it took us an hour to scramble under the rounded nose of the glacier to the Canyon entrance. We had not been hopeful about what we would find there but what we saw was daunting. The river had eventually narrowed to 30 metres or so, squeezed by the rock walls we had seen the night before. The channel twisted and turned through a series of S-bends, hurling the river from side to side. An enormous stopper wave guarded the entrance to the S-bends, its face twenty feet high. There was a sneak line round it which would put a paddler into a ferocious exploding hole. Careful timing might see him through but the destruction which lay below in the S-bends was formidable. For as far as we could see there were giant boils and whirlpools which would suck a kayak under and not even notice. Separately and collectively we compared what we saw with the rivers that we knew: the Frazer river, the Nile, the Colorado, the Corruh, the rivers of Europe, the Himalayas, North America. Turnback is five miles long and the S-bends are thought to be the easiest of the eight or so major problems. The next section we looked at was even more hopeless as the entire river smashed inescapably into a rock wall.

One by one we made our decision not to run the canyon. There was no discussion nor persuasion involved. Nor was this the place for democracy; there was no question of a vote. When first one person announced 'I'm going to walk,' the others took that piece of information and added it to all the others being turned over and over in their minds. What are the chances of a capsize. What are the chances of a swim? What are the chances of surviving a swim? A little later, someone else said, 'I'm out. If you're going to do it, it's going to be just the two of you.' Another piece of information for the two left: can it be run with two? Of the two, each felt he was prepared to follow: neither was prepared to lead. So the decision was made—we would all portage.

We had made guesses about the level of water we had seen in the Canyon and months after the trip the Canadian Water Authority records confirmed our estimates. The volume that day was three times higher than on any previous attempt on the Canyon, and more than twice as high as the level Klaus had described as the absolute cut-off!

We trudged back to our boats bitterly disappointed, each of us reflecting silently on our separate decisions; reasoning, justifying, composing phrases of self explanation. The rhetoric of failure is never easy. However we now had a new problem to fill our minds. How on earth were we going to cross the Tweedsmuir Glacier equipped as we were? Although it was longer by several miles it was much easier to cross the Glacier than to struggle along the precipitous banks of the river. However we were hopelessly under-equipped; for reasons of lightness on the river we had no rucksacks, let alone crampons, ice axes or ropes.

Leaving the kayaks on the beach we set off in trainers or kayaking boots carrying the rest of the gear in dry-bags or bundles tied together with whatever string we had with us. As it turned out the ice was the least difficult part. It was mostly covered with grit and stones which at least gave us a good footing. The main problems were the lateral moraines. Formed when two glaciers meet and flow together, these long ribbons of loose rubble running lengthwise along the Glacier were at times 100 ft high. We would sink and stumble in the unconsolidated rubble time and time again as we trudged through a landscape which was almost lunar.

Late in the afternoon we set up camp beside the river again and returned next morning for the kayaks. These at least could be slid over the icy sections but were infuriatingly unwieldy on the moraines. Progress was slow and we were worried that we might have to spend the night on the glacier. We reached our camp as it grew dark and collapsed there for a second night.

We returned to the river next day with a real joy. There was one final rapid of the Canyon remaining and we ran it with exhilaration and excitement. The river had widened again and beyond the rapid there was a calm safe area so we could paddle through and around the huge waves and plough into monstrous holes with comparative impunity. During the rest of the day the river widened more and the rapids became less violent. The mountains close to the river were steeper and higher now, more Alpine, rising to eight, ten, twelve thousand feet. We paddled quietly, dwarfed in their hugeness. The Vern Ritchie Glacier came in from the right but did not quite reach the river. We were flowing through forces of immense power, and with these basic elements I could enjoy again the happiness associated with the simplicity of just being on the river, living with it through rock and ice, sun and snow, racing cloud or still shadow. And I could easily abandon the crass assumption that the world was made for man.

The Tatshenshini River joined us from the left and once more we were in a maze of braided channels. Twenty rivers to choose from, each wider, faster, steeper than the river we had started on at Haines Junction. In the middle of this jumble of rivers and islands, three miles wide in places, we found the most idyllic campsite and we pulled in a little earlier than usual and basked in the warm sun. Far across the braids a magnificent North American Matterhorn towered above the river, 10,000 ft high, unnamed and presumably unclimbed, with glaciers tumbling from its slopes to the river below. In the midst of this otherwise untouched landscape a narrow straight clearing in the thin forest ran incongruously across the valley to mark the boundary between Canada and Alaska.

The banks closed in again and we found ourselves on a huge river, moving deep and fast through steep valleys shrouded in increasingly dense scrub and lush stunted pines. We were getting close to the sea and the climate was changing. The Walker Glacier sprawled in from the left almost to the river, and later we could see high above us on the right the tumbling branches of the Novatak Glacier which by contrast hung as though suspended amongst the massive peaks and spurs which flanked them.

Late in the afternoon we spilled out onto Lake Alsek. Several miles away across the lake great icebergs calfed off the Alsek and Grande Plateau Glaciers to float in the lake or to be grounded in the shallows by the wind. We played and jostled amongst these great water monsters unaware that they sometimes roll over without warning.

We found another beautiful campsite on a long spit of land forming an island. The mile-long beach was littered with driftwood and that night, our last on the river, we sat around an enormous blaze, occasionally wandering a few yards away to return with another tree for the conflagration. Out of the darkness came the distant boom of seracs breaking off from one of the glaciers.

As we paddled out of the lake next morning the river constricted and accelerated for the last time. Long vistas over flat ground and perfectly still water gave us distant reflections and reminded me nostalgically of the flat views of Africa that I had seen from yet another river. The river was now nearly a mile wide and only the occasional stranded iceberg made us aware of the river's great speed and power, as we broke in and out of the eddies formed downstream of them. Eventually the land flattened out completely into scrub and marsh. We spotted an old tattered flagpole on the bank and pulled ashore to confirm that this was the agreed pick-up point. We had reached the end of the Alsek.

There was little left to do now except dry out our gear, burn or dump what we did not want, and wait for the float plane which was due to pick us up the next day. It was then that Anna arrived. The put-put-put of an outboard engine drew our astonished attention across the river to where a small boat was now speeding across the river. 'Anna Breseman, and this is me granddaughter,' she said as she leapt ashore. Then by way of welcome, 'What are you fellers doin' here?'

We explained, 'Oh,' she said, 'then you'd better come stay with me.' It was said in a manner that left no room for argument, even if we'd wanted to. 'Mat won't arrive a day early, and he probably won't arrive tomorrow either. Get your gear together and I'll come pick you up in an hour.'

Anna had a small cabin across the river where she lived by fishing for salmon in the summer and trapping for fur in the winter. She was right about Mat not arriving that day or the next and we stayed with her and her granddaughter, as beautiful as the grandmother was amazing, for a couple of days. When Mat did arrive we strapped the kayaks onto the floats of his plane, bundled our gear inside the tiny cockpit and he whisked us away from Anna and her granddaughter, from the river we had grown to know so well and from the ice which formed it.

Journeys have no endings and so the rest is tedious. A noisy spectacular flight in the cramped cockpit of the twin Otter took us to Juneau. We had a few welcome beers in a tourist bar, then a few more, but it was all just a part of the slow return to reality. Ferries, aeroplanes, London; all that was still to come. More reality to come to terms with.

Yet if journeys have no ending then equally they have no beginning, becoming one long loosely defined continuous whole. And so as we sat around our beers in that tourist bar in Juneau we got to talking about other trips we would like to do in the future, either together or separately. South America, New Zealand, New Guinea or maybe Nepal.

'Yes, I hear Nepal is good.'

Journey Into Nepal
by Terry Storry

Monday 12th January 1987, Chatara Beach, Nepal.
'As children we played in mountain streams
As time grew you showed me your strength
As time flew you showed me your grace
From the high Himalaya
To the time rifted sands of the Nile,
River lead me on,
And lead me down to the sea.'

Marcus waxing lyrical in his diary at the end of our continuous unsupported eleven-day trip down the Tama Kosi and Sun Kosi, unconsciously expressed the general mood of the team. The changing river was for every one of us an allegory of our changing emotions. We began independent, highly charged, and nervous. We finished together as a group, relaxed and confident. Trying at first to master the river—a typically Western approach no doubt—we found in the end it was best to let the river lead us on. Slowly we fitted in, with the river and its moods and the people and their lives. We went to Nepal for the white water, and came back with something more.

Nepal was 'put on the map' as a canoeing venue by the twelve-man British expedition to the Dudh Kosi led by Mike Jones in 1976. It was Leo Dickinson's superb film of the expedition, *Dudh Kosi: Relentless River of Everest*, made for Harlech Television, that opened canoeists' eyes to the white water rivers of Nepal. In the decade which followed there was a wave of exploration. Groups from the United States, Europe, Australia and New Zealand, some large, some small, some sponsored and some not, had canoed most of the major rivers in the country, and by the 1980s commercial rafting was established on the Trisuli and the Sun Kosi.

In 1985, Graham Wardle and I, attending a British Canoe Union Coaching Course at Plas y Brenin, met Dai Richards recently returned from running raft trips on the Sun Kosi. He fired us with the ambition to

125

paddle in the Himalaya. There seemed to us two ways of achieving our ambition. The first was to do it the Dudh Kosi way. That was to find another desperate river flowing from a big-name mountain—the Marsyandi out of the Annapurna Sanctuary had been done,[1] but the Braldu from K2 was a possibility[2]—get sponsorship, and sell the film rights. It would inevitably mean a big team for bank support and filming, and this in turn meant porters. We would only paddle short stretches of river at a time. Many sections would be impossible—we would carry the boats round—and on other sections we would have to wait for the porters to catch us up. The attraction in all this was in doing a first descent.

Graham and I however, are nothing if not laid back. The thought of spending a year organizing an expedition (as Mike Jones had done), and then dealing with all the hassles of load carrying, porter strikes and film remakes, on top of the white water canoeing, was too odious to consider. So we went for the second option. That was to find a river, or combination of rivers, that had road access and egress, and could be canoed in a single push without bank support. If your pocket can stand it, this alpine style of canoeing is more rewarding.

Two is a little too intimate for a month in a strange country so we were pleased when Marcus Bailie decided to join us. Three became six as Marcus brought in his girlfriend Liz Colhurst, Graham recruited Chris Sladden, and I asked Gill Pile, a canoeing companion on many British rivers. Four or six seems to be the best combination for an unsupported trip, assuming that they are friends. It allows a subdivision into two or three pairs, but is still small enough, when together, to work as a team.

We arrived in Kathmandu in two stages, Marcus, Liz and Chris on 23 December 1986, and Graham, Gill, and I on 29 December. The early arrivals spent four days over Christmas on the Trisuli, a good warm-up river not far from Nepal's main road. Their comparatively short and easy trip from Trisuli Bazaar to Narayangat provided invaluable experience for our major expedition down the Tama and Sun Kosi. In particular, as Marcus notes in his diary for Boxing Day, a routine for life on and beside the river was established, and, at least by Liz and him, relished.

> 'We move slowly towards a routine—one which feels right is right. Up at first light (6.30a.m., but who needs a watch). Breakfast so far has been 'creamed rice' made up the night before. We are still slow in the morning, but getting better. It takes a long time to pack a kayak. Lunch is still variable. Today was

---

[1] A team led by Chris Hawksworth went high on this river in 1980.

[2] Mike Jones led an expedition to the Braldu in 1978. Tragically he was drowned on the river trying to save the life of a friend. At that point the expedition returned home.

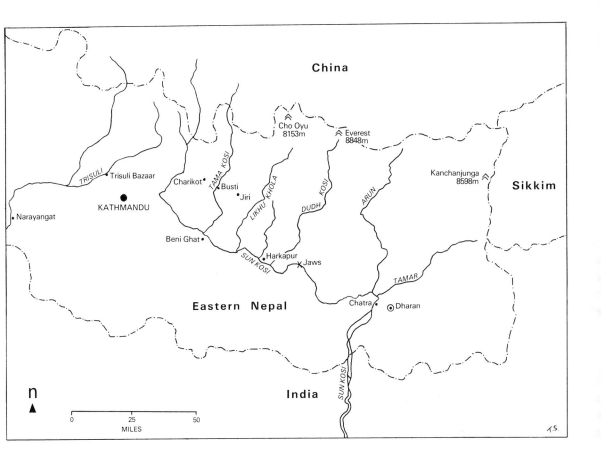

tea and excellent pan-bread, made with chapatti flour, sugar and dried milk over a driftwood fire . . . And the evenings. Off the river about 3p.m. or 3.30. Now we do need a watch otherwise we lose the light before we are ready for the dark (6.30p.m.). Lentils and vegetables poured over boiled rice is starting to taste really good.

'Fun watching Chris getting into the swing of things. And tomorrow? Ah tomorrow must wait . . . Everything seems so natural on the river, not ordered or confined. "Everything happens in time," Liz said.

For the untravelled youngster of the group, Chris, the Trisuli was a chance to get used to the 'un-Britishness' of it all. Liz on the other hand was much more cosmopolitan and, although the weaker paddler of the three, had relaxed enough by Boxing Day to enjoy some of the typical river life of Nepal.

'A better start, and pleasant days paddling with a couple of bigger rapids and more volume. Haven't a clue where we are. The bird life is wonderful; saw a brilliant blue kingfisher today—bright blue wingtops and tail, white throat

127

patch and red chest . . . Passed a couple of dugout canoe ferries, both about 30
ft long and very unstable-looking, but they seem to paddle them skilfully and
the passengers even have the confidence to make the crossing standing up! Our
lunchtime audience was very shy and only approached when we had finished
eating our chapattis . . . I took a wee lass on the back of my canoe who had a
wonderful smile when she laughed . . . Food is good although *daal bhaat*
(lentils over rice) could become tedious after a while.'

Marcus, Liz and Chris pulled off the Trisuli on 29 December at
Narayangat. It had been a good trip. They had settled into the country,
their boats, and each other. But the presence of the road was always there
to remind them that it was only a practice run. This lack of commitment
was most keenly felt by Marcus.

'I'm sure it must have been my imagination that made me think that the good
moments all occurred on the right bank, away from that damned road. We
finally accepted the road, but not easily, and not really at night, when the
stillness of the camps was jolted by the noise and lights of the lorries, and
ludicrously overloaded buses.'

And when the three had hot-footed, bussed, and rickshawed it back to
Kathmandu to meet us, it was Marcus who proposed that the united team
now go for a more serious expedition into eastern Nepal.

In the lounge of the Hotel Gaurishankar, after long discussion over
numerous cups of *chiyaa* (tea), we all agreed and then refined his plan.
This was to paddle the Tama Kosi (sometimes spelt Tamba Koshi) from
Busti to its junction with the Sun Kosi (or Koshi) and then continue down
the Sun Kosi to Chatra.

The Tama Kosi is the largest of the Sun Kosi's tributaries.[1] It flows
south-west from Panch Pokhari (Five Lakes) in the Siranchark region of
eastern Nepal. The Kathmandu—Jiri road, sporting a regular bus service,
crosses the river at Busti. Below Busti the Tama Kosi enters a deep
canyon, and for 6 miles drops at more than 200 ft per mile. To give some
idea of the steepness of this gradient, the Colorado, running through the
Grand Canyon, falls at 10 ft per mile, and the Olympic slalom course at
Augsburg falls at 50 ft per mile. In this canyon were many difficult rapids
of Grades IV, V, and VI. There is difficult canoeing for a further 12 miles
below the canyon (Grade IV, occasionally V) and then for the remaining
thirty miles to the confluence, the Tama is more gentle (Grade III). As far

---

[1] The other major tributaries are the Dudh Kosi, Arun and Tamar. The Sun Kosi itself
flows into the Ganges.

as we knew, the river was first paddled by the two Mikes, Wood and Devlin, in 1985, and had seen one or two descents since.[1]

The Sun Kosi rises high in Tibet to enter Nepal as the Bhote Kosi. When it joins the Indrewati Kola at Dolaghat, it truly becomes the Sun Kosi. Falling then over some 2,500 ft, it traverses eastern Nepal, reaching the *terai* (plains) at Chatra, and thence the Indian border at Bharda, travelling a total distance of 163 miles. At Chatra a jeep track leads to Dharan, from where there is a daily bus service to Kathmandu. Above Chatra and below Dolaghat however, the river is totally remote from road access, and has rapids of Grade IV. While not hard by modern standards, it is a serious undertaking for canoeists without raft support.

We estimated that it would take us four days to do the Tama, and a further six to do the Sun Kosi. The raft companies who ran commercial trips down the Sun Kosi told us that food was obtainable at one or two places on that river, but they had no knowledge of the Tama which was considered too hard to raft. We found a Sherpa who had scouted the Tama for a raft company, and he considered that purchasing food would be impossible along the way because of the poverty of the local villages. He also suggested that there would be hostility to us. He was right on the first count, wrong on the second.

To be on the safe side, we planned to take a minimum of six days' food in the boats.[2] We hoped to be able to buy sufficient rice and *dahl* for the final four days with our small denomination rupee notes—there is often insufficient money in the villages to change 50- or 100-rupee notes. Our food estimates were based on the assumption that each person needs about 1 kg or $2^1/4$ lb of food per day. Apart from 200 Mars Bars, donated by a generous shopowner in England, we had to buy all the food in Kathmandu—rice, lentils, porridge, dried milk, tuda, sugar, tea bags, flour, salt, some nuts, raisins and dates, and a couple of pots of honey. We divided the packages into six portions on our hotel beds, and then had a dry run packing our kayaks to see if it would fit.

We had been lucky with canoes. One of the major headaches in flying east is the 20 kg weight limit imposed by the airlines. Flying to or via the

---

[1] For an account of their trip see Mike Wood's article, 'A Car Crash Without the Glass', in *Canoeist,* June 1986.

[2] For *each* six-person meal, and we had two per day (with just a Mars Bar for lunch) the quantities worked out as follows:
$1/2$ kg of rice (breakfast and evening), $1/4$ kg of lentils (evening), $1/2$ kg of porridge (breakfast), 2 onions (evening), 100 grams of milk (breakfast and evening), $1/2$ kg of tuda (breakfast and evening), 200 grams of sugar (breakfast and evening), 6 tea bags (breakfast and evening), 400 grams of flour (breakfast and evening), 10 grams of salt (breakfast and evening).

United States with canoes is less of a problem, since 'two pieces' seems to be the only rigid limit, their weight and shape are open to 'discussion'. Taking boats to Nepal would have meant a hefty excess baggage charge which we could not afford. Just two months before we left I met John Taylor, co-leader of the 'Kites and Kayaks on Everest' expedition, at the Harrogate Trade Fair.[1] No sooner had I mentioned our problem than he offered to lend us the kayaks they had used, and had left out in Nepal. These boats, plastic successors to the Pyranha 'Everests' designed for the original Mike Jones expedition, were ideal for our trip because of their construction and larger volume. There was plenty of room back and front—once the foam buoyancy blocks had been removed—to take food, bivy and sleeping bags, 'land' clothes, spare split paddles, pots and pans, repair and first aid kits,[2] tarpaulin, and the *kukri* for chopping firewood. Moreover, being plastic (the original 'Everests' were fibreglass) the kayaks would not, we hoped, leave us 'shipwrecked' if they got wrapped around a boulder.

We set off from Kathmandu on New Years Day. Through Nima, the Sherpa we employed in Kathmandu to help us with the red tape, we hired a bus for the seven-hour journey. It was not without incident, as I noted in my diary.

> 'Set off from Kat at 9.30. Boats are tied on the roof—had to be careful of angle irons. Marcus thinks he has lost his return airline ticket. Dolaghat 12.30—Marcus eats with the drivers in an inn. Through three military checkpoints, at one of which we have to show our permits. At the 3rd Chris gets hit by the raised barrier, because he is on the roof. We search for 20 minutes for his glasses, knocked off in collision, and find them. Arrive Busti 4 p.m. Set up camp on the beach. Veg and tuna for tea. In bags by 7.30. Set up tarp, so we can keep heads out of bags despite heavy dew. We iodine and boil water ready for the morning.'

After crossing the Indrewati Kola at Dolaghat, we climbed steadily into the Himalaya. We seemed almost able to touch Gauri Shankar and Rowaling Himal, as well as innumerable other 7000-metre peaks, in the sharp clear mountain air. We should not therefore, have been surprised at the cold night which lay ahead of us, or indeed at the incredible amount of

---

[1] For an account of this expedition see Mick Coyne's article 'Kites and Kayaks on Everest' in *Canoeist*, April 1987. A book, no doubt, follows.

[2] Repair Kit: 1 roll duct tape, 1 roll denso tape, 2 pitex sticks, matches, evostik, needle and thread, Swiss Army knife.

First Aid Kit; Metronidazole 200 mgs (amoebic dysentry), Immodium (the runs), DF 118 (severe pain/shock), Codeine (mild pain, fever, the runs), antibiotics (two types in case of immune or allergic reaction), Mercurochrome (waterproof antiseptic), tincture of opium (not sure what for but *very* good), bandages, plasters.

moisture which condensed on our bags. Fortunately we all had goretex bivouac covers.

We were woken by the men of Busti coming down to fish. They carried long, 30-ft, bamboo poles, and cast silently into the morning mist. A few were accompanied by children, who dawdled wide-eyed beside our camp. I could not help noticing the relative poverty of this village and the people in it.

> 'The houses are all wood, not a stone or slate to be seen. They are perched on the river bank, and supported at the back (river side) by wobbly-looking stilts. The clothes on the men are old, frayed and worn, their hair and faces dirty. The children look thin and undernourished, seeming listless and lacking in energy.'

It was as Liz said 'a lonely village'. It reminded me of something Nima had told me before we left Kathmandu. The literal translation of Tama Kosi, he had said, is River of Copper, but it is also called River of Sorrow. In the reign of Ranabahadur there was a smallpox epidemic in Kathmandu, and the common people were expelled to the shores of the Tama Kosi. They endured great hardships on the journey, the children dying along the way, the people driven ever onwards by the King's soldiers. They were allowed no time to collect sandalwood for the traditional funeral pyres, and the children were simply cast into the waters of the Tama Kosi, River of Sorrow. Perhaps that was when the spirit of Busti was broken.

That is the stuff of myth and legend. But the reasons for the poverty of villages like Busti are the same as they ever were. There is no large-scale cultivation, the people being hunters and gatherers rather than farmers. They subsist on fish, on their animals and on the little they grow. Each house has hens, sometimes a cow, a few goats and maybe a pig or two. To gather food for their animals and to collect wood for the fires, the women have to go further and further from the villages each year. The topsoil from the denuded forests they leave behind is washed away in the annual monsoon (June–September), so regeneration is impossible. With fodder and firewood harder to find, the animals are less productive, and the dangerous practice of using animal dung for fuel has started, depriving any cultivated land of valuable nutrients. It is a vicious circle spiralling downwards, so much so that people are now leaving the high Himalaya for the plains.[1]

---

[1] For a detailed study of a river valley with similar problems—the Arun, also a tributary of the Sun Kosi—see *The Arun, A Natural History of the World's Deepest Valley* by E.W. Cronin Jr (Houghton Mifflin Co, Boston, 1979).

Given this background of hardship, which Nima had warned us about, we were prepared and indeed determined to be self-sufficient on the Tama Kosi. We deliberately did not tempt the villagers with money by trying to buy food at what would have been to them an exceptionally good price. If they sold food, it was food they could not eat, and the rupees in exchange are not a lot of good, pretty indigestible in fact. Where could they spend the money? On what? And who would sell it to them?

There was a fair amount of trade up and down the lower reaches of the Tama Kosi, and a flourishing economy beside the Sun Kosi, whose valley tracks were the major arteries of commerce in the region. But the people of the upper Tama Kosi just did not have a surplus of anything to trade, and despite the presence of the Kathmandu–Jiri road, still lived largely hand-to-mouth.

So we were a little sad, as well as excited, to wave good-bye to the little knot of grubby children gathered on the beach at Busti. I think it was fortunate, for my mood anyway, that after only thirty minutes on the river we hit the big stuff.

> 'A really great day's paddling. Set off at 10.00. Hit first big rapid at 10.30 where Graham and I rolled. 2nd rapid Graham, Gill, Liz and Chris portaged. It was a big two-tier drop (V), Marcus and I sneaked the first one on the right, but did the bottom fall through the guts. Next fall IV then stopped for lunch above another grade IV (15 ft angled drop). Then 200 m rapid (V). Liz and Gill swam. One more rapid, then stop for the night.
>
> Had problems with the boat's trim; stern heavy and leaning to the left. Repacked food into smaller stuff sacks at lunchtime, put them just behind my seat and shuffled them round until it felt right.
>
> It's so good to be on the river. After the long Christmas lay-off—suffering the effects of typhoid jabs and malaria pills—the ennervating flight to Dubai, then to Karachi, then to Kathmandu, the culture shock of Nepal, pleasant though it was, and the bus journey, here we are, finally doing what we had planned for a year and a half and saved for six months to do, canoe in the Himalaya.'

Liz, whose diary is predictably honest, would obviously have preferred a more gentle introduction to the river.

> 'Today we paddled. The river is maybe 40–50 yards across, clear blue green water, and has been technical and continuous all day . . . I found the adrenalin build-up quite hard to handle, and although I didn't paddle badly, I lacked a certain aggression and went for a swim. I let go of the boat and paddle and swam ashore à la beginner—that's what comes of being aware of what's coming up. An attempted roll would have been nice, but I didn't even think of it . . .

132

'The countryside here already seems less arid than where we launched . . .
Haven't eaten today, rotten stomach. Septic foot too; bashed my foot on the
roof of the bus. Can't afford to be careless on a long trip like this young lady.'

Considering the turbulence of the water in this Grade V rapid, it was
hardly surprising that neither Liz nor Gill managed to hang onto their
paddles or boats once they were swimming.

Liz was quickly reunited with her boat and paddle, but Gill, paddle in
hand, ended up on the opposite bank from her kayak. This problem could
be solved either by Gill swimming across the river, or by one of us towing
her boat to her. Neither solution immediately recommended itself, since
the water below the rapid was fast-flowing, bouldery and turbulent. Gill
did not have the confidence to leap into that sort of water again, even
accompanied by one of us in a boat; and the problem with towing the boat
to her, was that if it capsized it would quickly fill with water, and weighing
half a ton or thereabouts could drag the rescuer downstream or capsize
him or both. But by chance I was paddling with two spray decks (in an
attempt to get a more watertight seal round my waist), so I took one off,
put it over Gill's boat and tied the waist hole with a piece of string.
Hopefully this would allow us to continue towing it even if it capsized in
the current.

I balanced Gill's boat on a rock while Marcus attached his quick-release
tow line. He set off, ferrying across the river from one eddy to another, and
I tried to take some of the weight by nudging the gear-laden boat from
behind. We made it to the other bank some way downstream. I jumped out
and, releasing the bow toggle from Marcus' line, pulled the boat ashore.
Gill arrived, shaken by her swim and by her steep scramble through the
cliffs that hemmed in the river hereabouts.

We continued only a short way before stopping for the night. Liz and
Gill were exhausted. The rest of us had had enough as well, and we did not
know whether there would be good campsites downstream. Despite its
name (mine was the self-appointed job of naming campsites), Boulder City
was a level, albeit small, rectangle of soft sand hidden amongst the
house-sized stones. Looking at the map, after spreading our canoeing gear
out to dry in the last rays of the sun, we identified the spot as Chaite Ghat.
We realized later that neither of our maps were worth the paper they were
written on, and the village was almost certainly further downstream. In
any event we decided on the basis of this location that we had broken the
back of the hard paddling, and Marcus and I even had the presumption to
think we had canoed the portage the two Mikes had mentioned in their
first descent description.

These assumptions were way out of line as it happened, but it made

Boulder City a happy and relaxed place. Despite her nasty swim, Liz was enjoying the life going on all around us.

> 'On our first evening after paddling, Marcus and I saw an otter sitting on a rock, and then watched it swim upstream sliding over rocks and diving in pools for about three or four minutes . . . The butterflies are beautiful too. Most are the size of peacock butterflies and a little longer . . . We have seen a lot of egrets, mostly flying in flocks at dawn and dusk; the swallows appear then too.
>
>   'The local people look quite different from those further west, darker skinned and some even with long hair. I have been fascinated with how they cut planks of wood—a huge trunk is laid across a timber framework 10 ft off the ground, one man at the top, one at the bottom, and they simply pull a huge saw up and down. Wouldn't it be good if each plank in Britain took 3 or 4 hours to produce!'

It is easy on any river (or sea) trip to get lazy when you get off the water, particularly if you are feeling pleased with the way things have gone. But laziness means less fuel for the fire, less water and food in your stomach, and less sleep at night. To avoid becoming dehydrated (and therefore prone to heat exhaustion), and to maintain our strength, we needed a decent quantity of rice, *dahl,* bread and tea in the evening, and rice and tea in the morning. All the water had to be treated with iodine, boiled on a wood fire. We did not have the time or energy to boil the food and drinking water for the recommended ten minutes, and we hoped that the iodine would kill anything, particularly amoebas, which survived the boiling. We could not afford to have anyone fall ill with amoebic dysentery. Liz caught a mild dose which our anti-flagellate drugs held at bay; but it was bad enough to make canoeing a chore and eating a matter of survival rather than enjoyment. Anything worse and we would have had to rest up for a day or two, unsure whether to go for help or simply let the disease run its course. Unlike many expeditions we had no doctor, so prevention was always going to be better than cure.

Fuel for the fire was plentiful, dry driftwood which burnt easily. It was, however, often scattered far and wide across the beach, or, as at Boulder City, deep amongst the rocks, hard to see and difficult to retrieve. Our first job on arriving at a campsite was to collect the wood. While some did this, others erected the tarpaulin to keep the worst of the early morning dew off our sleeping bags. Our canoeing clothes never really had time to dry, except when we stopped very early, and putting on wet wetsuits became out morning purgatory. It was essential however, that all the gear in our boats remained dry even if we didn't and with dustbin liners, and a stronger outer covering to prevent them ripping, we made doubly, sometimes triply, sure of that. This meant that packing and unpacking took a long time. Even after a few days when the routine of setting up and breaking camp was established, it took us three hours every evening before we could think about sleep, and three hours every morning before we were on the water.

I felt good as we left Boulder City at 9 a.m. It was a feeling that did not last long. Marcus was the only one of us who could feel proud of the second day's paddling, and there was a hint of jealousy in my diary entry that evening.

> 'Today soon revealed how over-optimistic I had been in my predictions that we had paddled the hardest part of the river. Two hundred metres downstream of the campsite we came to a long section of technical Grade V, followed by a big drop of Grade VI. We scouted the rapid from both sides and all of us except Marcus decided it was too hard for too long, to risk paddling it.
>
> 'Marcus employed an interesting tactic in approaching this hard stretch of wild water. He broke it down into sections, treated each section as a separate rapid, and positioned us on the banks with throw lines in such a way that if he came out he could immediaitely be pulled into an eddy. The only problem with this approach was the time it took to set up, and the risk of losing his boat downstream because no one else was in their kayaks.'

An arm lifted in the air from behind a granite boulder 100 metres downstream. Gill was ready, her throw bag uncoiled beside the biggest eddy. Across the river Chris gave the thumbs up. He was standing just below a big stopper wave. I lifted my white yacht fender—home-made throw weight for my line—into the air, a signal to Graham and Liz that I was in position to guard the sump. Liz grabbed the line to Graham. Wrapping it round her waist, and bracing her feet against a boulder, she prepared to hold Graham should he have to dive in after Marcus or the boat. Above the roar of the water, we could not contact Marcus. We waited for him to look at Graham, who beckoned him down.

Marcus splashed his face with water, and moved out into the current. He dropped over the first fall, braced to the left, recovered and drew the boat sideways for the second drop. He hit the tongue perfectly and swept on down past Graham and Liz. Concentration written all over his face he broke out into a small eddy just above where I was standing. Facing upstream and looking over his shoulder he picked his line past the sump. A couple of powerful sweeps on his left sent him across the current above the huge undercut boulder. But as he passed, almost clear, a surging boil twisted his kayak sideways. In this most vulnerable of positions he slipped slowly over the waterfall below me. Only Chris and Gill could reach him now. I jumped onto a boulder to get a better view. He was stuck, broached sideways onto the boulder below the fall. He only managed to stay up by leaning all his weight, through the paddle, onto the rock towering above him. We had to get to him. But as I started down the bank, the adrenalin surging through my system, Marcus slid backwards out of his prison. Keeping his balance and his cool, he let the boat take him out, slipping sideways into the eddy next to Gill. It was a magnificent display of kayaking skill and nerve.

Marcus decided that to do the rest of the Grade V in a similar manner would take too long, even if he could work out how to paddle it. So after a cursory inspection, he joined the rest of us in portaging the rapid. No doubt he cursed that decision many times during the course of the long portage. We had to carry the boats one at a time, on a shoulder each, up a steep terraced path and down through the forest on the other side, resting every hundred yards and passed by nimble-footed Nepalese men carrying twice the weight in baskets on their backs.

It was lunchtime by the time we had finished the portage; the heat was stifling and we had an audience of local villagers to see us eat our Mars Bars. Amongst them was an old man with a painted face and long hair, some sort of guru we supposed. He remained with us for the rest of the day, watching our slow progress from the bank, grinning knowingly now and then. His ageing yet agile nakedness seemed to mock our fraught progress, and his secret smile seemed to say, 'I see the game you are playing, but that is not the way to fulfilment.'

The final hard rapid of this stretch was at least Grade VI and out of the question in our position. With careful scouting and bank security we managed to sneak it on the left, but by then it was 4.30 p.m. and we had less than two hours before dark to set up camp. It was already too late to dry our sleeping bags from the morning dew, and we were a little pushed collecting enough firewood. Some local kids bothered us, begging for gear, and someone spilt half the rice. A herd of cows trampled over our clothes laid on the bushes to drip dry. This then was Cow Camp. It was not a happy place, full of hurried and wordless activity. We had paddled or portaged just one kilometre that day, and we would no longer be sure where we were on the river. Was there harder canoeing still? And if so did we have enough food to last?

A night's sleep and some good Grade IV canoeing the next day sent these blues away. Liz, who, with Gill, was still finding the paddling hard, obviously relished the challenge.

'A gentler start thank goodness, or so I thought until we rounded a bend and went immediately into a long complex rapid which seemed to get bigger and bigger. I began to feel quite nervous and consequently paddled badly. We inspected another rapid which was big and in which I had a couple of full support strokes. Then some lovely Grade III rapids that went on and on. One

136

was harder than the rest and I went sideways into a pour-over and had a nasty swim. I was trapped in the stopper, first supporting and then swimming. For a little while I thought I wasn't going to come out. After that more fun rapids, another hole sideways—which I survived—and a near capsize with a spin out. Marcus and Terry ran one nasty-looking sump which the rest of us walked.

'An early stop for the night, but everyone well ready for it. Feeling tired now, but we are at a good camp, our things are dry and I'm full. Possibly the best day's paddling of my life.

'And what of the scenery? Well, with a little more time to look, what I saw has been really good. Occasional glimpses of mountains in the background, small houses dotted along bank, and a good trail on river right. The locals were friendly although understood little. Lots of fishermen'.

It takes two days or thereabouts to become part of a wilderness river. After a couple of days, all the minor problems have been sorted out—the numbers of layers to wear, the hole in the spray deck repaired, the dry-bags balanced in the boat, the seat padded, the footrest adjusted, and a practical rhythm to the day established—when and where to stop for lunch, and for the night, which wood burns best and how much iodine to use, who prefers cooking and who would rather wash pans, where to pack the sleeping bag and where to leave the spare jumper. And so it was on the third day on the Tama Kosi, when all of us, except Gill who swam three times, visibly relaxed. There seemed more time to enjoy the scenery, to revel in the paddling—many Grade IVs and one Grade V—and to deal with a couple of problems in a fairly relaxed way.

We stopped for lunch with Gill in tears saying that she had had enough. Everyone took something from her boat, and with it 20 lb lighter she had no further problems. After lunch it was Liz who had the upset, her boat getting jammed on a boulder midstream. We held Marcus' boat in the eddy behind the rock, while he climbed out to free the other. Once levered off it floated downstream, and Graham attached his tow line to it. Concentrating on clipping the bow loop, he did not see the stopper until too late, and dropped into it sideways. Liz's boat followed him in, and for a couple of seconds he was sitting in the hole with 500 lb of waterlogged boat on his lap. Fortunately Graham had the presence of mind to reach for the velcro release on his tow line before paddling out of the stopper. Had he not done so the jerk on his waist would surely have capsized him, and probably pulled him out of his kayak. And trying to release the tow line while swimming with the boat would have been awkward to say the least.

An old man wandered into our camp on the third night. He carried a short stick in his hand along which were pierced five fish heads. He offered them to us for sale. It was the only food we were offered on the Tama Kosi.

Unappetizing though they were I think I would have marginally preferred them to the pills that Chris popped every night. We first spotted this habit at Fish Head Camp, and because we were feeling relaxed and had plenty of daylight, a lively exchange ensued, as I noted in my diary.

> '"They're to make my beard grow;" Chris was trying to divert the obviously justified criticism of hypochondria that every doctor's son must face.
>
> '"The way to make it grow is to pluck it." Marcus was teasing his equally miserable growth with fire-blackened fingers. I reached across and pretended to pull a hair out of his chin between thumb and forefinger.
>
> '"Is that what you are searching for?" He continued plucking, and after a short pause concluded mysteriously, "It takes it into its second stage."
>
> '"I wish my bowels would move into their second stage," Liz moaned.
>
> '"Graham's already have I reckoned," Chris mumbled between bites of vitamin A and iron. "It's like trying to sleep below North Stack Fog Warning Station." Chris disappeared bottle in hand. Was it Bonington who said that, two days into every trip, the same three subjects come to dominate casual conversation, and they are all to do with food, namely ingestion, digestion, and evacuation.'

Leaving Fish Head Camp we quickly put the steep ravine of the upper Tama Kosi behind us. The hills still climbed thousands of feet on either side, but they were obviously made of softer material than the mountains above, because beside the river a flat flood plain gave room for more cultivation and larger settlements. Dugout canoes were positioned every two or three kilometres down the bank. Loaded to within inches of their gunwales, a dozen people squeezed between baskets of fruit, rice, cloth, pots and pans, these canoes looked about as stable as tree trunks, which, of course, is what they were. Only the ferryman sat high in the stern guiding his craft with smooth forward strokes and stern rudders, his passengers huddled as low as he could make them up front. A few of them looked prosperous, and some of the houses in this lower valley were made of stone, indicating a degree of wealth unknown upstream. The biggest village of all—Aakashee—even sported a landing strip, its streaming windsock visible to us across the flat lands beside the river.

After the exciting paddling of the last three days, making progress in these flat reaches was tedious. A cold easterly wind which sprang up in the early afternoon depressed us. And then suddenly round a bend we merged with another river. It had to be the Sun Kosi. We paddled into its browner flow at 1.30 on our fourth day. Our spirits soared; we had thought the Sun Kosi was two days away. Now, it seemed, we had time in hand. We could slow the pace down, start later, stop earlier, and fool around on the water. The Sun Kosi helped us into this relaxed mood by being almost totally flat for the first 15 kilometres after the confluence. We stopped for the night at 2.30 p.m. opposite the village of Beni Ghat.

Rafts came this way fairly often and we had been told by Encounter Overland that food was available in Beni Ghat. I recorded our trip into town in my diary.

'We bought six kilograms of rice in the local supermarket (mud hut), had our *kukri* knife sharpened in the ironmongers (same mud hut) and had a cup of *chiyaa* in the local café (neighbour's mud hut). Still the town is a metropolis by the standards of eastern Nepal. There is no road, but a suspension bridge for pedestrians links both banks, and a helicopter landing zone is marked out in the school field. Two smartly dressed girls clutching 'English Readers' asked Liz which one of us was her husband. To avoid an impossible explanation she pointed at Marcus. The information was greeted with much nodding of heads. Gill whispered in my ear, "Old Nepalese proverb say grey hair, wispy beard, and wrinkled brow, sign of man long married."'

'Grandpa' was not the only one to receive admiring glances. We had already had some trouble getting Graham into the viewfinder when taking pictures of him with the Nepalese, but it was not until our walk round Beni Ghat that I realized quite how big he must have appeared to them. They stared in awe as he passed the houses, some of the more adventurous children moving their hands in and out as though playing an accordion. I would not have been surprised to find a touch of envy in their hearts, as well as surprise in their eyes, for no Sun Kosi villager could hope to earn the money that had gone into making Graham's fifteen stone of muscle and fat. (Although we would never admit it to him, it was mostly muscle—he was the only one amongst us who could lift a loaded boat alone).

Buying food took time. We tried to find out the going rate, offer less and then bargain towards the normal price. Nepalese, like many poor people, relish a bit of bargaining. Many food items had a fixed price; eggs were two rupees, a kilo of rice six to eight rupees. (We received 23.5 rupees for one of our U.S. dollars on the black market.) Some items like chicken however, fluctuated in price between thirty and sixty rupees, the variation and high price probably caused by the influx of rafters in the 1980s. We couldn't afford these tourist prices, but in any case paying over the odds was bad practice. It inflated the price of goods beyond what the locals could afford, and created divisions in the community.

Another problem caused by the tourist raft trips down the Sun Kosi was begging. To give away gear or food—particularly if, as was likely, it held little value to the river runner—was hurtful to the pride of the Nepalese, and would in the end destroy that very quality of self-sufficiency in a harsh environment which most visitors to the country admired so much. We only gave gifts such as screw-top plastic bottles, a lighter or a whistle, in return for assistance, such as the collection of firewood by young children, or the help given by a young student in Chatra in looking for our bus.

Leaving Beni Ghat next morning our boats were heavier again with extra food. Our fifth day on the river was not particularly memorable, and my diary was terse and to the point.

> 'The paddling was flat and boring until lunchtime. There were six good rapids after lunch however. A play wave on the last one was a photo call. We camped some way below at a beach well stocked with wood ('Woody Cove'), but also accessible to the local village. Old woman and child squatted beside our camp for an hour, always an unnerving experience. I took pictures of the stickers on Chris's boat for our main expedition sponsor—a Leicester manufacturer who gave us thirty pairs of socks!'

Looking at the map in the morning it was clear we were somewhere in the section marked 'jungle corridor,' but exactly where we were not sure. All became clear however, when we passed under another pedestrian suspension bridge followed by a tributary entering from the left. We were above Harkapur, a village where we had been told food was obtainable, and where apparently there were 'serious' rapids. John Wilde, leader of the Australian Sun Kosi Expedition in January 1981, reported 'problems in a deep hole', with one of his expedition having 'an epic back loop'. As is often the way, those you are warned about seem easy. There were three rapids near the village, and only the second warranted a brief mention in my diary.

> 'Just before paddling into the huge haystack at the bottom of Harkapur 2, I saw Marcus, who was sitting in the eddy, bang his deck with delight. I guessed the wave must have a bite, and sure enough it had me in. I rolled up to see Marcus trying to keep his breakfast down, choking with laughter.'

Liz was equally laconic in her reference to the Harkapur rapids. Indeed, like the rest of us, she was more impressed by the village, where we pulled in to buy supplies, than by the white water.

> 'Paddling today was flat initially. Then a few bouncy rapids, but the biggest and bounciest were at Harkapur, a small village where we stopped to buy sugar and flour. Terry and Marcus both got munched in a hole. I took the chicken run.
> 'Harkapur was different to our first stop, Beni Ghat; much smaller, much fewer supplies, although very clean again. I was struck by the genuine friendliness of the people. We had chiyaa at a lovely shop, where I warmed

140

myself beside the stove. The owner's standards of cleanliness were pretty scrupulous. We watched him kill, pluck, eviscerate and spice a chicken, washing his hands after each stage.'

It was hard to tear ourselves away from the relaxing scene around us; women carrying pitchers of water up from the Sun Kosi in bronze and pewter jugs—was it my imagination or were the girls with bronze jugs better dressed?—a cow and goat snuffling in their stall next to the café as a boy threw in a pile of vegetable trimmings. I thought I would try out some Nepalese by way of farewell. *'Yasko kati chiyaa,'* I asked.

'Pachaas paisaa ko ek chiyaa,' our host beamed.

Thumbing through our Nepalese phrasebook I searched for 'Can you write the price on a piece of paper'; but there was nothing between, 'Can you make sure you are not late? *(Dhilo nagarrios?)*, and 'Can you tell me where is the toilet?' *(Chaarpi kahaa chha?)*, phrases which do not get much use in Nepal.[1]

'We'll let you handle this one, Prof,' Graham yelled, strolling off to the boats. Marcus however, came to my rescue with a *non sequitur*. *'Yo gaau raamro chha* (this is a fine village),' he said and, under cover of the 'conversation' that followed, I sorted out the money.

I agreed with Marcus, Harkapur was a fine village, poor, but not desperately so like Busti and with a fine spirit quite unlike that village. Four or five shops sold the basics—flour, *dahl,* rice, salt, tea, matches, soap, pots and pans—and a few luxuries—torches and batteries, mirrors, biscuits, pens and paper, combs, cigarettes. Close to the village were vegetable plots, and further afield, seen from the river, wheat. Goats, cows, pigs and chickens were much in evidence. The village had meat and eggs, and enough wheat and skins to trade for rice and salt. Firewood and animal pasture were still available close at hand. Just after arriving at camp that evening, a kilometre below Harkapur, a group of women and children herded thirty goats through our campsite. They were returning to the village, and had bundles of wood in their arms.

The extended family seemed to form the basic economic unit; there was no evidence of, and seemingly no need for employment in the Western

---

[1] With regard to their toilet arrangements Marcus wrote in his diary: 'Regrettably a lasting impression will be the approach of the Nepalese towards crapping—particularly near the river. Children shit on the street, adults along the paths leading to and from the village—men after sunrise, women before. I can not see how this can be healthy, nor is it consistent with their otherwise meticulous approach to hygiene. There does not even seem to be the concept of a 'crapping field' (Sudan style), where the sun reduces all to dust. There is only (occasionally) a village toilet *(chaarpi)* which merely concentrates the problem. The subject remains a mystery to me.'

141

sense of the word. Poverty may be the inevitable result of such small economic units, but the pay-off seemed to be a more relaxed way of life.[1] No one looked at a watch—few had one to look at—so they made their own time. The men stopped for twenty or thirty minutes to talk to anyone who went by, and when we did, to watch us. The children were let out of school early, bouncing across the rocks to see us leave the village.

Our camp that night was tense and lonely by comparison. Blackstorm clouds rolled in towards dusk, and although we had no rain, it still looked ominous when we awoke. The miserable weather made me yearn for some greasy protein-rich food, but of course it was rice pudding again for breakfast. Then I saw something which depressed me still more. As I climbed into my kayak one of the little goat girls who had passed through the camp the night before came through again laden with a huge log, her lovely face contorted by the effort. Strangely Liz too was down in the dumps.

> 'Now it is the end of the day, and I find myself feeling tired and more than a little wound up. I'm wondering how to relax my head for tomorrow. A much heavier build-up of clouds in the evening than we have seen; maybe even no stars tonight.'

I am not a great believer in premonition, but perhaps we both sensed that there was something more than a storm brewing below Harkapur.

A 'stopper' is the movement of water most feared by canoeists and rafters. Otherwise known as a hydraulic, pour-over, keeper, souse hole, or simply hole, the stopper wave is formed by a vertical or horizontal constriction in the river bed. The vertical constriction suggested by the name pour-over can be boulders on the river bed, or bedrock, or the concrete sill of a weir. Water flows over these obstacles and, accelerated by the drop, drives deep into the slower water below creating a 'hole' in the surface. Surface water on the downstream side of the constriction tries to fill the hole by moving back upstream, falling into it in a tumbling foaming stopper wave. A waterfall, unless it is of Niagara proportions, is dangerous not so much because of the fall as because of the stopper at the bottom. Less dramatic, but also less easily seen and avoided, are stoppers formed by horizontal constrictions, in gorges, in between landslips, or between areas of hard rock. Again water accelerated by the squeeze will tend to dive under slower water whenever the narrows open out, creating an upstream flow on the surface.

---

[1] How much the Nepalese attitude to work, to each other, and to strangers is also the product of cultural and religious factors, I do not know.

Objects which float, such as people and boats, will tend to be stopped by a hole. Some stoppers are relatively safe because they will release objects quickly. There may be a way out at the sides where the wave is less big, or in the middle where the current is passing through. Even a 'safe' hole however, will often circulate objects two or three times before spitting them out, and needless to say, the feeling of being in a washing machine is unpleasant, and may indeed be positively harmful if there are boulders, bedrock, concrete sills or metal spikes in there with you.

Other stoppers are definitely 'keepers'. A powerful downstream return flow or 'tow-back' prevents escape from the hole. The stopper is uniform across the river, and the sides blocked off by natural rock walls, or artificial concrete pillars as in weirs. Even if there is surface flow out at the sides, it may not be possible to get there if the stopper is horseshoe-shaped with the wings pointing upstream. The only way out in such a keeper is down; but the inherent buoyancy of a canoe or a canoeist, as long as they both contain air, will prevent them from being sucked down and out. This is why some have suggested removing buoyancy aids or life jackets as a last resort when stuck in a stopper. Of course eventually everything will come out, but by then it is too late.

The place from which to judge whether a stopper is dangerous or not is the bank.[1] I was in the river and ten metres upstream of 'Jaws' when I saw it. It was our seventh day on the water, our third on the Sun Kosi, and I was leading. Swollen by the Dudh Kosi which had entered from the north that morning, the Sun Kosi was pushing me at the incredible rate of sixteen thousand cubic feet of water per second towards the very teeth of the hole. I did not have time to judge whether it was a keeper or not, but it was time enough to want to be out of there. I had long enough to consider several strategies of escape—a reverse ferry glide, a sideways draw, a punch through under full power—and time enough to realize they were all too late. Fragments of a description whirled through my mind—'very serious . . . by far the longest rapid . . . well worth scouting . . . monstrous hole . . . capable of flipping rafts . . .'

The fragments were from Dai Richards' description of Jaws.[2] His guide to the Sun Kosi was difficult to follow—he had not mentioned the confluence with the Dudh Kosi which we had passed that morning for

---

[1] Side-on it is possible to see the extent of the surface tow-back, and if necessary measure it by throwing in floating objects such as sticks.

[2] 'Name: Jaws. Grade 4. Very serious, especially in high water. About 500 yards past Pre-Jaws is Jaws. This is by far the longest rapid and well worth scouting. In high water there is one monstrous hole and several very large holes easily capable of flipping a raft.' From *Sun Kosi: A Rafting Report* by Dai Richards, 26 April 1985. Printed and distributed by Encounter Overland, 267 Old Brompton Road, London SW5.

143

instance—but we had guessed when we stopped at a bridge for lunch that it was Nabaltar, and that the rapids which followed were therefore Pre-Jaws and Jaws. None of us munching on our Mars Bars however, had been unduly concerned by the description or indeed the name. We had, after all, already canoed a rapid described as 'serious due to the nature of the three or so holes' (Harkapur 2), and one entitled High Anxiety ('a serious rapid'), both without great incident, and both, like Jaws, Sun Kosi Grade IVs. We had canoed Grade V on the Tama Kosi and the Sun Kosi was low by post monsoon standard. But, as it says in the film, 'Just when you thought you were safe . . .'

Not only did I think I was safe, but my mind was about as far from watery things as it could be sitting above a rapid on the largest river in Nepal. The reason was a collection of villagers clustered around us and the kayaks, like flies round dead meat—which we must have smelt like after wearing Lifa Wear for seven days. Normally I ignored this daily visitation, but the paddling that morning had been particularly flat and boring, so our congregation was, for a while, distracting. As they watched us, I watched them, trying out a few smiles every now and then, and observing, as I wrote in my diary:

> 'They sit and watch, sometimes passing comment to one another—usually ribald I would guess by the cackles of laughter which follow—but more often silent, simply staring at our exposed white bodies (trying to get a tan), or fingering our discarded skins of wetsuit and cagoule, helmet and buoyancy aid, or tapping the plastic or our *dongas* and peering inside to see how we could kneel on the seats.'

I don't think I'll ever enjoy zoos again. I know how those caged animals feel, to have their every move watched even while they are eating, and why they pace up and down, restless to be away from those prying eyes. After twenty minutes I had to get up. I had to do something. I walked down the beach and climbed onto a high rock, looking down the river. I could see big waves and a few stoppers, but I could also see a route through. Later I realized this must have been Pre-Jaws. If I had continued down the beach I would have seen Jaws. But I was only looking because I needed air, rather than seriously inspecting the rapid.

Back at the zoo I kept outside our ring of watchers, sat down on a flat boulder, and did some sightseeing myself. The Nepalese women were flat-faced with high cheek bones and a Mongolian slant to their eyes. The older ones wore more jewellery, both ears and nose pierced with silver and gold. A few had bangles of the same metals on their wrists. These however, were their only ornamentation, for almost without exception their clothes were drab browns and greens, worn and frayed from constant use and caked with dirt. These women went barefoot. In some of the larger villages flip-flops were common. Only once on the river did we see women with brightly coloured saris or washed and combed hair. Perhaps this was because we did not see them at night. Certainly during the day most mothers and daughters were involved in heavy manual labour—hauling fodder for the animals, carrying water, fetching firewood, planting and harvesting crops. Overburdened and often malnourished the beauty of these hill women faded quickly.

If the worn faces and shabby clothes of the females were immediately noticeable, it was the legs and particularly the calf muscles of the men which quite literally stood out. The rivers of Nepal, and particularly the Sun Kosi, form natural highways for commerce through the country. There is not only no road access, but the tracks that follow the rivers are not even wide enough for carts or trolleys. So everything must be carried on foot into the hills, or rather on legs for the paths do not so much go along as up and down. Men do this long-distance carrying. They lift loads of up to 100 lb in baskets with shoulder straps and a headband across the forehead. A T-shaped stick like a wooden ice axe is carried for balance, and for resting on. A journey of six days is sometimes necessary to take the rice, *dahl,* vegetables, fruit, chickens, pots and pans, tea, salt and sugar down to the market towns or back up into the hills. So the men are immensely fit, and very strong in the leg. Their feet are splayed from constant walking under load, in barefeet or flip flops, and their diminutive bodies are spare of any fat.

Lack of protein, as much as hard work, was the reason for their leanness. And without adequate clothes the men, and the boys particularly, suffered from the winter cold. Sometimes they would come down to our beach in the morning, or stay late into the evening moving as close to our fire as they dared, and trying to drug their shivering undernourished bodies with a cigarette or two. Tobacco was a prized possession, and the youngsters copied their fathers in searching for and hoarding the minutest piece of shag.

These people could not expect to reach their fiftieth birthday (the average life expectancy in Nepal is 49), and indeed they were lucky to be alive in the first place (infant mortality in Nepal is amongst the highest in the world). These statistics are not surprising given the daily struggle for existence in the hill villages. But this apparently grim picture is not the one I have taken with me from Nepal. It is rather the open and friendly faces of the people, and their well-centred way of life. The men in particular seemed to enjoy themselves enormously, a joy in life that embraced friend and stranger alike. For a westerner like myself in whose society the strange male is typically hard-faced, and brought up amongst Orientals (my father was a Professor of Japanese History) where the male face is typically polite but inscrutable, I found the Nepalese men quite bewildering with their smiling eyes, casual touches, and eagerness to help.

It seemed to us that the Nepalese are so at one with themselves that they still fear nothing from foreign contact, or is it invasion? Certainly in the villages their poverty means they have little to guard, but there seems little meanness of spirit or guarded generosity even in the bigger towns. The fact that Nepal has assimilated 40,000 Tibetan refugees since the Chinese invasion of Tibet in 1949 says something for friendship, although who can say looking from the outside what subtle discrimination goes on? I only know that every time we stopped and searched the eyes of our river-bank audience for signs of envy, greed or fear, emotions that would spell danger for our possessions or even ourselves, we found none. I carry with me the image of the young Nepali running, tripping in anxious haste down to the river bank, calling urgently with voice and arms as though he wanted to warn me off his land, or perhaps sell something, or even get help for his sick mother. And when I pulled nervously to the shore, my face set grimly against banditry or begging, I was confronted by an enormous melon outstretched in eager arms. 'Excuse me sir,' he smiled, 'is this your first time in the country of Everest?'

I was nudged out of my thoughts and observations by the approach of two giggling boys who peered at my white body with big brown eyes. Disconcerted by their stare I went over to Marcus still lying supine in the sun. 'Do you think it's time we got going?' I did not want to tell him my thoughts. I knew he would think I was being 'quaint'.[1]

'I was afraid you were going to say that.' Yawning, he managed to open his eyes, just, and stretched his body into an even more relaxed position. Like many small people he is hard to stop when he is on the go, but once stopped he needs extra choke to get going. 'I am beginning to think your idea of a midday siesta is a good one.' Unusually our lunch beach the previous day had been deserted and I had fallen asleep in the sun. Now however, I was jumping, and I chivied the others into movement.

The 'B' team, Graham, Gill and I, were first on the water. We were, I think, still more river hungry than the others having arrived a week later in the country and having missed out on the Trisuli. Unbeknown to me this had already caused a minor split in Kathmandu. I had been keen to arrange a pick-up at the end of the Sun Kosi, at some extra cost; I thought

---

[1] Marcus was to write later in his diary:
'I struggle with the idea that there can be no improvement, no real improvement, as long as the West sees only quaintness, here in Nepal as elsewhere. I wonder how long it will be before the West writes off Nepal and looks somewhere else for an 'unspoilt experience'.

146

this would save us time. Marcus, representing the 'A' team, was only just convinced.

> 'Nima was our direct contact and for a price he arranged transport to and from the Sun Kosi. The "socks and prayer flags by *dunga*" team were a bit concerned about the cost of all this five-star treatment, but it seemed to work out O.K. and we went along with it.

Well, it didn't work out O.K. in the end, and I lived to regret using my Sherpa contacts. I also regretted not being sensitive to the 'us' and 'them' feelings. 'Why don't they share their biscuits?' Liz moaned in her diary at Harkapur, and with equal justice she probably thought, 'Why don't they wait for us?' as I led the 'B' team down the river. Still, what happened next, if it did nothing else, brought us back together as a team. 'At last we are six,' Marcus was to write that night.

The Sun Kosi was about 50 yards across hereabouts. It was muddy brown and monstrous. Strong sweep strokes forced our kayaks into midstream. Graham followed close behind, Gill further back, still nervous after her swims on the Tama Kosi. Big waves 7 or 8 ft high swept us down Pre-Jaws, the stoppers snapping ineffectually at our paddle blades.

The water in Jaws looked no different from Pre-Jaws. There was, it is true, a prominent rock wall on the right constricting the flow of the river and piling up giant cushions of water, but elsewhere there looked to be nothing worse than haystacks and small stoppers with everything flowing through. I kept high in my boat trying to spot the best line. It was only when I was two-thirds of the way down the rapid, still confident of an easy run, that I saw it.

Jaws was aptly named from the position I found myself in. I was 10 metres above a cavernous hole, floating towards the gnashing stopper that rolled across its back. The wave itself looked about the size of a small bungalow, and I knew that if I visited that house I might be a permanent resident. My first thought was to reverse ferry glide. Five metres nearer the hole I realized that it was useless. My only hope was to punch through the hydraulic. I levered on two or three powerful paddle strokes and entered the utility room.

Most of Sun Kosi was going into this particular washing machine. There was a dribble going past on the left, sufficient to paddle in if only I had inspected the rapid, and somewhat more going past on the right, up against a small cliff in a confused and turbulent froth yet also providing a way past, had I but known. In the middle of the river however, the main current was pouring over huge boulders forming an extremely energetic and powerful keeper. My attempt to paddle through it was like trying to run through a brick wall.

The front of the kayak buried itself and stopped dead. Water from behind pounded down on the rear deck forcing it downwards, and 25 lb of plastic Everest with 60 lb of gear stood on end like a top. For half a second I was paddling in the sky, and then I fell backwards into the hole. Out of habit I crouched forward into a rolling position, paddle beside the kayak reaching for the surface. It must have appeared on the face of a stopper wave because I was up again before I had hip-flicked. And that is when I began to wonder what it would be like to take my first breath of water.

Normally when a stopper capsizes a canoeist, the effect of his or her body upside down in the water is to throw a drogue into the downstream current, flushing the canoe and canoeist out. In a keeper however, the downstream current may be so far below, or continue beneath the surface for so long, that even a submerged canoeist contains too much 'surface' buoyancy to be flushed out. This is what was happening to me. I rolled up to find myself being pulled back upstream towards the boulders at the front of the hole.

Conscious thought became increasingly difficult. I remember trying to roll three or four times. I was desperate to stay in my boat. Even though I was better off without it now, I didn't have the sense to commit myself to the water. I couldn't reach the surface so I didn't know whether I was still in, or out, of the stopper. Instinct took over, forcing my body from the boat in the search for air. My thinking brain felt helpless and hopeless, except for one thing. On one of my half-rolls I thought I had seen Graham coming towards me. Surely he wouldn't try to help me if I was still in the hole?

I emerged gasping and retching into the bright sunlight. I could stand, or thought I could stand until I tried. Staggering and collapsing in small semi-circles 40 metres downstream of Jaws I felt stupid and embarrassed, a beginner out of his depth in the shallows. 'Glad you showed us what was there,' Gill smiled sympathetically; the others dabbled in the eddy anxious not to rub it in by helping me empty my boat.

Eventually I gave up. 'I can't lift it,' I said. 'It must be cramp or something.' Graham jumped out and did it for me. Then I found I could not even lift my paddle with my left hand. I seemed to want to hold the arm across my chest. 'I'll just have to sit down for a couple of minutes.' But seeing their looks change from smug amusement to real concern I began to realize there might be something wrong.

'I think we should have a look at your arm,' Liz said, easing my buoyancy aid off. The cag, jumper and top half of my wetsuit followed with difficulty. 'Can you raise your arm like this?' she said, lifting hers. I could not, and a strange dip in my shoulder appeared when I tried. 'The step in the shoulder was obvious,' Liz wrote later in her diary, 'and luckily

I knew what to do.' Liz had realized that my shoulder was dislocated.[1]

Sitting on the bench with my clothes scattered around me I only had the haziest notion of what was going on. Fortunately the pain was not bad, so I co-operated with Liz while she wedged my right side against a boulder, placed her feet against the left side of my chest, and pulled my right arm out at right angles. 'I did not quite pull strongly enough when I tried to reduce it,' she wrote with the benefit of hindsight, but looking into her eyes I saw that she was afraid of doing more harm.

Chris started to panic. He suggested paddling to Chatra to get help, while I waited there. The feeling of fright was contagious. We were many days' paddling or walking from anything remotely resembling a doctor or hospital, and I did not want to travel that far with a useless arm and increasingly painful shoulder. I wondered aloud whether any of the local villagers might know something about dislocations. Marcus meanwhile replaced Liz in the rowing position, and feet against my chest tried pulling. Graham leaned his weight back on Marcus' shoulders. Suddenly there was a crunch of muscle and bone, like a dog chewing on a rib, an ugly and beautiful sound. The thing at the top of my arm was a shoulder again.

My first thought was to get going again as though nothing had happened. Fortunately I was now—and remained for the next few days—in no state to make any leadership decisions, and Marcus' relaxed realism held sway.

> 'Terry was amazing—very little fuss. He didn't even want to stop and set up camp, but we insisted—'Dislocation Camp' needless to say!'

My lack of fuss was partly due to the paralysis of shock. On the rebound from that state of stupor I felt an exaggerated need for haste. We had arranged to meet Nima in two days' time, and by present reckoning it would take four days to finish. Having arranged the pick-up I was concerned to be on time. I found I could not switch off from the time pressure which is so much part of Western life. On the water the river took

---

[1] Shoulder dislocations are a fairly common injury amongst canoeists, although I had never seen one before. For the purposes of physiotherapy I learnt much about them on my return home. An anterior (forwards) dislocation, which this was, is most usual, caused by rolling in surf or stoppers, or by striking the arm, through the paddle, against a boulder while moving. Early reduction of the injury—returning the humerus ball into the shoulder socket—is recommended, because after about half an hour muscle spasm makes relocation much more difficult and often impossible without anaesthetic. It is preferable that a doctor reduces the dislocation since temporary or permanent damage can be done to the arm's nerve supply in relocation. Shoulder dislocations are typically painful and can be shocking. It is normal to reduce forward dislocations by pulling down more than out, often using a wedge under the armpit.

over, forcing its own pace, but every evening my diary contained phrases like 'still a long way to go' (Dislocation Camp) and 'perhaps we will make Chatra tomorrow' (Nameless Cove). In the end however, like all the others, I had to accept that old man river would get us there in his own time and not before. Liz, despite the constant worry of dysentery, was coming to the same conclusion.

> 'We don't really know where we are on the river—although we can make an educated guess which still leaves three days to Chatra. Chris is getting a little agitated. I have calmed somewhat, although I find this flat/huge wave contrast hard to relax in. I am amazed at my own lack of concern about time deadlines, and where we are on the river. It's all I can do to keep pace with one rapid at a time, one day at a time.'

Leaving Dislocation Camp the following morning the euphoria of shock and recovery had worn off and I was left with a bunch of torn ligaments. Liz helped me on with my gear and Marcus distributed the contents of my boat amongst the others. I was self-absorbed, anxious lest I put my shoulder out again. And I did, not by a wild support stroke on the left, or by a desperate attempt to roll, but by sunbathing at lunchtime. Gingerly raising myself off my stomach, I angrily kicked a sandy trail across to Marcus, arm held at high port. 'I've done it again, just by lying with my arm like . . . wait a minute . . . I think it's gone back in again.' So it had, as much to Marcus' relief as mine.

Now I was feeling really sorry for myself, my paddling tentative in the extreme.

> 'I avoid all high strokes. The range of movement in my left arm is about one foot, so even low strokes on that side are impossible. I must float broadside down all the rapids, including the Grade IVs, so that I can lead and lean on my strong side. I now know what it is like to be a C1 paddler and what Pat Kingman must have felt like in Crystal.'[1]

Liz too suffered that day from a recurrence of her stomach problems.

> 'Woke with a sore throat and croup after a sleepless night. Difficult to concentrate today. Now in bed early, not feeling good; exhausted and sick. More continuous rapids . . . but I didn't enjoy the day except for a shopping jaunt for food. They only had eggs and rice . . . $3^1/_2$-inch cat prints in the campsite tonight.'

Had she been well, Liz would have written more about 'Tiger Bay'. Even without the leopard prints padding a soft spoor across the monsoon

---

[1] Pat was one of the C1 paddlers on our Grand Canyon trip. She missed her line in Crystal rapid and turned sideways to try and cope with what followed.

high tide mark, this strip of sand on the edge of the jungle was an eerie place. In the gloaming Marcus had us urinating round the campsite to 'mark our territory', and after the first noises of the night started filtering through the trees we needed no encouragement. I tried in vain to remember the advice of an old Burmese hand, who had fought with my father in the Indian army, concerning the three deadly jungle animals—tiger, bear, and buffalo; one you must frighten, one you must hurt, and one you must run away from. Halfway through the night I still wasn't sure, so I continued to doze in my trainers, a whistle in one hand and a rock in the other.

The only animals we ever saw in Rhesus Gorge were appropriately monkeys. The canoeing below Tiger Bay, however, was exciting enough, particularly if you were a three-limbed mammal.

> 'Started 9.30. Shoulder felt much better which was fortunate because I had to roll in the third of a series of five big rapids in Rhesus Gorge. I made a half-hearted attempt the first time to test my arm; it felt all right so I went full bore on the second attempt. The gorge was impressive, thick green jungle coming down through rock bluffs to a churning river.'

Adding to the excitement was our anxiety over a rapid called the Black Hole. Dai Richards described hitting this rapid at 3 p.m. on the penultimate day of his trip, but since we did not know exactly where we were—the locals had been saying *Chatra dui din* (two days)' for the last four days now—we expected to see it round every bend. His description of the rapid was as follows:

> '*Name:* Black Hole
> *Grade:* Hole—impossible to run safely. Route down IV or chicken shoot in high water.
> The Black Hole can be identified by the colour of the left-hand bank. It is the second large black landslide. Investigation especially in high water is very important. The hole occupies at least half the width of the river, and is a definite *keeper*. To see it in high water is a very awe-inspiring sight.'

We never saw the Black Hole, but needless to say we saw hundreds of black landslides. We were still looking for that keeper in the plains of India as we passed over a mirror-flat Sun Kosi on the bus. I subsequently discovered that it was quite innocuous in low water, but a boat-eater in flood.

Lunch on a hot flat beach was succeeded by hot flat paddling. A ferry crossing offered *chiaa*, and we joined those waiting in the shade. A disjointed collection of dirty thatch huts sold tea, biscuits, beads, cigarettes, pans and cotton cloth. Nobody was buying, except for the odd cup, and I made the mistake of watching them wash up, so I couldn't even fancy that. But beauty is in the eye of the beholder, and Marcus saw a different scene.

> 'And the tea stop at the ferry crossing—one of the magic moments. Earth stove and grass houses on a flood plain beach. Transitory, changing naturally with the seasons. And earlier a higher more permanent ferryman's house, so reminiscent of Sidhartha.'

Despite my jaundiced view of that particular spot I was beginning to enjoy life again. My arm seemed to be working, the elusive Black Hole was keeping us all on our footrests, and I took time out in front. Loping contentedly round Nameless Cove that night I wondered if I was finally catching Marcus' Eastern fever.

> 'A new place every night. Somewhere new, yet familiar, to find a clothes line, a fireplace, a flat piece of sand to lie on, and a bunch of driftwood to burn. How good it is to travel and not to arrive.'

A middle-aged man came down to the beach in the morning, and after much prodding and tapping, knelt in Graham's kayak. Before we could reach him, he was off, ferry gliding across the river, shouting unintelligible joy to us. He brought it back smiling, and waved good-bye.

Still eyeballing every black slip on either slope—well, Dai might have been looking upstream when he described that 'aaaaaaahhhh'—we paddled two more rapids in the 'landslide series' quite without incident. Then we were into another gorge.

It was a copy of Rhesus Gorge—or perhaps it *was* Rhesus Gorge—and Chris, accompanied by Marcus, determined to get some pictures of the monkeys whooping through the trees. The rest of us pushed on and became involved in another form of monkey business.

I looked down on the Sun Kosi being squeezed through a 30-ft wide slot and felt weak. I tried to think 'Black Hole' so that I had an excuse to wait for the others, but although the rapid had been caused by a landslide, it was made of concrete grey boulders fallen from the right bank. They first dammed the river so that it had to fall 15 ft to gain its old level, and then, where it fell, pushed the water left into a blank wall of schist. The waves were steep and confused, rebounding and folding off the rock wall, but a big pool below meant that one way or another it would be over with fairly quickly.

I had to run the rapid facing right to avoid the diagonal stoppers and clapotis, but this meant supporting and paddling on my weak side. A wave slapped, a muscle popped, a nerve jangled, and I was down. Gill however, did not get such a good line. She was flipped over by a wave doubling back

152

and failed to recover. Still in the main flow she was swept out of her boat and, leaflike, downriver. Both Liz and Graham were on the bank taking pictures. I did not have the strength to tow her to the bank. Suddenly, without any means of rescue, we were in trouble. 'Swim for it,' I cried hoarsely, hoping she would let go of the boat that was dragging her downstream. Dazed and confused she floated on. I looked over my shoulder. Was there another rapid round the corner? Another 30 metres and we might both be wrapped round a fallen tree, or into the 'aaaaaaahhhh'. I looked back. It was as though she had been reading my thoughts. Mark Spitz would have trouble keeping up with her. The Olympic dash took her to a small haven of rock jutting out from the jungle. One-armed I helped her empty her boat, and keeping an eye out for cat prints, scrambled up the rock to look for watery foe. There was nothing, just a few lazy meanders that laughed at my panic.

The hills relented after this, allowing in shafts of sunlight to warm Gill at our lunch beach. Two major tributaries, the Arun and the Tamar, poured in from the left swelling the Sun Kosi to twice its former size. And then round a bend, no different from any other, a Buddhist temple appeared, throwing culture and civilization at us. Behind it was a one-street village, and below a tented market on the flood plain. We bought some rice, smelt the incense, watched the tall women with round eyes and long black hair, and felt India all around. Surely we were close now, but how close none of us could have guessed.

The end was painfully swift as Liz noted in her last diary entry.

'Terry has a muscle in his arm which appears to keep popping in and out, but otherwise manages to keep going. The ease with which he is prepared to lighten his load in the morning suggests that it is quite painful still. Paddling was fun. The elusive Black Hole remained elusive for the remainder of the trip. A couple of really fun rapids and some monkeys close by, and then on to the confluences first of the Arun and then after 500 yards the Tamar . . . confluence followed by a gorge and then a surprising town with a temple and women in saris. Suddenly different influences and we are near the plains. The contrast when it came was instant and stunning. From lush green terraced gorge to seemingly nothing but flat sand, heat haze and an isolated tree on the horizon. Suddenly and unexpectedly the trip is over. As if down a drain all our energy disappeared.'

A beach at Chatra, a small and unbelievably dirty town where the plains of the Indian subcontinent meet the foothills of the Himalaya, was our home for the next two nights. For a hefty fee we had arranged for Nima to meet us with a bus, but he had waited only twenty-four hours and left three hours before we arrived. Was Nima Sherpa infected by a Western sense of urgency? We felt let down; he had not behaved by the rules of our river. In the end we gave him up, and found our own way out by Land Rover and public transport.

Waiting for Nima on the baked beach we dried our clothes and sleeping bags—there was no dew for the first time in eleven mornings—and let our minds wind round the trip. It was here that Marcus wrote his poem—'River Lead Me On'—and the postscript to it.

> 'After all these years a second verse.[1] Still I guess
> the exit gorge was just the kind of place to inspire
> song-writing. The little town in the middle, Buddhist
> temple and *daal* houses, so different to the clustered huts
> and naked beaches of the past eleven days. Then so suddenly out
> of the hills . . . pouring onto the plains, as though
> we had come to the end of the world. I have this
> memory of sitting on the rocks with Liz in the sun
> watching the monkeys and talking. A passing porter
> told us they were called Diru, as he stopped briefly
> from places unknown to places only imagined. How
> little we know of this country we have passed through.
> But the moment was good—and the talk too.'

---

[1] For the first verse see page 41.

Stormwrecked—In the Hudson Strait and Faroe Isles by Nigel Foster

The Faroe Islands, which lie midway between Scotland and Iceland, are one of the sea's great playgrounds. Eighteen islands stand solid and bold against the elements. In the narrow sounds the North Atlantic Ocean swell and the tide streams, which reach up to 12 knots, meet in a frenzied dance of wild white phantoms, echoed off every prominent headland and point. Even when the sea seems to sleep it is never still. When calm water entices the unwary towards the towering headlands and inviting islands, the deception is all-too-soon realized as a rumble like distant thunder reaches the ear and the boiling turbulence of a tide race rushes into view. Mile upon mile of towering unbroken cliffs, the massive rollers of the tide races and the screaming hordes of seabirds make a dramatic and challenging playground for the advanced paddler.

I visited the islands three times before advertising an 'expedition course', to the area as part of my 1987 'Nigel Foster Canoeing Ventures' programme. The intention was to explore an area of the west and north of the island chain, an area boasting some of the highest vertical sea cliffs in the world, and to sample, if possible, some of the spectacular tide races. By now I had come to realize that the islands have a knack of producing the unexpected, but the unexpected is always a surprise.

The five of us were camping in a lush valley bottom beside a bright tumbling stream that dropped noisily over rocky ledges into the sea. Above us and all around were the typical Faroese striated basalt crags rising steeply to the mountain peaks. We shared the area only with the eider ducks and black guillemots and the ever-watchful terns that had a colony nearby. During the strong winds of the past few days we had enjoyed some spectacular cliff and mountain walks and had made one short trip in the kayaks beneath the shelter of the cliffs to the north. The nearest headland was split by a precipitous cleft through which the sea ran, isolating the massive grass-topped stack; home for thousands of puffins. Nearby, a dark cavern plunged deep into the headland, and on exploring

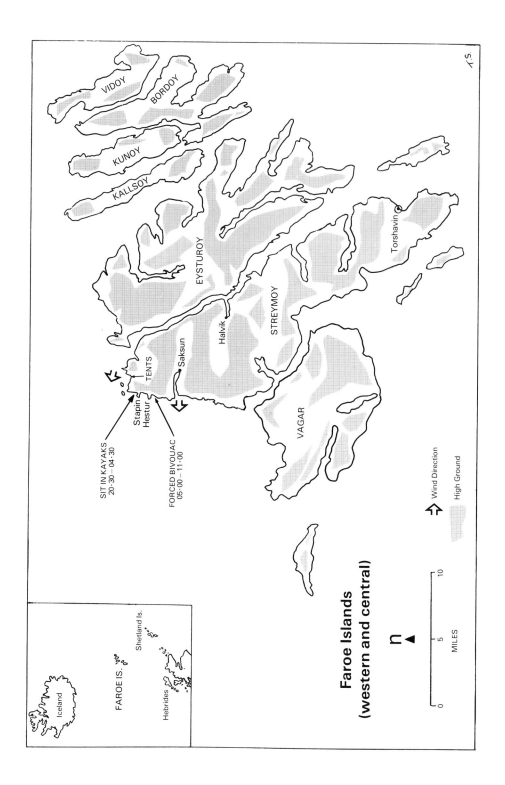

**Faroe Islands
(western and central)**

its echoing depths we spotted a glimpse of daylight and paddled right through to the other side of the headland. As the tide began to ebb, a powerful stream ran through the narrow passageway and this had given us a good deal of fun, running the underground tide race in our sea kayaks and making a break-out behind a rock pillar towards the exit of the cave. Then we would battle our way slowly through the tunnel against the tide to prepare for another descent. The Faroe Islands were living up to expectations. There was certainly magic here! However, we were all eager for the wind to ease to allow us to continue our journey.

The wind buffeted the tents and twists of spray raced across the bay. We were idle. The previous night my dreams had been cut abruptly short by a visit from Anne. A sharp noise had woken her and from her tent she could see that our kayaks were being taken by the wind. We hurried down to find them still tied together but dragged to the very brink of the rock ledge on which we had left them. The three lightest kayaks dangled in space like a huge grotesque bunch of bananas. At any moment the whole fleet could be on its way to the sea! Quickly but with great care we unfastened each kayak in turn and set it down at the back of the ledge. Then we ferried them one at a time up to the lush grassland and into the shelter of a stone sheep fold. There at last they ought to be safe. Sadly there was a little damage; a few chips and scratches and one broken compass, but we considered ourselves lucky under the circumstances.

During the following afternoon the wind eased, as forecast, and as everyone was itching to get afloat we decided to go for an evening paddle. To the south ran an impressive line of vertical cliffs rising to over 2000 ft. About four miles away, a narrow cut in the cliff led into a sheltered haven, with a tiny church and a couple of farms surrounded by meadows brilliant with flowers. I had visited this place called Saksun once previously, by land, and was eager to arrive by sea. With the last of the southerly tide stream to help us, we expected a short but spectacular journey, with time for a stroll and a cup of coffee before returning to our tents with the help of the new northerly tide stream. I brewed up a pot of fresh coffee, filled my flasks, then, tempted by the gorgeous aroma I brewed a second pot and drank it all. I little thought that I might later regret my self-indulgence.

The scenery was as impressive and dramatic as we had anticipated. Gigantic buttresses seemed dwarfed beneath the tremendous height and verticality of the main cliffs above them. Sudden gusts of cold wind swirled draughtily around corners and clouds of puffins and fulmars drifted and circled on the air currents. The stacks and fins of rock that rose so high above us were capped with dripping green vegetation and peppered with tiny white specks that on scrutiny turned out to be thousands of puffins. Way above, the cliff edge was darkened with sombre swirling cloud, and on lowering our eyes we would suddenly focus on the seemingly tiny shapes of seals, perched on top of boulders that had obviously fallen from the cliffs. The seals' wailing cries added to the heavy atmosphere.

There were moments when the wind seemed quite strong in our faces, especially when we rounded some of the prominent buttresses, but I saw no reason for concern until we reached the corner beyond which lay the channel into Saksun. It was plain that the wind was strong there. Blowing out from the gap, each gust was lifting a curtain of spray and driving it relentlessly in racing pursuit of the previous gust. Tucked close beneath the cliff we were sheltered from all but the noise of the wind, which was loud even here. 'It looks a bit breezy!' I said, stating the obvious. The others made no comment. They were a very capable group of paddlers, and I felt we should continue unless conditions proved too bad. However, I had grave doubts about reaching Saksun and I was aware that in the event of a capsize, a rescue in these conditions could be tricky. A wind like this could roll an empty kayak across the water. 'I'm not sure about this,' I explained, 'but I'll go and have a look to see what it's like. I think we'll probably have to give Saksun a miss.'

I eased out into the wind. My hair pulled tight against my scalp and my eyes streamed. It seemed as though the skin on my face was moving around to the back of my head! I paddled powerfully but steadily against the wind, ferry-gliding out from the cliffs. Here the wind was stronger. The gusts ripping across the water at me shook and twisted my paddles against my grip and suddenly lifted or pressed against my paddle blades. I made the switch from one side to the other as rapidly as possible so that I only ever had both blades out of the water at the same time for a brief moment. Nevertheless, balancing was still not simple. I increased my paddle rate and noted that I could now make slow progress against the wind. Ahead of me lay nearly two miles of wind-swept water without a single sheltered spot to rest in. It really was not on. I swung my bow back towards the cliff and by bracing sideways against the wind and paddling forwards I regained the restful shelter of the cliffs.

'Well! I think it's a wee bit too strong!' I said when I had joined the others. Happily, nobody disagreed with me. Not wishing to deprive anyone of the chance to feel the strength of the wind, I suggested we might try a short circuit; out across the wind, a turn downwind, which the Nordkapps the others were in would do automatically in this wind, and then a retreat into the wind-shadow of the cliff. The first paddler moved out, but although she remained upright and apparently unruffled, the wobbling and the evident struggle to keep control of her paddles in the violent gusts made me change my mind about the wisdom of the exercise. We turned our backs on Saksun and headed for home.

By now the wind was blowing quite strongly behind us and we scooted across the water with very little effort. From time to time a particularly malevolent gust would hit us from an unexpected direction and I joined the others in trying to keep upright. Nobody capsized. We passed a point where a waterfall had been tumbling down the cliff. No water was reaching the sea now. The stream simply disintegrated into spray as it came over the top of the cliff. We finally neared Sjeyndir, where we were camping, and the wind died away completely. The cliffs seemed to give us complete protection and we were able to relax again. 'Well, Nigel!' said Graham as we cruised along gently on the still water. 'Is that all you've got for us? I mean, haven't you got anything really exciting up your sleeve, like 15 ft walls of spray or something?' I laughed. Graham has an insatiable appetite for being taken into harder and harder conditions. However, I knew him well enough by now to read into his words that he had found the return journey with the mischievously tricky wind at our tails quite exciting enough. Not that that would deter him if another challenge lay ahead. 'There's just no satisfying some people!' I said in mock reproach.

'I found that quite—'Rosemary paused for a moment to consider her words, then continued, 'quite tricky at times. I felt sure someone would capsize, and I wasn't sure it wouldn't be me!'

'I know the feeling!' I said, grinning.

We cut in closer to the cliff and through the gap inside of Skedid; a stubby stack only sixty feet high. Ahead of us lay a second rock, Navarin, and a mile beyond, around the corner in the cliff lay Sjeyndir, the valley in which we were camped. We were almost back already. As we entered the gap between Navarin and the cliff, I felt a light breeze brushing my face. Suddenly a violent gust slammed into us. I clung on to my paddles and was blown rapidly backwards, enveloped in a cloud of stinging spray. 'I'm over!' came an urgent cry from behind me. I glanced back to see Graham's upturned hull. His paddles struggled at the surface as he attempted a roll. He must have been unsuccessful, because when I next glanced he was out, clutching his boat but without his paddles. Without hesitation Anne crossed towards him and picked up his paddles only to be bowled over herself by the next screaming gust. I had almost reached them when another gust slammed into me. In a moment I was over, sculling frantically for support on the water. I tried to flick upright and failed. I tried again and failed. I had difficulty even remaining at the surface. The wind had now blown me within reach of Graham's stern, but I found I was in the wrong position to be able to make use of it so I let go and sank beneath the surface. Somehow everything was calm and peaceful down there! I brought my paddles into position and rolled up. Relieved faces were watching me. 'A real pig's ear you made of that one, Foster!' I thought to myself, as I leant a hand to help Rosemary who was struggling with Anne's kayak. Graham had found a corner of the rock to cling to and having righted his kayak was in the process of pumping it dry. Jean clung sensibly to the rock.

As soon as everyone was back in their boat again, we crossed cautiously back into the shelter of the cliff nearby. I had a final look around the corner. A continuous billowing cloud of spray was streaming out from where the bay lay hidden by the curve of the cliff. Billowing clouds between 20 and 40 ft high scudded along as if chased by demons! I had never seen anything like it! I felt stunned by the demonstration of the sheer power there, and feeling suitably sobered, I followed the others.

As I paddled I considered our position. We were trapped by the wind. We could neither reach Saksun nor return to Sjeyndir where we had left our tents. Between these two points lay four miles of vertical basalt cliffs. There was no possibility of climbing the cliffs to safety; they rose vertically from the sea to heights in places of over 2,000 feet. While the wind blew this strongly we would be unable to go anywhere.

We had to decide whether to try to make a landing on the boulders that lay heaped at the base of the cliffs. At face value it might have seemed a reasonable thing to do, but knowing the sea conditions that prevail around the Faroe Islands it was quite likely that the swell would increase. At present it seemed exceptionally calm, but if we managed a landing at all, it would be an awkward one and it might be impossible to launch again if the swell did increase. On one of my previous visits to the islands, the swell have been massive for a whole fortnight. For the time being it would probably be better to stay afloat and wait for the wind to abate. Surely it could not keep up at this strength for very long.

By this time I was beginning to regret my earlier greed for coffee. Much earlier, on our paddle south towards Saksun I had become aware of the urgent pressing of my bladder. Now I could ignore it no longer. I just had to have a pee! Unfortunately my wetsuit long-john hampered my first attempts as, rafted up against the other kayaks I tried to balance on the back of my kayak and pee into the water. As the kayak lurched and tipped I realized that I really needed two hands for holding on. The fact that there were three girls in the group added to my embarrassment and in the end I climbed back into my kayak determined to find a rock to climb out on. This possibility was not very promising either. In the event I did find a rock which seemed to have enough suitable holds for me to be able to climb to the top, but getting onto it in the first place was not so simple. I rafted up again for assistance and tried again and again to stay against the rock for long enough to leap out and climb up. Each time I was poised ready, the kayaks would surge forwards on the swell and be out of reach.

160

In the end, the raft was steady for a moment and I quickly stepped out and began to climb. Immediately I was aware that the holds were much more greasy than I had expected, and as I climbed higher I found them just as slippery but also sloping outwards. Suddenly both of my feet began to slide. I clung on with my fingers but they too started to slip. Moments later I was falling. A narrow gap appeared between my kayak and the rock and with relief I dropped into the gap, catching my arms with a crash on my kayak as I passed. There was a muffled cry of surprise nearby, before I scrambled back into my kayak. Defeat! Oh well, I would resign myself to urinating in my wetsuit. The last time I had needed to do this, I recalled, was six years ago in the middle of the Hudson Strait.

I thought back to that crossing. It had been the most committing stage of the most committing expedition I had made. It was a solo journey, and I had flown to Frobisher Bay on Baffin Island, north-east Canada, intending to paddle south from there to the Hudson Strait, across the Hudson Strait to northern Labrador and then down the coast to Labrador's northernmost village, Nain. This would be a journey of about 650 miles, in uninhabited territory, and I needed to carry sufficient supplies in my kayak to last me at least one month.

I was nine days out from Frobisher Bay before I reached the southern end of Resolution Island. There I prepared to cross the Hudson Strait to the Button Islands which lie off northern Labrador. It is 40 miles from Resolution Island to the Button Islands. I carried an empty tin in my kayak in which to have a pee if the sea conditions were calm. In rougher weather it would have been foolish to remove my spray deck and so I would be forced to pee in my wetsuit. It was unthinkable that I could paddle 40 miles without needing a pee!

I pondered over Jean's predicament again. She was zipped neatly into a one-piece dry-suit, sealed at the neck, wrists and ankles. Should I ask? I thought it rather unfair so I kept quiet.

Rafted up again beneath the cliffs, I found questions worming their way into my mind. Would the wind drop? Would the swell increase? What if the wind changed direction? Should we try to land, or how long should we be prepared to sit on the water before deciding on that course of action? We opened a flask of coffee and someone produced some chocolate bars. 'Fancy climbing out?' Eyes turned upwards at the vertical face. 'With our kayaks on our backs, of course!' someone else chipped in. I got out my hat. Rosemary produced hers. Just two hats tonight. We passed them round, not for a collection but to give each person in turn a spell of cranial warmth. Silence fell. Now the waiting began.

Time drifted slowly by. The swell increased steadily until we found it hard work holding a raft of five kayaks together. We split into two rafts.

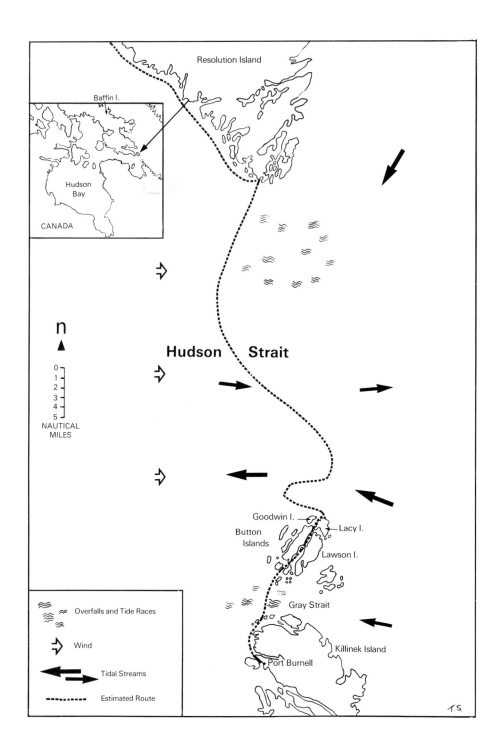

Resolution Island

Baffin I.

Hudson Bay

CANADA

n

0
1
2
3
4
5
NAUTICAL
MILES

Hudson   Strait

Goodwin I.

Button
Islands

Lacy I.

Lawson I.

Gray Strait

Killinek Island

Port Burnell

≋≋ Overfalls and Tide Races

⇨ Wind

← → Tidal Streams

•••••• Estimated Route

T.S.

Still the billowing spray poured out from the bay and the downdraughts out from the cliffs created explosive patterns and twisting phantoms of spray. My mind drifted again back to that solo trip in 1981 from Baffin Island.

That trip had begun inauspiciously. My personal luggage had been mislaid by the airline by the time I reached New York, I had missed my connecting flight as a consequence and had been forced to spend the night in the airport. The following morning brought the start of an air traffic controllers' strike, and in the end I had to travel overland to Montreal where I finally caught a plane for Frobisher Bay the following morning. I had been forced to wait for two weeks for my missing luggage and by that time I was concerned about the lateness of the season. It would be late August before I was likely to be in position for a crossing of the Hudson Strait, and by then the weather has usually turned windy and unsettled. I would also find my days rapidly shrinking in length in the change from 24 hours of daylight to the dark winter conditions. Without even a village for 300 miles either way, I would be unable to obtain any sort of weather forecast.

I had left Frobisher Bay anyway, fully prepared to return there if things seemed too risky, and had experienced a few problems with tricky landings and awkward launches before reaching Resolution Island and the Hudson Strait. Icebergs, a 40-ft tidal range, steep rocky shores, mountains; they all added splendour and a sense of bare power to the area. Solitude heightened my senses and I felt more than ever before an understanding of various aspects of my own thought processes, and learned to work with them rather than cutting across them. An example of this was after a particularly awkward launching from a rocky island I had been trapped on for two days because of difficulty in finding a launching place. I had taken over an hour on one unsuccessful attempt before I tried to seal-launch down a ramp of rock instead. The attempt went badly. Having launched myself down the rock, my kayak had spun around before it hit the sea, and I found myself swept by a foaming breaker into a vertical crevice in the cliff, from which I emerged unhurt but very shaken. My confidence was somewhat ruffled and although I could have set off across the 40 miles of open sea towards the Button Islands on the very next day, I listened to the tensions in my mind and spent the day relaxing, eating and painting. The following morning I had set off with a clear and calm mind.

My mind did not remain calm for very long. I was beyond sight of land within ten minutes of launching. The Hudson Strait is notorious for its fog which is present on one day out of every two throughout the summer months. This did not worry me too much, although I hoped that the

163

conditions might clear before I reached the Button Islands so that I could approach the land confidently and accurately. I always feel a little anxiety when I am approaching land in fog. Somehow there always seems to be a little devil in the back of my mind telling me that my calculations are wrong, or that my compass paddling is not accurate enough. Then with a suddenness that startles me, the strange shapes of land tower above as they launch themselves out of the fog at me. A sense of awe mingles with relief.

What was more ominous than the fog, however, was a breeze that sprang up from the west and grew quickly stronger. First small white-caps, then a criss-cross of breaking crests and steep waves were whipped up. My fog-encircled world seemed to be closing in on me. How much stronger would the wind get? I had no way of telling. How long would it last? Would I be blown off course?

My navigation was reduced to the simplest and most foolproof method I could devise. The tide streams run strongly through the Hudson Strait at rates of up to five knots in the middle. Closer to land the rates are greater. Unfortunately the rates are very approximate if applied to the total width of the strait: 40 nautical miles (46 English statute miles). It is likely that the rates in different parts of the strait vary at any given time. A variation of only one knot over two hours could deflect me enough for me to paddle straight past the Button Islands in conditions of fog. It was a risk I would not take. So, to start with I assumed that the tide would be even, and having estimated the time it would take me to cross the Strait, I balanced out the hours of westerly tide against the easterly tide stream. The compass bearing I would then need to follow would be that of a straight line from Resolution Island to the Button Islands; the shortest possible distance. Then by adjusting my departure time I ensured that at the end of the day I would not arrive at the islands, but at a point to the east. Then, if there was any error, I would still be confident of reaching the islands by paddling west. The only uncertainty would be exactly how far to the west I would have to paddle. There was no reasonable doubt in my mind about my calculations, but could my plans be thwarted by a strong westerly wind that would carry me further to the east than anticipated? Would I be able to gain the islands at the end of the day, paddling against a strong headwind?

I maintained my compass course. A broken wave crest swept across my deck and I braced automatically against the icy water. My kayak lurched as the next steepening wave passed underneath, and as I dropped into the following trough I could see that the next crest was about to topple. A couple of rapid paddle strokes as I rose to meet the crashing water and my kayak shot sideways and forwards, gaining speed from the wave, yet running off downwind in the process. Bitterly cold water gushed down my neck and up my sleeve. A dull cold weight dangled at my elbow. I lifted my elbow, dropped my wrist and pulled my cuff open with my other hand. Much of the water drained away again. The relative comfort was short-lived. The next breaking wave forced more water into my sleeve. Despite my rapid paddling I was getting cold.

My kayak crunched against rock and I opened my eyes. The raft had drifted against the buttress beneath which we sheltered. 'Do you want us to paddle, Nige?' asked Jean.

'No. It's O.K.,' I replied as I sculled my kayak away from the wall with my paddle crooked in one arm and my free hand holding her kayak. 'It's getting cold now!' I shivered. The movement seemed to have drawn cold draughts into my anorak. I looked across the water. White racing clouds! But these were no ordinary clouds. This was salt water driven from the sea by the extraordinarily strong wind. I looked up. Dark shapes of cloud twisted and cavorted 2,000 ft above me at the cliff edge. At least the cloud was racing out from the cliff and not towards it, I thought. As a child I had once been terrified by the illusion caused by cloud moving towards the steep Sussex chalk cliffs; it had appeared to me as though the cliffs were toppling over onto me, and no amount of reasoning could fully reassure the little boy. It's strange how events can trigger memories from long ago.

I rafted up against Jean. 'Are you warm enough?' I asked.

'Yes, actually I'm not too bad, thanks,' said Jean cheerfully.

I looked across to Anne. "How about you?'

'I'm all right,' she replied.

'There doesn't seem to be any drop in the wind yet,' I said. 'But it can't blow like this forever!'

There was a loud rattling noise followed by a series of explosive crashes. We all looked around sharply. Falling rock! Graham's voice carried across the water to us. 'I'm glad we decided not to land there, now!' he called. The rocks had fallen into the jumble of massive boulders that formed a beach of a suitable scale to the cliffs. Boulders the size of houses formed the pebbles and jagged rocks the size of cars formed the sand. The sea broke and foamed into the base of this ramp, forcing up into the many galleries and tunnels, frothing out from dark corners and cascading back down the bare rock. It was the sort of shore that would give a seaman nightmares. The chances of a shipwrecked seaman climbing out of the sea onto the rocks were slim, but the prospect of being stranded beneath the towering cliff with no way out would be worse. Yet the sea conditions tonight were still very gentle by Faroese standards. Even a moderate Atlantic swell would have made our sheltered haven completely untenable.

The swell was definitely bigger than it had been earlier. The thunder of waves breaking into the cave at the base of our buttress and rebounding around the pillars and rocks to the side of the cave was quite unsettling. What would we do if we were forced to abandon our shelter from the wind because the swell had become too great? Perhaps I should try to find a landing place. I weighed the possibilities with their advantages and disadvantages yet again and concluded that we would probably still be better off waiting where we were for a while longer. If only the wind would drop! It was cold but not unbearably so. If the weather did not improve, then I would have to think of something else. In the meantime, we were drifting slowly away from the buttress. Fingers of wind were gently tweaking us out towards the storm. I crooked my paddle in my arm again and sculled slowly back to within feet of the rock. Graham and Rosemary were sat close to us now, their heads resting against one another and their eyes closed. I hunched my neck down as far as it would go into my collar, shut my eyes and tried to conserve heat.

Back in the Hudson Strait nothing had changed; fog, strong wind, breaking waves and the constant hard work of fast paddling. I cursed the wind. It was difficult for me to tell whether it was getting stronger or not, but the sea was certainly rougher now. The sun gleamed through the fog like a full moon and I wondered how deep it must be. If I could only poke my head up through, I would probably be able to see for miles. I paused for a moment and grabbed a piece of cheese from my anorak pocket, peeled back the wrapping with cold fumbling fingers and took a large bite. The kayak lurched alarmingly and I grabbed my paddles. Steady again for a moment I pulled the wrapper back over the cheese and dropped it back into my pouch pocket before paddling on. I sucked the cheese to savour it for as long as possible. Surely I must be further east than I had intended to be? Should I alter my course so that I would end up close to the Button Islands? If I altered course by just a few degrees I would not have to head into the wind for the final stages of the journey. The problem tormented me for a while as I battled on, my face and hands now thoroughly chilled by their exposure to the wind.

I was by now needing a pee. There was only one way to solve that problem in a sea like this. I braced my paddle on the water for a moment while I squirmed in my seat. My close-fitting wetsuit long-john did not make things easy. I tried to lean back to alleviate the pressure, but as the kayak lurched and tipped with every wave I found myself bracing tightly with my legs inside the cockpit. I laughed. I just could not relax sufficiently! Finally a trickle, then a steady warm stream began to pour around my thighs. What a relief! As the warmth spread pleasantly down

166

my legs I straightened them to let it out at the ankles. 'Phew!' I exhaled loudly. 'That's one hell of a lot better, Foster!' As I paddled away again I worked my feet on the Lendal foot pump to drain the cockpit. I considered again the question of whether I should alter my compass course, then made the fateful decision that nearly cost me my life. I changed course.

Seven hours had passed and the fog had melted a little. I fumbled with crinkly hands for my tube of honey, but discovered that it had set so solid with the cold that I could not squeeze it from the tube. Not that I could encourage my fingers to grip very strongly. I pushed the tube back into my pocket and pulled out some chocolate instead. 'Come on land! Where are you?' I thought. 'Surely I should be able to see the islands by now? Well, maybe not. What's the visibility now? Ten miles?' I tried to compare in my mind the visibility now with other situations I had been in where I knew the distances involved. It was hard to judge, but I decided that 10 miles was probably over-optimistic. Three miles would probably be more accurate. If that were the case I might have another two hours to go before sighting land. 'Come on now! Keep paddling!' I encouraged myself.

Another slow hour had passed when my eyes focused on some dark shadowy shapes to the left of my course. 'Land?' I questioned. I felt uneasy as I turned my kayak in order to use my main compass to obtain a bearing. 'Hell! I can't be that far off course! What's gone wrong?' I tried to visualize the shape that the islands would present from that angle by studying the chart. When I looked back I realized that the shapes had changed. 'That's odd.' Then I realized that it might just be dense banks of fog that I could see. Although it was a relief to me that I had not been shown to be off course, I still felt a bitter disappointment. I was still out of sight of land. I looked around at the tumbling crests. The cold wind bit at my face. 'Come on land!' I shouted into the wind. If only the wind would drop it would make things a lot easier. I toiled at my paddles again until the kayak was speeding through the water once more. 'Bloody fog!' I muttered darkly.

Eventually more shapes appeared. I consulted my chart and compass. These shapes were on target, but I could not be sure they were not fog banks again. I studied the indistinct rounded shapes, memorising the sequence of humps and hollows, then paddled on with my eyes fixed on my compass. I waited and waited before looking up again. The shapes were still there and they appeared the same! 'Yahoo!' I shouted. 'Thank God for that!' I felt a great sense of relief. The growing tension I had been feeling had been released and I was smiling again. I no longer had doubts about reaching the islands. They appeared to be very close, but I made a pessimistic estimate and judged them to be between 6 and 8 miles away. I checked the time and this tied in reasonably with my estimate.

I looked down at my hands. The right one, more exposed to the cutting wind and icy water, was almost numb and the skin looked startlingly white and crinkled. My hands have always remained fairly dextrous even in cold conditions, providing I keep my arms and wrists well insulated. Consequently I seldom wear pogies or paddle mitts, neither of which had I found very suitable for slipping on and off in rough conditions. Now I was beginning to wish that I had taken the precaution of having mitts handy. 'Oh well,' I thought, 'I won't be much longer now.' I estimated that I would need another hour and a half. The sea was humping up dramatically, which, as the wind did not appear to have increased, suggested that the tide had now turned against the wind. The flood tide should run swiftly south-west through the Button Islands and generally sets into Ungava Bay to the south-west. This should help me on my way. But, as time went by, I did not seem to be drawing any closer to the land. What was the problem? Maybe I was getting closer. Perhaps I had been further away to start with than I had expected. Maybe the lack of visual definition was masking my actual progress. On the other hand, was it possible that the tide was being deflected by the islands in a north-westerly direction instead of running to the south-west as I had expected? I was beginning to feel very uneasy, but I had no alternative but to keep going and to trust that all would be well.

The cloud began to break up and although the visibility was still not good, it seemed as though the sun might appear for my landing. I paddled hard, surfing diagonally across the frenzied waves. There was still no noticeable change in my position, but land seemed tantalizingly close. Surely I must be getting closer. The waves steadily increased in size to about 8 ft and started crashing more heavily behind me. Green walls shattered into foam and thundered past with explosive fury, leaving the white surface spitting bubbles with a hissing sound against the background roar, and each time I was caught by a break I was carried bouncing sideways while the freezing water streamed maliciously into my tightly drawn anorak hood and down into my wetsuit. My water-filled sleeves swung heavily from my arms. 'Come on!' I shouted. 'Give me a chance!'

Waves generally break against a tide stream, and from the direction of these waves it seemed as though the tide was sweeping me to the north-west rather than the south-west. I snatched a glance at my watch and realized that I should already be ashore. Yet I seemed no closer! I could no longer ignore the possibility that I would have to wait until the tide turned again before I could reach land. That would mean I would be out here in this sort of sea in the dark! Could I cope? What if the fog returned?

'Nigel! It's your turn for the hat.' Anne's voice brought me back from my memories to our wait beneath the cliff. 'Thank you!' I said, gratefully taking the still-warm hat and pulling it over my head. I shivered involuntarily. It seemed that we were passing it around at just about the right speed. The cold was just beginning to gnaw painfully when the cosiness of the hat came along again. For a while I felt quite snug, but this 'short evening paddle' was turning out to be much longer than expected. It was nearly 1.30 a.m. now. We had been afloat for eight hours. I looked up. Although it was nearly dark I could still see the writhing clouds at the clifftop. Somehow they seemed to be moving more slowly now, and looking along towards Navarin the white clouds of spray were no longer visible. 'The wind seems to have dropped a bit,' I commented. 'I can't see the spray any more.' Jean and Anne agreed. 'I think we ought to go along and have a closer look. We might be able to sneak back into the bay,' I said optimistically. I called across to Rosemary and Graham who were cuddled together in the gloom. 'Do you think it's dropped a bit?' Graham called back.

'I'm not sure, but it looks as though it has,' I shouted. 'Are you coming to have a look?' We broke up our rafts and started paddling. I felt cold and stiff and, probably because I had been relaxing with the support of another kayak, I felt irrationally unstable. I did not voice my feelings, but I discovered afterwards that the others had felt the same. Perhaps it was the increased swell and the occasional blast of wind combined with the near-darkness.

As we neared Navarin I could see the spray again behind the fateful rock. The wind blew strong in my face and gusted unsteadily. My paddles jumped in my hands. 'Sorry!' I shouted. 'It isn't any better. I think it was just too dark to see from where we were. Let's go back!' In the darkness the silent shapes turned unsteadily and I followed them back to our familiar corner. Spirits were low. We ate some chocolate and withdrew into our own private worlds again.

The swell was still increasing. Both rafts had discovered the ideal place to be beneath the cliffs. A few yards one way and we would gradually drift in towards the crashing water and the cave. A few yards the other way and we would gradually drift out to sea and into the wind. I rested my chin against my chest and began to doze.

I awoke some time later and checked my watch. Strange, I thought. Up until now, every time I had consulted my watch another hour and a half had elapsed. This time my watch told me that only five minutes had passed since my last look. Time seemed to have slowed down! I closed my eyes again. Another hour dragged by before I opened them again. I looked at my watch and again it taunted me with only another five minutes passed.

It seemed as though half an hour could encompass a whole night-time of waiting. I shut my eyes again and thought back to the Hudson Strait.

The sun was sliding down from the clouds and cast a weak light across the waves. Then all too soon it was bulging and sinking across the horizon. I felt devastated. From now on it would get darker and colder, yet I had no alternative but to keep going. As the darkness settled I occasionally glimpsed a pinpoint of light on the islands. This must be the beacon on Goodwin Island marking the southern limit of the entrance to the Hudson Strait. 'Come on Foster! You've paddled at night before!' A splitting crash to my right warned me. A great white streak appeared in the dark above me and seconds later I was being carried in its freezing grasp. I hung on, bracing automatically as my kayak bucked and twisted beneath me. Then it was gone, and I was trying to steady myself. All around me the sea was hissing. Brilliant specks of greenish light gleamed in the water. I tentatively paddled forward again, peering into the night for the Goodwin Island beacon. Crash! The thunder of the next breaker demanded my attention. I felt suddenly glad of all the years of kayak surfing, and all the night paddling I had done in the past. Without my reflexes in the dark I would be finished.

Eventually land seemed to grow closer. The pitch-black shapes silhouetted against a slightly paler sky. 'Oh for a moon!' I thought. It was a new moon tonight; the darkest it could be. The tide streams would be at their strongest. Whoomf! A hollow explosion to my left startled me, and moments later a huge wave caught me from my left side instead of the usual right. Then as I bounded sideways, I could see a line of foam approaching from the right. Suddenly my kayak buried nose down in frothing foam for a moment, then slowly rose up again. Then to my horror a long horizontal white streak appeared in the sky above my bow with a splitting crash. I sprinted forwards and the kayak reared almost on end to greet the broken water. As the impact caught me in the chest I heaved on my paddle and the kayak plunged through to drop heavily into the water on the other side. 'What the hell's happening? Strong eddies at the edge of the tide race? Maybe it's a rock or shoal! Oh hell! If it's a breakover rock I've had it!' The awful thought of the waves pounding me onto an isolated rock chilled me more than the cold did. This was gut fear. As I struggled to control my kayak in the turbulent water I knew I had to move fast!

With the immediate danger over, and waves breaking only from my right side again, the next change although rapid and unexpected was rather less daunting. One minute I was being thrown around and the next I was on much smaller waves, my ears full of the prickling sound of rising bubbles. Around and behind me I could still hear the crack as each peaking wave toppled, and then the rumbling roar as masses of heavy water crashed downwards, only to blend into the background noise as the next peaking wave took the lead. I sprinted forwards towards the light, anxious to get as far as possible from the rough water, and as the sea grew progressively calmer closer to land I relaxed more and began to appreciate the shimmering stars of phosphorescence that danced around my every paddle stroke and clothed my wake with slowly dying sparks. Bright specks clung to my hands. It was a beautiful sight which brought back memories of one particular night crossing of the English Channel. The magic stars had returned.

For a while I thought my problems were over. I could picture myself slipping quietly into the channel separating Goodwin and Lacy Island, cruising gently along in search of an easy landing. 'There must be somewhere easy to land,' I thought. 'Maybe I'll not bother to try to sort out the tent in the dark. I'll just change, jump into my sleeping bag and then cook up some food. Shouldn't be long now!' I luxuriated in the thought of being warm and dry again.

My hopes were short-lived. I soon realized that I was being swept rapidly to the east. The tide must have turned again. I pointed my kayak into the current, hoping to ferry-glide into the channel between the islands, but despite paddling frantically, I was swept backwards past the light and my chosen channel, and finally out from land opposite Lacy Island. The tide was faster than I could paddle. I must get to land! What if I were swept past the islands? The horror of the idea filled me with dread and I cut across the tide towards the dark cliffs. Finally I reached land. The smell of wet rock filled the air and the damp dark presence rose from the dancing shapes of broken water into a slightly paler night sky. Risking close contact with land in preference to the possibility of losing contact with it altogether in the tide, I carefully skirted the cliffs until I could see what appeared to be a low shoreline jutting out. As this became separated from the cliffs I realized that it must be another island or offshore rocks. I could not gauge scale or distance in the dark.

Soon I could see another low shore and this turned out to be very close to me. I scrutinized it as best I could but there seemed to be no possibility of landing so I continued. Now on unbroken water and out of immediate danger I felt incredibly weary. I longed to be ashore. Shortly I found a place where waves were rushing up the shore with a sound like rolling shingle. A beach? I thought I could hear the sound of pebbles sucking down in the backwash. The white shape of broken water seemed to rush up and draw back on a reasonably shelving beach. I felt sure the waves were not dumping. It's amazing how deceptive things can appear in the dark! Tiredness and a gnawing feeling of cold made me anxious to land

and get sorted out. I had been working extremely hard without a break for sixteen hours now, and in my desperation to land I made a costly mistake.

Crash! The sudden jolt of my kayak hitting the cliff shook me awake. I looked round. Jean was moving our raft away from the cliff and Anne was trying to dodge her other paddle blade which was scything through the air. I turned my head. Graham and Rosemary sat huddled together just a couple of yards away. Behind me I could see the wild fleeing clouds of spray rising and changing shape with animal speed. Closer beneath the cliffs towers of spray were being lifted from the sea in the eddying downdraughts. The wind was not easing. It didn't seem to be so dark now. I looked at my watch. Half past four in the morning! We had been afloat for eleven hours and there was still no sign of the wind abating! I made up my mind. If there was anywhere that we could land, then we would land. We had waited for long enough hoping for a break in the weather. Even if it meant risking being stranded under the cliffs by increasing swell it was time to make a move before the group got too cold and tired.

I explained briefly where I was going, then I paddled stiffly as far as Navarin, half a mile to the north, without finding even a remotely possible landing place. I had not really expected to but I wanted to be certain. At Navarin I paused for a moment and watched with a sense of awe as the wind tore spray from the water to join the already dense clouds, 30 or 40 ft deep that were racing out to sea. What fantastic power must be unleashed here! I felt very small and humble. Turning I paddled gently back, aware of the chill that my movements were bringing to my body.

'Seen anywhere?' called out Graham.

'I'm going to check the other way first,' I shouted back, avoiding the question. Keeping my distance as I passed them I hoped that I would not have to admit that I hadn't found anywhere. Beyond the gigantic buttress was another 'beach' composed of huge boulders but where it rested against the cliff it was topped by green vegetation. It looked less stark than the area towards Navarin, and there were hollows beneath some of the larger boulders that might provide us with shelter from falling rocks. I scanned the shore as I paddled south. Shortly I came up against the wind. I braced suddenly as a massive gust nearly caught me unawares, and I realized I had gone far enough. If I had nearly been over again myself, then I would not bring the others as far as this. I turned around and retreated from the evil grasp of the wind.

I had seen two possible landing places. Now I needed to look at them both more carefully. The southern choice looked just as inhospitable as the first, and as I waited, wave after wave pounded onto the rocks, foaming and bounding this way and that until all the massive energy had been dissipated and the streaming webs of water drained into the foam-filled gullies to race noisily back to greet the next approaching wave. I imagined myself on the back of one of these waves, swept up towards my chosen gully. The rocks were smaller here and the backwash more straightforward. I would be moving up fast across those rocks, visible a moment ago but now well covered. Then I would be at the back of the gully and rising, rising too fast and far to even contemplate getting out. Now I would be dropping again and coming out backwards, dragging across those rocks, now uncovered . . . and into those rocks. The next wave was rearing up. I would be unable to get through that. Crash! 'No way!' I breathed.

A brief quiet spell came and for about fifteen seconds I could imagine a different scenario. I would be able to paddle in on the back of a wave into the same gully, leap out of my boat and scramble up those steep rocks. If my timing was good, I should be able to do it. What about the others? With me ashore to assist it should be possible. The waves were increasing in size again so I moved off to check the other alternative.

Here the problems were different. There was a scattering of offshore boulders over which the larger waves were breaking. Once through this mine-field the waves were foaming into a narrow area of boulders the size of tables and armchairs, reaching finally to the base of a huge flat-topped boulder to the left of which promised to be a good safe place to haul the kayaks. Here the foam piled up and then scoured to the right beneath an undercut in a boulder some 20 ft high, draining forcefully through a maze of boulders. We would have to be careful with our timing or we would be swept around by this sideways movement. I waited until I had witnessed several lulls during which I felt I might chance a landing. Between the lulls the waves were violent. My main concern was the shortness of the lulls with only ten or fifteen seconds of suitable conditions. If the sea got any bigger then landing or launching would be out of the question. Still plagued by doubts I returned to the others.

'I've found two places that might be possible,' I explained, 'but neither of them is ideal. I'd rather everyone had a good look before we come to any decision.' We paddled round. Everyone seemed pleased to be moving again. It was gone 5 a.m.

We stopped at the first of my suggested spots and everyone watched quietly while a large set of waves pounded in with great surges of white water savagely enveloping the rocks. Even when the lull came, the rocks looked inhospitable. The sideways draining movement away from my chosen route up the rocks seemed to leave little margin for error. However, as we sat in the blustery wind watching the second spot, I felt that I preferred the other, if only because it was sheltered from the wind. The others seemed to agree. Nobody really minded where we landed, but as

Graham pointed out, there seemed to be a better chance of shelter in the rocks once ashore if we took the first option. We returned again. I would go first. If I made it successfully I would be able to help the others as they followed. If I made a mistake, I was on my own. I felt uneasy. 'Graham and Rosemary, could I borrow your tow lines please?' Without questioning they unfastened them and handed them across to me. I stuffed the lines down the front of my buoyancy aid. I gave a few brief instructions and then added, 'Once you've started in, don't hang around, and please . . . please take care!' I was now ready. I just needed to wait for a lull. I thought back to my landing on the Button Islands.

Sitting off Lacy Island in the dark I had waited in uncertainty. I was not sure how far away the shore was, or how powerful the waves were. I approached gently, a few yards at a time, trying to gauge the steepness of each wave as it passed under me. Suddenly I was picked up and rushed forwards. I steered blind as the wave broke around me, then crunch, the bow of my kayak hit solid rock and jarred to a halt. Moments later, the bow lifted upwards and sideways, hitting again and again as the broken water roared all around me. I was being carried forward again. Confused but realizing that I had made a mistake, I freed my spray deck and bailed out into waist-deep swirling water. I had barely gained my feet when the powerful backwash swept me away and I found myself swimming, clutching my kayak and paddles. I had mistaken ledges of rock for a beach! 'Bloody hell!' I thought, and angrily kicked for the shore. Next moment I was overwhelmed by the next wave as it thundered up the rocks. I tried to stand but could get no grip on the slippery surface. In the dark I lost all sense of which way was up and which was down as my head dipped beneath the water. I surfaced gasping and clung on desperately to my boat as I was sucked helplessly into the sea again.

Once again I was thrown up and tried to stand, but was carried slipping and stumbling across the ledges into deep water. I kicked again for the shore and again failed to get a purchase on the rock. I felt utterly drained. The water no longer felt cold. I just wanted to relax for a while. I forced myself to try again. I kicked for the shore and as the wave crashed around me I was bounced across the rocks again, feeling no pain in my chilled body. I stumbled to my feet and careered across the slippery surface up to my knees in water, but was bowled over by my kayak. Struggling to my feet again I fell into a gully and was dragged back into the sea. The next time I managed to find a grip on the rocks and hung on grimly as the water drained noisily away. Drunkenly I stumbled across the slimy rock, automatically hauling at my kayak to follow. Then the next wave broke. The kayak was thrown at me, helping to push me further up the rocks where I came up against a steep step. I felt desperate. I had to haul the kayak onto this step but I didn't seem to have the strength. Each wave threatened to dislodge me as I clung to the edge. My kayak rolled over and over, snatching at my grip. Maybe if I could make it lighter by removing the deck bags, I might be able to pull it up. I fumbled to release the cam fastenings holding the square bag on the front deck, and they snapped open. At the next moment I was enveloped in churning water. I clung on desperately. As the wave drained away I reached in the dark for the bag. It had gone! I felt around in the water for it before realizing the futility of my action. In sheer anger I hauled at the kayak and dragged it inch by inch up onto the next ledge. Once on the level again I dragged it more easily from the reach of the sea. It seemed that will-power and anger had finally taken over where my strength had failed. I crouched down and ripped off the hatches from the kayak with numb hands, and started to pull out my gear. Clutching the first couple of bags I stood up, but lost my balance. Dizzily I stood up again but failed to keep my feet. Confused, I dropped the bags for a moment, abandoning them in the darkness while I concentrated on finding my sleeping bag.

I came across a box of Christmas cake and devoured a huge piece as quickly as I could, then continued to unload. When I found my cagoule and overtrousers I pulled them over my wet clothing, and eased my mittens over my numb hands. Then I turned to my kayak again. 'Sleeping bag! I've got to find my sleeping bag! I've got to get into my sleeping bag!' I muttered over and over again. I needed to be quick. I could not afford to get any colder! In the dark I squeezed the next bag between my palms, trying to guess its contents. My fingers had lost all feeling.

My heart beat rapidly. I tried to squeeze the vivid memory of that fateful landing out of my mind as I watched the waves creaming over the rocks. It was light now! I would be accurate and in control.

The waves were dropping in height. Now! Go for it! I shot forward towards the shore. I was quickly through the cordon of outer boulders and the wave was breaking around me. I was carried straight towards the flat ledge I was seeking. As soon as the hull of my kayak started bouncing across rocks, I slipped off my spray deck and in one movement lifted myself from my seat and dropped backwards into the water. My legs free of the cockpit, I pulled myself onto my feet and launched myself forwards towards the ledge. The water pulled at my legs but in a few more steps I had reached the rock, and lifting my nearly empty kayak by the cockpit I almost ran up to the top. Choosing a secure spot well out of reach of the sea I gently set my kayak down and placed my paddles inside the cockpit. I was ashore! I turned and looked out to sea, raising my thumbs to signal my success. However, instead of relief I felt only a mounting tension. I had to get everybody else ashore safely.

I unzipped my wetsuit and had a pee, then looked carefully around me. There was no better place that we could land. That question answered, I found a fist-sized stone wedged solidly betweeen two massive boulders. It was an ideal chock-stone. I unfastened my tow line and clipped it around the stone. Then, retrieving the two borrowed lines from my buoyancy aid, I joined all three together. Now I had a lifeline that would reach well out into the troubled water. Slipping off my buoyancy aid I tied it to the free end of the line. Now I had a line that I could use for throwing to someone in difficulty, or to use as a hand line if I waded in to help. I walked across to the edge of the rock and, passing the line through my hands to make sure there were no kinks, I made a loose pile with the buoyancy aid on top. 'That's it then! Nothing more to do! Let's get on with it Foster,' I muttered, holding up my hand to signal that I was ready. A few gestures indicated that Rosemary was to be the first.

As soon as I could detect the approach of a lull in the waves, I gave the signal and Rosemary came paddling in, faultlessly, I grabbed her boat before it could be taken away sideways, she leaped out and we were away, up towards the safety of the rocks. 'Well done Rosemary!' I shouted above the din of the sea.

'Perfect!' Rosemary smiled. 'Do you want to borrow my buoyancy aid?' she asked. I nodded. As I zipped it up I muttered, 'One down and three to go!'

The other landings proceeded cleanly and without any greater mishap than a few cuts from the barnacles and a few scratches and chips in the gel-coat of the kayaks. By the time the last boat was ashore, Rosemary and the others had passed most of the kayaks up onto a higher platform of rock in front of a substantial cave formed underneath a gigantic boulder. This shelter proved to have its faults, including a number of smaller entrances through which a chilly breeze seemed to blow, and a few nesting shags, but it was a good shelter. We were soon all huddled together inside passing around a cup of coffee from a flask and some chocolate. 'What about a fire?' asked Graham. Surprisingly he had a small amount of dry driftwood in his kayak that would serve as kindling. All we had to do was to find some more. Three of us went off to search while Jean and Rosemary gathered together vessels in which to collect rainwater. Until then I hadn't noticed that it was raining lightly.

I climbed carefully up the massive boulders, peering into every crevice in the search for wood. The others were by now out of sight. I spotted a long hollow angelica stem down inside a crack. I reached down into the gloom to pick it up. The darkness exploded towards me as two wildly flapping shags came hurtling out into my face and floundered noisily across the rock. I clung on weakly. 'Don't do that to me!' I pleaded quietly as my heart raced away. I looked down. My stick had been dislodged and lay some fifteen feet lower down in the crack. I'd lost that one!

Above me in a steep ramp reaching up the cliff was a muddy slope, bright with the flowers of sea mayweed. There was nothing burnable there so I descended gradually, picking my way carefully between and under the boulders back to our cave. The others had found no more than I had, and our pathetic little collection of hollow stems hardly had the makings of a fire. The water that had been collected was no better. The cups they had positioned beneath the drips from the rocks had filled with a dark yellow-green liquid—the filtrate from 2,000ft of bird cliffs. I decided I would prefer to drink my own urine than this!

We had all warmed up a little following our scrambling around, so we huddled together in the cave and tried to sleep. Although I certainly dozed off for a while, it was not long before I was awake again and shivering. I reflected that I had taken the prospect of a 'short evening paddle' far too lightly. Graham and Rosemary both had a few spare clothes, we had flares in plenty—enough to heat up a few meals—and we had two hats. Jean had about one week's supply of her dehydrated food. We had no stove, no bivvy or sleeping bags, and worst of all, no water. We had finished our last flask of coffee and now just had to wait and hope. At least our clothing should dry a little on us. It seemed ironical that if we had had our camping equipment with us, we could have lived in complete comfort here. As it was, all our gear was lying idle just a mile away over the cliff—at least it should be if the wind had not taken it! I tried not to think too much about that possibility.

Every so often I unwrapped my cold limbs and forced myself outside to check the weather. By about ten o'clock the wind seemed to have increased still further. Swirling towers of spray were dancing out over the water, and massive fleeing patterns raced this way and that as downdraughts slammed at the water. 'Sixteen and a half hours,' I reflected. 'That's about the time that it took me to cross the Hudson Strait and to get myself onto land again.' I thought back to the dreadful night I had spent huddled in my sleeping bag, so cold that I had shaken like a railway carriage all night.

In the morning I had picked up the pieces, and having lost my stove amongst the other items in the bag that had been swept away, I had gathered driftwood for a fire before being able to cook a meal. I also had to fashion some cutlery from driftwood before I could eat. I had discovered a mass of bruises and some badly skinned knuckles and thumbs—the result of my encounters with the rocks during the night landing. Worse, I discovered that all my fingers had been frostbitten. It was three months before I regained any feeling in my fingertips.

As the days followed, the weather repeatedly blew into gales. I had a particularly difficult crossing from the Button Islands across the Gray Strait, but eight days after crossing the Hudson Strait my luck changed. Still 300 miles or more from the nearest village to the south, I came across an oil tanker in Port Burwell and hitched a lift down to Nova Scotia. That trip had been just a little too close to the mark for comfort.

Checking again about an hour later, the weather seemed quieter. There were no signs of the strong wind at all. Everyone moved around cheerfully. It was time to move again and nobody was anxious to sit around here any longer than they had to. We passed the kayaks down onto the flat platform again and I stood and timed the lulls. It seemed that we would have between ten and fifteen seconds in which to carry a kayak from the ledge to where the water reached with the smaller waves, hold it steady on the water while the paddler jumped in, fasten the spray deck and then for the paddler to hurry clear of the rocks before the larger waves returned.

We were ready, poised. I detected a decrease in the size of the oncoming waves. 'Ready?' I asked by way of a warning. 'Right! Go!' I shouted, and the orange and white kayak was on its way. Everyone moved so urgently that Graham was in his kayak before the best of the lull had arrived. Three of us were not enough to hold his kayak and Graham was swept suddenly sideways onto Anne. She fell backwards into the water and the kayak passed right over her, coming to rest amongst large boulders with no easy line of escape. Anne was back on her feet, thankfully unharmed, and we all hauled Graham's kayak back across the rocks to where he had started. Nimble fingers fastened his spray deck and with shouts of encouragement he was launched on his way, paddling like a demon. He had almost reached safety when the first of the next set of waves reached the outer rocks. His kayak lurched sharply up and he was over it before it broke. 'Well done Graham!' came the chorus of shouts. Graham turned, satisfaction visible on his face even at that distance.

Jean was next. Now we had had a practice run, the launchings ran more smoothly, with the timing almost perfect. However it would not be possible to make an unaided launch. The positions of the rocks precluded a seal launch, and the sideways rush of water that had taken Graham would prevent a 'leap-in-and-go' approach. The kayak had to be afloat, and it had to be held. That meant that the last person was going to have some big problems.

Rosemary had now joined the others, leaving Anne. My mind, working around the problem had come up with a possible solution. 'Anne, are you a confident swimmer? I mean how would you feel about swimming in this?' We looked out as a particularly violent wave thundered across the rocks towards us. 'Well, I didn't mean when it's coming in like this one!' I added hastily.

'I don't mind,' said Anne. 'Do you want me to swim out?' I explained briefly what I had in mind, then we set to work. I joined two tow lines together to link my kayak to hers. Then taking her own tow line and the remaining line, we were able to fasten a long line to the stern of her kayak. 'Now then,' I explained again, 'if you can help me afloat, then come back and launch your kayak, I'll tow it clear. Then, if you hang on to this line, I'll tow you out. Hopefully we'll both be clear before anything big comes in.' I smiled, then added, 'Then I'll put you back in your boat! Honest!'

I glanced out. There was a lull on the way. The other three figures were bobbing on the water watching. This should be the last hurdle. I gave a nod and we were moving. With my kayak on the surging water, Anne steadied while I slid into my seat. Moments later I was paddling. The line snapped taut before I expected and there was the sound of Anne's kayak leaping across the rocks. I eased off for a moment to allow Anne to reach it, then paddled gently forwards until her kayak was afloat. Then I sprinted away. Anne was wading quickly through the water behind me. I was almost level with the outer rocks before her line came fully tight. I paddled as hard as I could and was relieved to see how quickly we were moving forwards. I glanced behind. The kayak behind me was through the gap and Anne was almost there. I carried on.

'No problems!' I had pulled up with Anne well clear of danger. I turned and brought the kayaks to Anne. She climbed lightly out of the water into her cockpit, 'Well done!' I said smiling broadly. 'That was brilliant!'

'It seemed to go really easily,' she replied. The others gathered round and we redistributed the tow lines before setting off towards Sjeyndir once again. The scene was very different now. Five paddlers cruising gently across calm water, through the now familiar Navarin gap and into the same quiet bay that we had left some $18^1/2$ hours previously.

We landed easily, but discovered a certain amount of wind damage to the tents. It took us nearly six hours to put right the damage that was repairable, but everyone was just happy to have survived. We encountered yet more wind, but finished our trip with a magnificent paddle around the north of Eysteroy, where we were captivated by a superb waterfall cascading from the cliff top to form a drifting curtain across the entrance of a cave. Curving through the sparkling water were two brilliant rainbows. To complete the spell, as we paddled through the waterfall the rainbows bent into perfect circles around us. It was a far cry from the ordeal of a couple of nights before.

Conclusion

'From whatever place that I write to you you can expect that part of what I tell you will be travels within my own mind.'

Coleridge.

Eccentrics are two a penny in North Wales. There is an old woman in Capel Curig who berates the bonnets of passing cars with her walking stick when they fail to give her a lift to the local shops. There is a man who lives in a rhododendron bush near Blaenau Ffestiniog; formerly he occupied an umbrella near Sayle, but he moved because of the lack of privacy. And there is Huw, canoeist of fortune, rattling around in a VW camper with WHITE WATER CONSULTANT written over a big blue wave on the side. Everything with him is 'on the side' and he is into water and debt over his head.

Consult him you might not; but he is a lovely man because he preaches, from the soap box of his eccentricity, what everyone else does not like to admit these safety-conscious days, namely that white water and sea touring, like every other adventure sport, is as much about risk-taking as it is about technique.[1] It infuriates some—'Well, do you feel a real man now?' the wife of a fellow-paddler fumed after Huw had canoed where everyone else had walked—and amuses others—'If Huw says there is a line down a rapid then you *know* it's a portage.' But this is jealousy masquerading as colour supplement pyschology, envy hiding under the guise of a responsible approach to the sport. However much we pretend otherwise, we like to have 'the right stuff', we do not like to 'bottle out'.

---

[1] We do not speak here of competition canoeing which is all about skill, training, and the achievement of goals, rather than risk. And there is an increasing divide between 'sharpies' (slalomists) and 'stumpies' (recreational canoeists).

Call it competition with yourself, or a struggle with the elements[1], but on every canoe trip there will be a time, sometimes many times, when there is a choice between doing and not doing, and that is the really memorable time.

So on expeditions to the Hudson Bay, while travelling in Africa, or simply during weekends in Wales, you will find us punishing our bodies, stressing our minds, nervously searching a blue horizon, or jibbering above some drop that before the days of plastic boats would have consigned the canoeist and his craft to the scrap heap, edging ever closer to the limit, not the limit of canoeing, for there is no such thing, but the limit in our minds beyond which the responsible adult takes over—the 'I have nothing to prove, family to consider, career to think about' adult. And if you want to know whether you have reached the limit, your limit, or have passed it, then listen to a war story from a crazy horse, let him talk you down his epic run, and see whether your paddle muscles are still twitching for a go, or you are unconsciously shaking your head.

> 'The first pin is no problem. You can lever yourself round. But then I didn't get enough speed over the second plunge. It sucked me backwards and sideways, and the boat went down the sump. I was jammed vertically in there, with the boat folding round my legs and water pouring over my face. I was shitting blue conkers. I thought my legs were going to break. If I'd had a knife I would have cut the boat. They must have heard my screams in the hotel . . . But you'll be all right youth. Go for it. Take no prisoners'

The place was Swallow Falls, North Wales, the fool, or hero, Steve Hartland. No one wants to be a fool and everyone wants to be a hero, but for us the end result was, and is, less important than the excitement of getting there. If you want the thrills you take the spills. Steve knew that my paddle muscles would be twitching. Like many climbers, rough water addicts share a need for fear and for the release from fear.

Oh you ego, you monster, you roughshod rider over natural instincts, how you insist on your risks and rewards. Are we then just adrenalin junkies, and the book merely a 'look what we have done'. The thought is unseemly—I can hear my mother now, 'Oh he's just showing off because he's got an audience'—but, like Huw, and despite the opprobrium of an 'adult' world, I would say yes, we are 'conquistadors of the useless' and the book nothing more than a celebration of life on the edge. I would . . . except for something that happened in Corsica. Let me tell you about the

---

[1] Why do we do it? My answer is comparitively homespun and simple. You conceive the idea, you plan it, you carry it out, and you get a great feeling of satisfaction. Happiness is struggling against the huge elemental pounding waters of some strange river . . .' Mike Jones in *Canoeing Down Everest* (Hodder and Stoughton, 1979).

incident. Trivial though it was, it brought home to me the other, more subliminal reasons we go for this canoeing (and writing) game.

Glass covered the pavement. Huw was slumped beside the Land-Rover parked on a Mediterranean shore. 'I've got bad news for you Terry. We've been robbed, and they've taken your briefcase.' It was a couple of seconds before I realized what he meant. My credit cards were O.K. I patted my pocket, my walkman and waterproof camera were gone, but that was an insurance job; the Fium Orbo film, with that morning's Grade . . .

'Oh no, Huw, the chapters.' He just nodded. He knew that two chapters of this book were in the briefcase, and he also knew that I had no copies.

'Loel saw some of our stuff in the back of a police car and has gone to the police station.' It was something to say. There was no hope in his eyes.

Trudging disconsolately through the streets of Ajaccio I was ready to give up. It was probably a sign. Even if it wasn't, I doubted that I had the will to start again, remembering all those hours at a desk writing about what I could have been doing. It had all been a waste of time.

Asking the way in halting French, I was directed down a boulevard lined with cafés. It made me think of Briançon, and Philippe, the town's fishmonger and leading white water canoeist.

'Comment ça se fait tu manges autant,' he used to say to me across café tables such as these, as I tried to replace some of the energy lost in following him down the Dauphiné desperates, *'quand tu fais si peu dans ton kayak. Tiens, bois encore et mange moins. Demain on fera une rivière qui vraiment te donnera faim.'*[1] Now he is dead, killed driving as he lived, close to the edge, down by a river, racing to collect his precarious living from the market. Perhaps I could start again by writing about laughter and friendship with Philippe in southern France; the effort would seem worth it.

Then there was, and is still, Basher Kelly, the thinking man's Hell's Angel, who travelled with me to the United States and gave me his trust, precious gift. The narrow street funnelled my eyes upwards to the jagged horizon of Corsican peaks. They could just as well have been the Rockies, and I thought of our trip down the Animus, 'the killer river'.[2] And like the river, the memory came pounding, swirling, overlapping, more poem than prose.

---

[1] 'How can you eat so much when you do so little in your boat. Here, drink more and eat less. Tomorrow we will do a river that will really make you hungry.'

[2] '"Absolutely unrunnable," claims one Durango raft guide. "A killer river pure and simple," says another. Yet, expert kayakers, since Ron Mason in 1966, have known otherwise and run the Animus frequently and quite safely.' *Rivers of the Southwest* by Fletcher Anderson and Ann Hopkinson (Pruell Publishing Co, 1982).

182

'Breakfast forced down for energy
In the dog hours; we drop the hire car
In the blackness of Rockwood siding
I forget the camera.

The scrambled changeover into the pick-up
Puts us facing each other
I the gleaming in the east—
"Oh, just a river I fancy,"
Marty the gloom in the west—
"I wasn't too keen to say the least."

"In years of above average snowpack
The river is considered unsafe,"
So said a guide, and I hope for a hard frost
To keep it in the Needle Peaks.
But beside a nervous yellow hole at 9,000ft
My jayboots sink hopelessly deep.

Marty rolls another as I rush to the water,
A bikers forced calmness before the ride.

The first five miles seem so hard and
The next twenty-two "are far more demanding".
Elk Park footbridge, and 2,500ft + 2 miles to U.S.550, says
This is the Animus man, and if you don't like it, you can go.
"Bugger that, but better keep an eye on me."
I am in awe of Marty using the long climb out
As a cover for dismissing this last chance.

Cataract Gulch and Deadwood Creek,
Kendall Gulch and Sultan Creek bring yet more water,
Tumbling down the black walls of metamorphic rock.
Lost in this huge landscape I have to pick a way
Down a melting drain. There is no chance to relax,
Or dibble dabble,
And I lead by instinct rather than design.

I see the great swathe carved through the pines
By the landslide from Mt Garfield and brace myself
For the dense stoppers of Slide Rapid.
Marty flips, fails to roll, and kicks
Out of his element; in the liquid mountains,
Grabbing for a straw boat and paddle,
Gasping the first breaths of water.

His kayak appears, but not he. I let it go
Paddling upstream close to the bank, in an eddy,
Searching for the body that told me yesterday
"You'd better look after me tomorrow."
In the corner of my vision a moving form on the other bank
Waves weakly, and I race after the boat.
Can we survive a night out here if it is lost?
Panting and pushing I force it to stop.

A skier at Needleton packbridge smiles at us resting
Beneath the ponderosa and scrub oak. He has time to relax in
The evening chill of the box canyons, watching muskrat and
Otter play. We envy him his measured progress
As we surge westward under Mountain View Crest.
An abandoned steel truss bridge offers views down another
Scary rapid, the line rushing past huge stoppers and over
Haystack waves. Tight lipped in the sinking sun
We salute each other with nervous thumbs,
Sharing the last drops of energy and courage.'

I staggered, catching my foot on the curb, tired after that morning's canoeing, and awoke to my surroundings again. Dragging myself through the backstreets of Ajaccio I remembered a similar weariness as Marty and I carried two miles out from the end of the Animus. Every trip has its price, for every high there is a low.

The problem is we never know how much we are prepared to pay, until we have taken the ride. Marty's diary makes it clear first, that his Animus swim was a big price but second, that it was worth it.

'I had managed a quick breath but I knew it wasn't really enough. I started to set my paddle for another roll when I began to get really knocked about on some rocks. Shit, here we go. I knew I was in for a rough one. Struggling for breath I surfaced, coughing my lungs out, getting a beating all the time from the rocks beneath the surface. I was in the middle of a good Grade IV desperately holding on to my boat and paddles. Then I lost my grip on the Taiphun . . .

. . . I can remember the last 5 miles being just as continuous but I felt a lot happier. I was starting to read the water at last (after 23 miles!). I was able to relax and pick out rocks, stoppers, and holes a long way ahead. I was enjoying the paddling.'

Nigel Foster, on the other hand, almost payed more than he could afford in the Hudson Strait. He hardly reflects on it at all in his chapter, but I know it slowed him down somewhat. These bad times give us all pause for thought, and we do well to remember and record them. And that is another good reason to start writing the book again, I thought, stumbling towards the police station.

184

Inside the Gendarmerie there was a bench worn smooth by the wronged and wrong-doers of Ajaccio. Lying on it was my briefcase, knifed open to reveal an empty space, empty except for a pile of papers. I fumbled with the battered and twisted locks, dropped it, and my book tumbled out. Why the robbers had left it I have no idea. More sensible surely to throw it into the sea where the water would mask any traces of their identity. Could they have guessed the value of the words to me? Whatever the reason I was hugely happy to have them back, their return producing a catharsis of sorts. For now I realized that although the book could be dismissed as the work of an unfulfilled ego, or ignored as the ramblings of a philosopher *manqué*, to lose it would have been like forgetting a dream in the morning, the sense of loss deep and abiding even though the details mattered little.

The problem with remembered dreams is that they contain repressed undercurrents of feeling as well as satisfying wish-fulfilments. Whether this more emotional, less dramatic side to the stories should be told I am not sure; occasionally we let it all hang out, more often we leave the dead of night well alone. We have our excuses. Some things are too hurtful to print, others are too embarrassing to admit, while yet others are so difficult to understand that only a psychoanalyst could make sense of them. Yet knowing that there is something missing makes us dissatisfied, as Marcus suggested in a letter sent to me with his chapters.

'We can no more describe a memory than we can share a dream. Now that I have written these accounts I realize that I have destroyed them. Each was real, alive, filled with people, laughter, arguments, and uncertainty of outcome. Now the tedium of rereading them upsets me. There is so much missing!'

Still despite the feelings left unstated, the emotions left unexplored, I hope there is enough to suggest motivations beyond the admitted desire to 'do it'. Friendships found in deed and forged in need, the enjoyment of nature in all its watery forms, the relaxation of living by instinctive demands (principally food and sleep) in the rhythm of night and day (rather than the 9–5), gaining wisdom in the confluence of cultures, all these and more draw us back time and time again. We all share Nigel's sense of sadness as he finishes the circumnavigation of Iceland and realizes his reason for being there is gone. We search for beginnings rather than endings, for experience more than achievement, for adventure, not the telling of it. And if, in the writing, you are left wanting more, that is how it should be.

Amongst the papers the Corsican robbers left me was a hastily written letter never sent. Reading it again I see that I was tired and lonely that day, living in the past. But to make a history out of nostalgia is no bad thing if it serves to strengthen our dreams for the future. Perhaps I will send it after all.

'I have just finished the last chapter of my book. It was saying good-bye to New Zealand. We do a lot of that in travelling. And one good-bye leads to another until the search for new experiences becomes a way of life. I am addicted to the intensity and the movement; but sometimes I want to stop and reach out for a more permanent hold. Which is why I am writing, the book, and to you. Help me if you can. Write me a letter, tell me how you feel and what you think. Even if I have to read between the lines, it might last beyond the good-byes.'

Appendix 1

Selected Glossary of Canoeing Terms

Access   Embarkation point. Way down to the river or to the sea.

B.D.H.   Plastic screw-top container for storing emergency gear in a canoe.

Backtow   Water flowing upstream below a stopper wave. The longer and deeper the backtow, the more dangerous the stopper.

Boil   An upsurge of water spilling outwards from the centre in the shape of a mushroom. Prevalent in high-volume rivers with vertical banks.

Bongo-slide   Sideways surfing on breaking waves after the canoe has been broached.

Bow rudder   Paddle stroke used to turn a canoe; placed near the bow.

Brace   Paddle stroke used to support or right a canoe; placed out to the side.

Break-in   A manoeuvre taking the canoe from an eddy into the main stream.

Break-line   The area close to a shore in which waves are first breaking.

Break-out   A manoeuvre taking the canoe from the main stream into an eddy. Also used to describe the eddy or resting place.

Buoyancy aid   A flotation device worn by canoeists to aid swimming.

Canoe   Canoe is the generic name used in Britain for both the kayak and the (Canadian) canoe. Kayaks have their origins in the Eskimo kayaks which have covered decks and are paddled in a sitting position with twin-bladed paddles. Canoes have their origin in the dugout canoe used by Indians all over the world for hunting, fishing, trading and warring. It is paddled in a kneeling or sitting position, with a single blade and has an open deck. Some canoes now have closed decks for white water use. To differentiate canoes from kayaks the former are often called Canadian canoes.

C1   Canadian canoe paddled by one person.

C2   Canadian canoe paddled by two people.

Cfs   Cubic feet per second. A measurement of the volume of water moving down a river.

Chart   Map of the sea.

Clapotis Rough sea caused by waves rebounding from a steep shore and colliding with incoming waves.

Cockpit The area in a closed-deck canoe where the paddler kneels. Many plastic kayaks now have large 'keyhole' cockpits to ease exit in the event of a pin.

Current Movement of sea water produced by wind, thermal differences and salinity variations. Not to be confused with tidal streams.

Deck lines Rope or elastic on the front and rear deck of a canoe. Used on the sea to locate charts and carry emergency gear (food, flares, spare paddles) and on rivers to aid lifting, lowering and rescue.

Draw stroke Paddle stroke used to move a canoe (or raft) sideways; placed at the side of the canoe.

Drive force The force of the paddle blade that will pull against the water in normal forward propulsion.

Eddy Area of still, or upstream moving water, which forms on the downstream side of obstructions in a river or the sea. Used by canoeists to stop, rest, manoeuvre from one side of the main stream to another, and (less common) to make progress against the main stream.

Egress Disembarkation point. Way out from the river or the sea.

Eskimo rescue Method of self-righting a capsized canoe while staying inside, using another's canoe or paddle for support.

Eskimo roll Method of self-righting a capsized canoe while staying inside, using a paddle stroke for support.

Ferry glide Manoeuvre to take the canoe from one side of a stream to the other. The canoe is set at an angle and paddled upstream.

Fetch The distance across open water which the wind blows without hindrance. This together with the speed of the wind and the action of any tidal streams, will determine the height of the waves.

Fibre pile Synthetic fluffy material favoured by canoeists for trousers and long-johns — when not wearing a wetsuit.

Fishing rights Rights secured by an unjust and peculiarly British law that gives a few riparian owners control over British rivers, the banks, the beds and the water as it passes over them. Unless there is a public right of navigation canoeing in Britain on non-tidal rivers is equivalent to walking over private land without permission.

Footrest Adjustable plate or plates in the front of a canoe against which a paddler wedges his feet.

Grab loop Loop of rope on the bow and stern deck of a canoe to aid carrying and rescue.

Grade Defines difficulty and seriousness of a river. See Appendix 2.

Harness Quick-release webbing system worn on the chest by some paddlers on difficult and dangerous rivers, used to attach, or be attached to, a rope.

High cross Manoeuvre used to take a canoe across a fast shoot of water.

Hoist Rope pull using a mechanical advantage. Often set up with the aid of prussiks, pulleys and karabiners.

Hole See Stopper.

Karabiner Metal snap link used with static or running ropes.

Kayak See Canoe.

K1 Kayak paddled by one person.

K2 Kayak paddled by two people.

Lee shore The shore onto which the wind blows.

Line Good or best route down a rapid, avoiding difficult or dangerous water.

Loom The paddle shaft.

Loop Action of the canoe after it has been ridden or taken down the face of a breaking wave into the trough. The buoyancy of the boat sends it back skywards, the stern then 'looping' over the bow.

Paddle hook Device which can be attached to a paddle and used to extend the reach of a rescuer. Used for hooking boats and paddles, and (occasionally) paddlers.

Pinning Horizontal or vertical jamming of a boat in an obstruction.

Pop-out Similar to a loop except that the canoe does not topple over itself, but lands upright behind the wave.

Portaging Carrying the canoe along a bank in order to avoid an obstacle.

Prussik Short loop of (relatively) thin rope that can be attached to a (relatively) thick rope (e.g. throw line). A prussik knot will grip under load, but can be moved when not under tension. It is useful for climbing up ropes, and for hoists.

Pulley Small wheel that allows a running rope to move through a karabiner with reduced function.

Seal launching Entering a river or the sea by sliding down bank or shore.

Spray deck Nylon or neoprene skirt worn around the paddler's waist to seal the cockpit of a closed-deck canoe.

Split paddle Paddle cut in half to allow ease of storage on the deck or inside a canoe. Habitually carried as spare paddles on trips.

Standing wave Stationary wave forming over an obstruction or constriction in a river bed. The stream passes through the wave.

Stopper Otherwise known as a hole or hydraulic jump, a stopper is a vertical eddy current. When moving water is accelerated over or through an obstruction, there is low pressure created on the downstream side of that obstruction. This hole is filled by water coming back upstream forming a tumbling, breaking stopper wave. The main downstream current passes underneath the stopper but floating objects such as canoes or canoeists may be held in the hole by the return current. Man-made weirs are notorious for forming such in 'keeper' stoppers.

Sump An underground passage in which there is no air space.

Sweep stroke Paddle stroke used to turn the canoe; moved from bow to stern.

Tidal stream The horizontal movement of sea water produced by lunar (and, to a lesser extent, solar) attraction in an (approximately) six hourly cycle.

Throw line Rescue rope carried stuffed in a bag ready for throwing.

Tidal race A tidal stream accelerated by horizontal or vertical constrictions — such as a shallow sea bed, a narrow channel, a jutting peninsular.

Tow line Quick-release line carried by canoeists for towing tired or injured paddlers, or capsized boats.

Wetsuit Neoprene long-johns habitually worn by canoeists next to the skin to restrict water movement (and therefore its chilling effect), and to protect against bumps and scrapes.

Weir A man-made obstruction in a river particularly dangerous to canoeists and swimmers due to the powerful and uniform stoppers which form on their downstream side.

Notes

1. On or about rivers, *left* and *right* is taken to mean when looking downstream.

2. On the sea, a wind described as westerly comes *from* the west; a tidal stream described as westerly (or 270) goes *to* the west.

Appendix 2

International River Grades of Difficulty

1   Easy: Here are rivers with beautiful united waters flowing in peaceful meanders. There are no obstructions in the river and the canoeist (or swimmer) may float any which way he pleases.

2   Moderate: The river is already quicker. The occasional rock, overhanging branch, or bridge pillars may cause problems, but the channel is always clear and obvious.

3   Fairly Difficult: Now things are more complicated. The current is swift and the river narrows in places producing waves and stoppers. Obstructions force the canoeist to manoeuvre in and out and across the current. Nevertheless the best channel is easily recognized and remembered. A swim is more likely to hurt the pride than the body.

4   Difficult: This is challenging water. Rapids follow each other in quick succession, and are continuous and difficult to 'read'. The route is not obvious from the water and inspection from the bank is the norm. A swim is usually unpleasant and occasionally injurious so rolling is important. Obstructions and stoppers may hold canoes.

5   Very Difficult: Even after inspection from the bank it is difficult to recognize a route through Grade 5 water. There are pressure waves, whirlpools, boils, and small waterfalls. Stoppers hold swimmers as well as canoes. The water is always fast, often heavy, with tight bends and large boulders in steep ravines. To swim would be dangerous so rolling is essential.

6   Extremely Difficult: Grade 6 water is a playing field of foaming chaos. To all but the most experienced (and inexperienced) canoeist the river appears impossible to negotiate. It may be canoed only at particular water levels. The paddler can expect at times to disappear completely and at other times to be hurled skywards by a prodigious force. Rolling is problematical in the turbulent water and rescue and evacuation from gorges presents severe problems. Mistakes may be dearly payed for; there is a definite danger to life and limb.

191

Notes:

1. This is only one of a number of different descriptions of the International Grading System, but in essence they are all the same. I have based this one on a French description, a full translation of which may be found in my *Alpine White Water* guidebook.

2. The grades are necessarily broad to cope with a variety of rapid and river types and with fluctuations in water levels. It is the convention to grade a river when it is bank full, so a drought or flood may alter (usually, but *not* always, lower and raise respectively) the grade of a river.

3. Rivers are graded by their hardest section. Thus on a given river with an overall Grade of 5, there will be many sections of 1, 2, 3, and 4. There *may* also be a rapid of Grade 6, which, while being noted as such, does not affect the overall grade because *it* is the exception (Grade 5 paddlers will portage it). Three or four rapids of Grade 6 however, would warrant a grading of that number (no one goes canoeing to carry their boats round falls).